A Western Horseman Book

NATURAL HORSE-MAN-SHIP

By Pat Parelli

With Kathy Kadash

Photographs by Karen Parelli

NATURAL HORSE-MAN-SHIP

Published by
Western Horseman Inc.
3850 North Nevada Ave.
Box 7980
Colorado Springs, CO 80933-7980

Design, Typography, and Production
Western Horseman
Colorado Springs, Colorado

Printing
Publisher's Press
Salt Lake City, Utah

Ninth Printing: September 1997

ISBN 0-911647-27-9

DEDICATION

This book is dedicated to all
those seeking to experience what the world of
Natural Horse-Man-Ship has to offer the horse and
human. To those who want fun, excellence, truth,
and results in their equine partnerships. To those who
love the feeling you get from the Natural approach to
teaching and learning versus the Normal approach.
And to the horse.

• PAT PARELLI

ACKNOWLEDGMENTS

I would like to thank these people, past and present, for their inspiration, stimulation, support, or faith in me, which has influenced me greatly over the years and which I credit my success. All I added was perspiration and imagination.

I did not list them chronologically, alphabetically, or in order of importance.

Fred Ferrara
Jess Tharp
Shorty Freeman
Troy Henry
Monte Foreman
Casey Tibbs
Dr. Bill Linfoot
Ed Connell
Glen Burns
Pat & Marion Humphrey
John Hawkins
Tony Ernst

Tom Dorrance
Bill Dorrance
Ronnie Willis
Ted Ashworth
Dr. Robert M. Miller
Ron & Joan Crevalin
Mike Bridges
Ray Hunt
Freddie Knie
Linda Paterson
Jeff & Kat Hobson
Johnny Jones
Clint Johnson

Billy Flournoy
Gerry & Sharon Blanks
Al Dodds
Donny Wright
Dave Carlson
Bob Berg
Gerry Westfall
Bill Wildes
Joe & Arlene Aguilar
Maurice Wright
Jack & Doris Parelli
Karen Parelli

PREFACE

THERE ARE many books that should be read again and again, and this is one of them. It's easier to grasp the principles and goals behind Natural Horse-Man-Ship after the second and even third time you read this book. Each time you do, you'll get more out of the words on these pages and understand completely what Pat Parelli is saying. This book is a blend of concepts and exercises. The exercises or maneuvers are designed to help you more fully comprehend the concepts and help you communicate effectively with your horse on his level.

The book is divided into three sections: 1/ Natural Horse-Man-Ship—An Overview, 2/ Natural Horse-Man-Ship—On the Ground, and 3/ Natural Horse-Man-Ship—In the Saddle. Each section uses the six keys Pat has identified as vital in the development of a Natural Horse-Man—Attitude, Knowledge, Tools, Techniques, Time, and Imagination. Like the petals of a flower, each key unfolds in the three sections until the heart of Natural Horse-Man-Ship is presented in its entirety.

—Kathy Kadash

Update:

Since this book was first published, Pat Parelli has moved to southwestern Colorado where he has established his International Study Center and a mail-order business for his equipment, videos, and books.

The address for both:

P.O. Box 3729
Pagosa Springs, CO 81147
Ph. 1-800-642-3335 or 970-731-9400
FAX: 970-731-9722

Philosophy

THIS IS not a horse-training book; it's a people-training book. Don't think you have to only train your horse. What you've probably got to do is train yourself to be more principled, and therefore, more effective.

What I plan to offer you in the pages of this book is a philosophy I call Natural Horse-Man-Ship. Natural horsemanship has been around a long time. It is not something I invented, but it is something I'm excited about. As a matter of fact, it's so old, it's new again.

Over 2,000 years ago, one of the first great riding masters was a man named Xenophon. He said that communication is the key to horsemanship. Learning to communicate with your horse is vital if the two of you are to be on the same track as partners. And helping you to learn to communicate with your horse is going to be a large part of this book.

The first person who sat on a horse didn't have anybody to use as an example.

"Natural horsemanship . . . is not something I invented. . . . As a matter of fact, it's so old, it's new again."

He had to study the horse, the animal's nature, and how it works. I don't know how he did it. Maybe he found a foal whose mother had been killed, and he raised the young horse. Somehow, he got the horse's confidence. Then, he thought about putting his leg over the horse's back, and he got this great feeling. He felt like a horse; he could run faster and jump higher than he could before. That was the dawn of Natural Horse-Man-Ship.

NATURAL HORSE-MAN-SHIP—A DEFINITION

The dynamics of horsemanship can be obtained naturally through communication, understanding, and psychology. This is what I hope to share with you. In contrast is normal horsemanship, which is sometimes obtained through mechanics, fear, and intimidation.

Natural Versus Normal

I should define what is natural and what is normal. Natural is what Mother Nature provides for us and allows us to work with. As far as I'm concerned, a horse is one of Mother Nature's finest creations.

Normal is what everybody does that everybody else is doing when they have half of a mind to. The only reason everybody does what everybody else is doing is because everybody else is doing it. In other words, peer pressure.

But what's normal changes every 60 miles and every 6 months. I've been all over the world, and I've found there's a line every 60 miles where normality changes. What everybody does in one location is different than what everybody does north, south, east, or west of them. So normal is not worldwide or universal. It changes, not only from month to month and season to season, but from location to location.

We go through life being pressured to become normal. If everybody is doing it, we think it must be right. One thing that normal does is put a thick shell on our imaginations.

Normal has synonyms like good, common, average, ordinary, usual, conforming, typical, and mediocre. What we should want to do in Natural Horse-Man-Ship is stay away from normal. Normality is our adversary.

Some synonyms for natural are native, instinctive, inborn, inherent, and intuitive. Have you ever seen somebody who is really natural with horses? When they work with horses, they're not really working with them, they're playing with them and things seem to happen naturally. This type of person usually has what is described as knack.

I would like to be able to help people obtain knack through knowledge and skills. Knowledge is something you can share, and skills are things you can develop. The object of this book is to help you gain natural knowledge about horses and develop your skills naturally.

Traditional and Progressive Thinkers

Just like there are two types of horsemanship, there are two types of thinkers: traditional and progressive. In normal schools, people are taught systematically in traditional teaching methods and it takes forever.

Traditional thinking is what normal people do. However, it's traditional for tradition to change. It has for centuries. In fact, the only constant thing in life is change.

A progressive person is a person receptive to new concepts and techniques. This is a person who wants to key into the big picture, not just the details.

I'm a progressive thinker, and that's what I hope you strive to become. I've learned to isolate, separate, and recombine properly, and I do this with the elements of horsemanship. For example, I take each ingredient of a maneuver individually and work on it, not the whole maneuver at once. This is why bending a horse with one rein, as I do in lateral longeing and flexion exercises, drives people crazy. It doesn't look at all like the big picture they have in their minds of doing a half-halt. If a maneuver has six ingredients in it, I try to get really good on one ingredient at a time. Only later, when I've perfected each ingredient, do I put them all together to form the complete maneuver. That's what isolate, separate, and recombine means.

Horse-Human Relationship

If you are to obtain Natural Horse-Man-Ship through progressive thinking, you must first realize that a horse is not just a horse. He is an attitude with four feet, and he thinks differently than you and I.

The type of intelligence people have is based on reasoning power. We use logic to figure out things and to get what we want. Horses, however, base their thinking patterns on comfort. Horses want to feel safe and comfortable. Anything that interferes with that can cause fear and anxiety in horses.

Most people are inadequate when it comes to horses because they think like people. My goal is to get people to think like horses.

The best way I know to do that is to play with horses on the ground through lateral longeing techniques. This is a way for you to understand horses and for them to understand you. In this book, I'll explain theories and techniques for exercising your horse on the ground as well as in the saddle.

Why do people get into horses in the first place? I've asked this everywhere I go. Nobody gets forced into liking horses. People get into horses because they have a dream. The dream starts off with them and their horses riding off into the sunset harmoniously. Then they get involved with horses and something happens. Eighty percent of people who get into horses get out in the first year. I estimate that 80 percent of the remaining 20 percent get out in the next 5. They do so for the six Fs: Fear, Frustration, Feeling like a Failure, lack of Fun, and lack of Funds.

These fears are founded on three lies that have been told to all of us when we first got on a horse. 1/ Just saddle a horse and get on. 2/ Kick him to go. 3/ Pull the reins to stop.

I guarantee you that if you just saddle a horse and get on without any prior and proper preparation, you won't get any extraordinary results. If you just kick the horse to make him go, he'll go, but it will be with a terrible taste in his mouth. And if you just pull on the reins to stop, he'll push on the bit and you'll get everything wrong that you've ever wanted. The best you'll ever get is mediocrity.

I have a program that I like to share with people and it comes in 41 words that begin with the letter "P."

"Pat Parelli proudly presents his programs and the proclamation that prior and proper preparation prevents P-poor performance particularly if polite and passive persistence is practiced in the proper position. This perspective takes patience, from process to product, from principle to purpose. The promise that Pat plans to prove is that practice does not make perfect, only perfect practice makes perfect, and it is peculiar how prey animals perceive people as predators and not partners."

103 Ingredients

Excellence with horses and a partnership for life is what we all are striving for and rarely get because normal horsemanship gets in the way. I've identified 103 ingredients in Natural Horse-Man-Ship, and these concepts are the basis of this text. I list them in a particular order: 1, 2, 4, 6, 8, and 10. Added together, they equal 31. There are two sets of these numbers (1, 2, 4, 6, 8, 10). 31 + 31 = 62. Add the 41 "Ps" as mentioned above. 31 + 31 + 41 = 103.

Here is how the 1, 2, 4, 6, 8, and 10 break down.

1/ There is one thing that everyone is after with horses: a natural partnership for life.

2/ There are two types of horsemanship: natural and normal.

4/ There are four areas of study: colt starting, foundation, refinement, problem solving.

6/ There are six keys: attitude, knowledge, tools, techniques, time, and imagination.

8/ There are eight principles: 1) Horse-Man-Ship is natural. 2) Don't make assumptions. 3) Communication is mutual. 4) Horses and humans have responsibilities. 5) The attitude is justice. 6) Body language is universal. 7) Horses teach riders and riders teach horses. 8) Principles, purpose, and time are the tools of teaching.

10/ There are 10 qualities of a Natural Horse-Man: heart and desire, respect, impulsion, flexion, attitude, feel, timing, balance, savvy, and experience.

The second set of numbers (1, 2, 4, 6, 8, and 10) go as follows:

1/ One rein for control.

2/ Two reins for communication.

4/ Four goals of the Natural Horse-Man-Ship network: 1) Get people interested in Natural Horse-Man-Ship enough to take it up as a hobby. 2) Have people live through their experiences with horses. 3) Show people how to have fun with horses. 4) Have people excel with the knowledge of Natural Horse-Man-Ship.

6/ There are only six things a horse can do: go forward, backward, right, left, up, and down.

8/ There are eight responsibilities of the partnership: four for the human and four for the horse.

10/ There are 10 levels of Natural Horse-Man-Ship.

When you add the top 31 ingredients and these last 31, you get 62 ingredients. Add these to the 41 "Ps" and you have 103 ingredients in Natural Horse-Man-Ship.

6 Keys

The six keys are especially important in the scheme of things, and it is within these six keys that this book is outlined: Attitude, Knowledge, Tools, Techniques, Time, and Imagination.

It's important that you have all six and not just one or some. When you observe someone who is working with horses, don't only look for the techniques or tools he is using. Look for all the key elements; they all have to be present in a Natural Horse-Man.

1/ Attitude

You have to have a natural attitude. An attitude is a multitude of actions and interactions at any given time; therefore, every action and/or interaction represents an attitude. Natural Horse-Man-Ship is an attitude for people who are positive and progressive, and who believe in the natural point of view of the horse.

2/ Knowledge

You have to have the knowledge of how horses think. Most people think like people, and that's a whole different type of knowledge.

3/ Tools

You have to have tools that work naturally. You should be able to tell a Natural Horse-Man by the tools he uses, and also by the tools he doesn't use or those he wouldn't use.

4/ Techniques

You have to understand natural techniques. For example, most people saddle a horse and get on, kick to go, and pull to stop. Instead of these normal ways to make horses go and stop, use natural techniques that produce snappy departures and graceful transitions.

5/ Time

If you take the time it takes, it takes less time. Most people don't have the time to do it right, but they always have the time to do it over and over. With respect to time, we have to understand the relevancy of time, the meaning of short-term time and long-term time, and the word "timing."

6/ Imagination

You have to exercise your imagination. Imagination is something children have that adults do not, or at least they lost the ability to use their imaginations effectively. Einstein said that imagination is even more valuable than knowledge.

These are the ingredients that are necessary to achieving excellence through Natural Horse-Man-Ship.

This book is divided into three sections: 1/ Natural Horse-Man-Ship, an Overview; 2/ Natural Horse-Man-Ship, on the Ground; and 3/ Natural Horse-Man-Ship, in the Saddle. Each of the three sections is broken down into the six keys and explained as it relates to that key. For example, what you need to know about your attitude, what knowledge you need to have, and what tools you require for "playing" with your horse on the ground are detailed in Section II. By the same token, what techniques you use and the time it takes to do things with your horse while you are riding are detailed in Section III. Each section is a development or further unfolding of the section that precedes it. In other words, you should understand more about tools and their uses when you read about them in Section III than you did when you read about them in Section I.

Instead of excellence with horses, mediocrity is what most people get and don't even know it. For example, someone who goes to the show, wins the blue ribbon, yet has difficulty loading his horse into the trailer to go home is a perfect example of a person accepting mediocrity as a good result. Often, people put their efforts and energy into becoming great riders or showmen, instead of becoming great horsemen. Most people are looking for the winning edge. In reality, what they really need is the natural foundation.

A foundation is something that is rock solid, something that can be tested, something that is true. We are talking about the foundation between horse and human, a partnership for life. What I offer you in this book is the foundation for that partnership —Natural Horse-Man-Ship. On the pages of this book, I'll explain the 103 ingredients in the hopes that you and I will become better horsemen.

I would like to suggest that the first time you read this book, you put most of your efforts in understanding the six keys and the eight responsibilities of Natural Horse-Man-Ship. If you get these, the rest will come naturally.

CONTENTS

NATURAL HORSE-MAN-SHIP

AN OVERVIEW

ATTITUDE

AN OVERVIEW

SINCE A LOT of a person's attitude, opinions, and beliefs are vital to a relationship with horses, attitudes are the first things we must examine and try to understand in Natural Horse-Man-Ship.

There tend to be two distinct ends to the spectrum when it comes to a person's attitude in getting a horse to doing something. There's the stick attitude, used by the person who is going to bash the horse with the stick and make him do it. Such a person uses force and intimidation to make a horse perform.

Then there's the carrot attitude, used by a person who is going to sweet-talk the horse into doing something. Such a person is usually ineffective and begs the horse instead of asking for and getting respect from the horse.

In between the two extremes is the person who is assertive. Such a person is neither aggressive nor wimpy, but balanced somewhere between the two.

With horses, the natural attitude is to be as gentle as you can, but as firm as necessary. When you're gentle, be gentle without being a sissy. When you're firm, be firm without getting mean or mad.

The attitude of Natural Horse-Man-Ship is to do things for the horse and with the horse rather than to the horse. The idea is to use your imagination beyond the

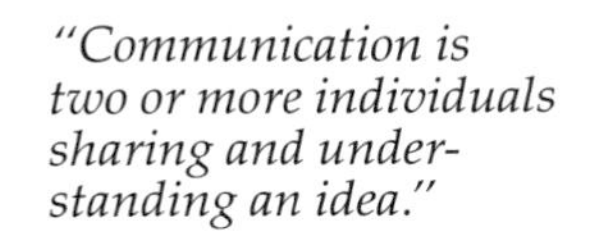

"Communication is two or more individuals sharing and understanding an idea."

boundaries that normal people do.

The attitude of a Natural Horse-Man is that the principles are more important than the purpose—that adjusting to fit the situation is more important than rules.

Natural Horse-Man-Ship is an attitude for people who are positive, progressive, and who believe in the natural point of view of the horse. They have taken their quest to become natural horsemen as a passion and want to move up through the 10 levels of achievement naturally.

In Natural Horse-Man-Ship, there are no rules, only principles and goals. Since principles are more important than goals, I'd like to identify the eight Principles of Natural Horse-Man-Ship.

8 Principles of Natural Horse-Man-Ship

1/ Horse-Man-Ship is natural.

Horse-Man-Ship is three words linked together. It's a horse and a human going willingly together. Horse-Man-Ship is for horses as well as humans, and the horse comes first.

In this regard, it is important to understand that the horse is a prey animal, and that he is driven by three major instincts: a/ to be perceptive to danger, b/ to fly from fear, and c/ to be gregarious. He is a born coward, a born claustrophobic, and a born "full-throttle-aholic" by varying degrees.

By varying degrees means that some horses are more sensitive than others. For example, some are more cowardly than others, although they are all cowards to some degree. In the same sense, some are more claustrophobic than others. In other words, some can stand confinement or restraint better than others. "Full-throttle" means all out forward. "Aholic" is usually referred to as a person who can't help himself or who has an addiction to something. With regard to horses, full-throttle-aholic means the horse reacts first and thinks second. He runs from fear at full speed, and only looks behind when he thinks he's safe.

In applying this to horses, let's use a typical scenario as an example. When a horse gets his foot caught in a fence, because he is a born coward and a born claustrophobic, he doesn't calmly think, "Oh, darn, my foot is caught." Instead, the horse panics. He doesn't think logically, and he automatically goes into full-throttle. He tries to escape his entrapment any way he can, even if he hurts himself in the process. This is usually the case unless the horse has been taught to stand still when his foot is caught. I'm not saying that all horses have these sensitivities to an extreme degree. Some are quieter and less panicky than others. They are all born with their own degree of sensitivity.

When someone buys a horse, he mistakenly thinks he owns the horse—heart, body, and soul—and that the animal should succumb to his wishes. A horse is an individual, not simply a possession. He has wants and needs, too. He wants to become comfortable, and as long as you can prove to him that you're not a predator, he'll be comfortable.

It is important to understand that the human is the horse's biological enemy; in other words, a predator. Most people get upset when their horses act like prey animals instead of partners. And most horses get upset when their humans act like predators instead of partners.

People who think like people (and not like horses) think that when a horse is following his instincts, he is being naughty. We need to understand that a horse is programmed by nature to act like a prey animal.

Horses are easily recognized as prey animals because of three distinct characteristics:

1/ They smell like what they eat, which is grass.

2/ Their eyes are set on the sides of their heads, which means they have bilateral vision. This gives them great peripheral vision and the ability to see predators sneaking up behind them. But it also gives them the disadvantage of not having great depth perception.

3/ As a prey animal, the horse is perceptive to danger, people, places, changes, and things; particularly dangerous people, places, changes, and things.

People are easily identified as predators because of three major characteristics:

1/ Humans smell like what they eat, which is meat.

2/ Humans have eyes in front of their heads, like predators. We have great depth perception and the ability to focus on a moving object. But we lack good lateral vision.

3/ The human is sometimes not perceptive to danger, people, places, changes, and things.

When Horse-Man-Ship happens, the human becomes half horse and the horse becomes half human. Our job as the horse's leader is to get him to be braver, less claustrophobic, and less of a full-throttle-aholic. In other words, for Natural Horse-Man-Ship to truly happen, the horse must want to become a Horse-Man first. He has to become braver, less fearful of tight places, and more willing to stand his ground rather than panic at what he perceives to be danger. And the human needs to become assertive enough to be viewed as the "alpha" member of the horse's society, rather than being viewed as a predator or a wimp.

2/ Don't make assumptions.

The word "assume" is made up of three little words: Ass, U, and Me. It is easy to assume and to teach the horse to assume. Don't assume today that your horse is going to wake up on the same side of the corral as he did yesterday, whether he was good, bad, or indifferent. A horse lives moment to moment. He wakes up on a different side of the corral each day. This is why it is important to have and to understand the ritual of pre-flight checks (a series of steps that are detailed later in this book).

On the other hand, teaching the horse not to assume is also significant. For example, if you were to ride your horse 3 days in a row in an arena and stopped everyday at the gate just before you got off, you would teach your horse to assume that when you got to the gate, it's time to stop. By the fourth day, the horse would take over and when you got to the gate, would probably stop and wait for you to get off. Instead of teaching him to assume when you are going to quit, teach him not to assume by varying the time and area in which you stop. Mixing it up will keep the horse guessing and not assuming.

Here's another example of teaching your horse to assume: If you went on a trail ride for 3 days in a row, rode out a mile or two, then turned around and trotted back home, on the fourth day your horse will start jigging home. You will have taught your horse to assume that when you got to a predetermined distance, he is supposed to turn around and trot home. This is how he would make an Ass out of U and Me.

In order to obtain horsemanship through communication, we must learn not to assume.

3/ Communication is mutual.

Communication is two or more individuals sharing and understanding an idea. If I pat my leg and the dog comes, we've communicated. But I can talk to a post until I'm blue in the face, and I'm just talking. Communication is a mutual affair between two or more individuals.

A good example of a horse trying to communicate with the human is when a rider kicks his horse to go, then pulls him to stop, and the horse opens his mouth. Instead of listening to the horse who is trying to say, "Your hands are too heavy and you're not communicating down to my feet," the rider ties the horse's mouth shut with a cavesson and says, "Shut up and do what you're told."

4/ Horses and humans have responsibilities.

If horsemanship is going to be a partnership, both the horse and the human have got to have some responsibilities. There are eight responsibilities: four for the horse and four for the human. (A detailed description of each responsibility is in Knowledge—An Overview.)

Four responsibilities of the horse:

1. Learn to act like a partner, not like a prey animal.
2. Don't change gaits.
3. Don't change directions.
4. Watch where he is going.

Four responsibilities of the human:

1. Learn to act like a partner, not like a predator.
2. Develop an independent seat.
3. Think like a horse.
4. Use the natural power of focus.

5/ The attitude is justice.

Your attitude toward your horse should be a just one. In other words, you should cause your ideas to be your horse's ideas, but understand what his ideas are first.

Then it's up to you to cause the undesirable things to be difficult and allow the desirable things to be easy. If the horse is doing something you don't want him to do, create a situation in which it's hard or uncomfortable for him to do those things and also one in which it's easy for him to do what you want him to do. It'll soon become his idea to do whatever is easiest.

I use the words "cause" and "allow" when it comes to creating situations for your horse. I don't use "make" or "let." The word "cause" is less commanding than "make" and "allow" is more respectful than "let." Some people "let" their horses do incorrect things, and then they get angry with them when they do. To correct the problem, they then try to "make" their horses do things.

Some people by nature are makers. They're always mean when they ask their horses to do things. Other people are beggars, always gentle when they ask. They just let the horses do anything they want.

You need to be assertive. Do something about the situation when it needs to be done. Assertive is somewhere between being aggressive and being a wimp. Be as firm as necessary without getting mean or mad; be as gentle as you can without being a sissy.

Trust that your horse will respond to what you ask; but be ready to correct, no more one than the other.

Try to become a natural leader for that natural follower, the horse. You've got to be mentally, emotionally, and physically fit so you can be just at all times. You've got to have your act together. You have to become collected in the human sense.

The horse has three systems: respect, impulsion, and flexion. Everything I'm talking about so far has to do with getting the horse's respect so he will give you his impulsion, which is controlled forward energy. Then you learn how to keep him flexible in the mind and body.

The attitude is justice, and to be just, you have to be assertive, be a causer, and not a maker. You have to allow, and not let.

6/ Body language is the universal language.

Body language is universal. I've got it. You've got it. Horses have got it.

This horse's body language tells you his attention is split. One ear is trained on what's in front of him, and the other is cocked to his right and what's happening there. He's got his mind on two things at once.

There are things a horse does to let us know what he's thinking. For example, when he puts his ears back, he's irritated. Watch out! If he's blinking, he's thinking. If he licks his lips, he is probably digesting a thought; he understands and accepts the situation. If he's cocked a hind leg, he's relaxed; but if his ears are back and he lifts a hind foot, he's ready to kick. There are many postures that key us in to the horse's state of mind.

The body language of humans is just as important or more so. Most people don't key in to their own body language. The way they look at horses, their body posture, their actions, tells horses what they are thinking. You can easily misrepresent yourself to the horse through inappropriate body language. When some people approach their horses, their body language or posture makes them look aggressive or sneaky; like they have the look of the lion. On the other hand, there are those people who have the look of the lamb. They're sheepish or submissive.

Other examples of misrepresentation are: Walking into the pasture just to say hello, but with a grain can in one hand and a halter behind your back. You look like you're intent on catching the horse, and the look on your face is strong and scary to the horse. This is where the predator needs to be aware of how he represents himself to the prey animal, the horse.

7/ Horses teach riders and riders teach horses.

This is such an important principle. Many good horsemen say that horses are their best teachers. There's a reason for this. For example, if you want to learn how to cut cattle, buy a trained cutting horse to learn from. He'll teach you about the sport and what it feels like to cut a cow so you can understand it better. Then, once you've got the feel, you can offer it to other horses you ride. If you already know how to cut, then buy a 2-year-old horse and help him along.

One of the more common fallacies is buying a young horse for a young or green rider. An example is when parents buy their children young horses. So many times you hear about the parent who buys a 2- or 3-year-old horse for his youngster, thinking the two will grow up and learn together. That combination is usually a disaster. The horse needs to learn what he's expected to do from an experienced rider. The child needs to learn what it takes to cause a horse to move properly and also gain confidence from a steady mount. Green riders on green horses does not make sense. It can be a deadly combination.

On the other hand, it's important to learn from the horse who knows his job well. There are many things he can teach you, and then you can become a teacher of horses.

8/ Principles, purpose, and time are the tools of teaching.

Think about principle as being the horse, and that must come first. Purpose is the cart, and time is the driver. Now, we've come back full circle. We're talking about principles again, and now we have to go through each one of these principles and add in purpose so the horse knows the meaning.

First, we teach the horse principles; we build a foundation of things we want the horse to know. Then, we add purpose or a reason for doing what we want the horse to do. For example, we teach the horse to side-pass because someday we might want to open a gate while on the horse's back.

10 Qualities of a Horse-Man

There are 10 identifiable qualities of a Natural Horse-Man, half horse, half human. In this sense, a horse has to become a little bit human and a human has to become a little bit horse.

It's interesting, but I've met only six natural horsemen in my entire life. I've shaken hands with millions of horse owners and lovers, even people who were good riders, but who weren't horsemen. And I've shaken hands with hundreds of equestrians. Equestrians are good riders and have true knowledge about horses; but they still aren't horsemen.

I've even shaken hands with many good horse hands. A horse hand is somebody who is a good rider, as well as a horse lover. He is as knowledgeable as an equestrian, and he can share his knowledge with any horse he rides. That's what I believe I am.

The 10 qualities of a Natural Horse-Man are: 1/ Heart and Desire, 2/ Respect, 3/ Impulsion, 4/ Flexion, 5/ Attitude, 6/ Feel, 7/ Timing, 8/ Balance, 9/ Savvy, and 10/ Experience.

Of the 10 qualities, horses need to have the first 3½, and riders the other 6½. This means they both share one of the qualities. The first quality, that of Heart and Desire, is needed by both horse and human.

3½ Qualities for the Horse

½/ Heart and Desire

In legends and stories, we've all heard about horses who ran faster and jumped higher out of heart and desire. A natural horseman does everything he can to cause a horse to perceive that he needs and loves his human.

1/ Respect

Respect for the human is one of the most important qualities a horse can have. Respect has no fear in it. It has a willing, cooperative attitude about it. In order for a horse to respect you, he must not fear you and must see you as the leader. He must see you as the alpha horse in the herd. He's got to see you from his point of view.

All horses know that there are only six things they can do: go forward, backward, right, left, up, and down. In a herd situation, they yield to each other in these six ways. So, for a horse to respect you, he must yield to you and from you in those six ways, whether you are on the ground or on his back.

Respect is something you get on the ground or you don't. If your horse doesn't respect you on the ground, he won't respect you much in the saddle either. Respect is hard to get and easy to lose.

When you are mounted, you get the horse to respect you by having an independent seat, controlling his hindquarters, and riding with a focus.

I like to view respect as mental collection because the horse gives me his mind.

Once I have his mind, I can start to gain control of his emotions. This, to me, is where impulsion starts.

2/ Impulsion

Impulsion is controlled forward energy that comes from behind (the hindquarters). Impulsiveness is uncontrolled or wild energy that comes from behind. At the other end of the spectrum is non-responsiveness or a lack of energy. Impulsion lies somewhere between impulsiveness and non-responsiveness. It's when "go" equals "whoa," and "whoa" equals "go." That means the horse is balanced somewhere between moving forward and standing still. He harnesses the power of his mind and body and uses it to perform.

A rider uses this impulsion when he asks his horse to perform. If he can't get impulsion from his horse, it's because the horse is emotionally out of control, and he's emotionally out of control because he does not respect the human. This is probably one of the most frustrating problems humans have with horses. Impulsion comes from respect. In the physical sense, it is controlled forward energy; but in the abstract sense, it can be viewed as emotional collection.

We get impulsion from the horse by balancing the six yields: forward, backward, right, left, up, and down.

I like to think of the six yields in terms of a weight scale. Since most people understand the difference between an ounce and a pound, this provides an easy reference point to understand the concept of yield.

If you were to measure a yield, how much would it weigh? To me, a yield has a maximum weight of 4 ounces to still be a yield. Therefore, forward, backward, right, left, up, and down are equal and should take no more than 4 ounces of effort to obtain.

Think of it as asking the horse, telling the horse, then promising the horse. Ask, tell, or promise. When you ask the horse to do something, he should do it with a minimum of effort (i.e., 4 ounces) on your part. This is a relative scale and depends on whether the horse responded to your request willingly or grudgingly. Anything between 4 ounces and 4 pounds of effort, you are telling the horse. After that, anything from 4 pounds and beyond, you are promising the horse he is going to do it. The secret is to match the horse's resistance.

For example, if you pull the rein to the right and the horse resists with 4 ounces of effort, you respond by using 4 ounces of effort or strength in your pull. But if he resists with 4 pounds of effort, you respond with a 4-pound pull to counteract his resistance.

The idea in Natural Horse-Man-Ship is to get the horse to yield in all six ways equally, 4 ounces apiece. Here's a scale to point out the differences in yields. In a normal situation, it takes less than 4 ounces of effort to make a horse go forward (since going forward is natural and easy for a horse), up to 400 pounds to stop (especially if it takes a strong pull to make the horse stop), 4 pounds to turn to the left, and 40 pounds to turn to the right (since most horse are stiff to the right), 4 pounds to rear in the air, and up to 4,000 pounds to get him to lie down (one of the hardest things to get a horse to do).

3/ Flexion

There are two types of flexion: mental and physical.

A. Mental flexion comes directly from the human. Humans who are rules-oriented usually do not have flexible horses. Humans who have attitudes that adjust to fit situations usually build flexibility into their horses.

B. There are two types of physical flexion: lateral and vertical.

Lateral flexion is a submissive head position combined with disengagement of the hindquarters to control the horse. With lateral flexion, you use one rein at a time to bend the horse's neck right or left and to cause the back legs to step under the hindquarters. If you bend the horse's neck to the left, the left hind leg should step under the right side of the hindquarters and vice versa.

Vertical flexion is a submissive head position used to engage the hindquarters for propulsion. Here, two reins are used for communication.

Contrary to popular belief, collection is not achieved when a horse tucks his nose in and down. That's only vertical flexion. True collection is when respect, impulsion, and flexion are naturally combined. Respect is mental collection. Impulsion is emotional collection, and flexion is physical collection.

Now your horse can be mentally, emotionally, and physically fit enough to be the calm, cool, and collected partner that you've always wanted.

6½ Qualities for the Human

½/ Heart and Desire

Heart and desire applies to humans in that a horse does not care how much you know until he knows how much you care. One of the natural secrets to horse handling is to show your horse how much you care before and after you show him how much you know. Put your heart in your hand; rub him with your heart.

Good judgment comes from experiencing and learning from your own bad judgment.

1/ Attitude

The attitude of the human is probably the most important thing to the horse. The human should be positive and progressive and believe in the horse's natural point of view. Learn how to be a natural leader, a partner for your horse. Be assertive; don't act like a predator or a wimp.

2/ Feel, 3/ Timing, and 4/ Balance

Feel, timing, and balance are three separate qualities, but they are linked together. With these three things, the human can communicate with the horse.

The quality of feel is something that needs to be developed in the human and is probably one of the things most lacking. The horse feels everything. The human usually only feels the things he doesn't like.

But what gives you feel? There is a four-letter word that starts with "F"—Focus. I say "four-letter word" to get people's attention and make them think. Focus gives you feel. Most people look at their horses trying to get them to do what they want, rather than focusing on where they want to go or what they would like to have happen—getting the feel to go down to the horses' feet.

Feel gives you timing. Get in time with your horse. You shouldn't be 2 seconds late in responding to his actions. Your body should synchronize or mesh with your horse's movements on a consistent basis.

Feel and timing give you balance. If you are in balance with your horse, you are in tune or time with his actions.

The horse is the best teacher of feel, timing, and balance.

5/ Savvy

Savvy means to understand. Every jackass thinks he has horse sense. Most people think like people and so they don't savvy horses. You have to savvy "horse savvy." This means you have to think like a horse. You need to learn from the horse because he's the one who thinks like a horse. In other words, when in Rome, do as the Romans do. And when in the horse corral, do what horses do.

Feel gives you timing, and feel and timing give you balance. Your body should synchronize or mesh with your horse's movements.

6/ Experience

You have to experience experience, and it takes both good and bad experiences to put it all together. Good judgment comes from experiencing and learning from your own bad judgment.

Time in the saddle is one of the best ways to experience horses. How many hours do you have in the saddle? 1,000, 10,000? If you have ridden 100,000 hours on a horse, think how much you'd know. I cannot experience experience for you, but I can share my experiences with you, for secondhand gold is as good as new.

The horse is a natural follower; he is looking for a natural leader, somebody who has the natural attitude, feel, timing, balance, savvy, and experience. As you mature in Natural Horse-Man-Ship, you will find your attitude, feel, timing, balance, savvy, and experience also will mature.

AN
OVERVIEW

KNOWLEDGE

"You should first get a horse's respect while on the ground."

ACCORDING TO Webster, knowledge is familiarity, awareness, or comprehension acquired by experience or study. In Natural Horse-Man-Ship, we experience, learn, and study the "natural" knowledge about horses. That means we understand how horses think, act, and move naturally. This chapter offers you the guidelines for that natural knowledge.

Prey-Predator Relationship

First and foremost, humans need to think of horsemanship from the horse's point of view. We need to think like horses in order to understand and communicate with them.

The main thing to understand is that horses are prey animals and people are predators, and each thinks differently. This is the critical biological distinction between the horse and the human.

Predators usually think in direct lines while prey animals think laterally. Here are definitions of the two types of thinking. A predator (human or animal) is using direct-line thinking when he makes decisions based only on his wants or needs of the moment. A prey animal uses lateral thinking when he considers all the factors and angles before adjusting to fit the situation.

As an example of the difference between prey and predator types of thinking, let's use a mountain lion and a horse who are both thirsty. The predator mountain lion, with direct-line thinking, has no fear and goes to water by walking directly to it. The prey-animal horse, on the other hand, goes to water with a step, look, listen, and smell attitude, always concerned that there is a predator nearby before he puts himself in a vulnerable position. He moves cautiously forward until he perceives there is no danger.

As another example of direct-line predator thinking, most humans don't walk into the pasture with a halter and a lead rope in their hands until they're in the mood to ride. When the horse sees the human predator coming toward him, he perceives the danger of being caught and runs away.

Prey animals, such as horses, cattle, and deer, are programmed by nature to make predators fail. If they weren't, there wouldn't be any around. They need to know how to survive and out-think predators.

Basically, prey animals are born cowards, born claustrophobics, and born full-throttle-aholics. They are born this way in order to survive. They have got to be perceptive to danger, fly from fear, and remain herd-bound.

Do you know what we look like to horses? Predators. We smell like what we eat (meat); our eyes are on the front of our heads; and our ears are back all the time, which, to a horse, is an aggressive expression. We use direct-line thinking, and often we focus on our horses like a mountain lion stalks a foal.

If you don't prove to your horse that you're not a predator, he'll carry that feeling with him through everything you do. For example, if, when riding, you become assertive and try to get your horse to do something, he thinks the predator that has been sleeping on his back all of a sudden has come alive. Then the horse becomes anxious and fearful.

Until you realize what you look like to a horse (a predator), you can't begin to have a communication system with him. You need to know what kind of behavior you should have to get a certain kind of behavior out of the horse.

First of all, you have to prove to the horse that you aren't as bad as you seem. Then, once he accepts that, he becomes gentle. Gentle means he no longer perceives you to be dangerous. After that, he decides to put you in a pecking order to see where you belong in his world: high or low on the respect and authority scale.

A horse is more than just a horse; he's an attitude with four feet. Since the attitude of the horse is one of a prey animal, he is supposed to act the way he does. But in order for a horse to become a horseman, he has to act less like a prey animal. You've got to get him to be perceptive to your cues and communication, rather than to danger. You have to turn his flight from fear into impulsion. And, you've got to get him to want to be with a human, rather than being gregarious just to the herd. You have to take the herd instinct and turn it into bonding with the human.

This is what Natural Horse-Man-Ship is all about. It's easier said than done because horses think in lateral terms and humans think in direct lines, and this is often a source of conflict.

As a prey animal, a horse is a born coward, a born claustrophobic, and a born full-throttle-aholic. With Pat in the saddle, this gray horse has learned to put Mother Nature aside, even though his natural enemy, a mountain lion, is directly above him. Through Natural Horse-Man-Ship, a horse can learn to be braver and less claustrophobic, and he's better able to control his flight from fear.

Three Systems—Respect, Impulsion, Flexion

To me, the horse is very simple. He's got a respect system, an impulsion system, and a flexion system. Throughout this book, I'll try to explain my philosophies of working with and controlling each system.

When I look at a horse, I try to be a diagnostician and a psychoanalyst at the same time. I look at a horse much like a mechanic would look at a gasoline engine with its three systems: air, fuel, and fire. In diagnosing the problem, it's important to know the root of the problem, and which system is causing the trouble.

This horse is definitely having a problem with a rider being on his back. Ninety percent of the time it's a mental problem that causes an emotional problem, which causes a physical problem. In this case, the horse's mental problem was probably that he didn't understand what was being done to him. This, in turn, caused him to be frightened. His fright then caused him to buck to get the "predator" off his back.

Photo by Valerie Michael Ross

As I said, horses, too, have three systems: respect, impulsion, and flexion. The respect system is mental collection; the impulsion system is emotional collection; and the flexion system is physical collection. If you look at the horse in that way, then it's easier to diagnose where the problem is. Ninety-nine percent of the time it's a mental problem that causes an emotional problem that causes a physical problem.

With human beings using direct-line thinking, by the time they notice what is really happening, they only see the physical side of the problem and they diagnose it as such. For example, a horse starts to become unruly. The human feels that if he can just get the horse's nose tucked in, get the head to be vertical, he can get control of the horse and get him collected. He usually uses physical or mechanical means to get this to happen. Rather than engaging in a conversation with the horse, he ends up engaging in a battle with him. That is direct-line thinking.

In lateral thinking, you get the horse's respect and impulsion first, and by doing so, he will be mentally and emotionally collected. Therefore, you won't have to find ways to get him physically collected. You can save that for the time when you refine the basic foundation of his development into advanced communication.

How do you get a horse's respect, impulsion, and flexion? Each will be explained separately.

1/ Respect

You should first get a horse's respect while on the ground. He either respects you and what you ask him to do, or he'll disrespect you. In Natural Horse-Man-Ship, we use lateral longeing techniques to establish respect on the ground. These techniques are described in later chapters.

Respect is hard to get and easy to lose; therefore, you should strive to maintain it.

You must also get and maintain a horse's respect while riding. But first, however, you get a horse's respect by proving you're the alpha animal (primary or superior animal, the leader) while on the ground. This is where the relationship starts. This is the first and foremost way to get a horse's respect. But before you get his respect, you have to get his heart and desire. If you're dealing with a horse who does not want to be around you, then getting his respect is a shallow or meaningless thing. Because if he doesn't want to be around you, he won't respect you or want to perform for you either.

There are many ways that a human can cause a horse to want to be around him. One way is to provide many of the little niceties of life, such as grain, carrots, sugar, and a good scratching. Often, you'll get advice not to give the horse these treats for fear you might spoil him. I suggest there are ways you can learn how to provide these nice things, yet still get the horse's respect through your relationship with him. This relationship should be one with you as the leader and the horse, the follower. You establish this relationship through the six yields.

The six yields are the six basic movements that a horse can do: go forward, backward, right, left, up, and down.

These are the same movements we direct through lateral longeing. There are three attitudes the horse can take in doing these six things: a/ He can escape from you in these six ways. b/ He can disrespect you in these six ways; or c/ he can yield to and from you in these six ways.

It's important to understand the difference between escape, disrespect, and yielding to and from pressure. Escape is usually out of fear or confusion. Disrespect comes from contempt or disregard for the human. And yielding to and from pressure is caused by respect for the human as the leader.

The horse will give the human respect if the human upholds his four responsibilities, which are: 1/ to not act like a predator (be mentally, emotionally, and physically fit); 2/ to have an independent seat; 3/ to think like a horse and not a human; and 4/ to use the natural power of focus. (Read more about horse and human responsibilities later in this chapter.) With the latter, if you focus on where you're going and what you want to do, your horse will sense your decisiveness, respect you for it, and follow you as the leader.

I will give you $1,000 if you can show me someone who has these four things under control, provided you give me $10 for everyone I can show you who doesn't. I can show you thousands of horses who don't have respect for humans because the humans haven't shown the horses (through lateral longeing) that they should respect them on the ground.

2/ Impulsion

How do you get a horse's impulsion? Impulsion is probably one of the most difficult concepts to grasp, since it is essentially emotional collection. A lot of people think that they have impulsion when the horse's motor is running, when he's going forward. Actually, impulsion is controlled forward energy that comes from behind (the horse's hindquarters). It stems from mental collection or respect which, in turn, harnesses the emotional collection of the horse.

We've all ridden horses who were emotionally scattered. Scattered is a word that is the antithesis or just the opposite of collected. An emotionally scattered horse drives from behind and is going forward, but it's through escape. It's not a yield. Escape is impulsiveness.

Through the six yields, impulsion happens naturally because the horse already has it. All we have to do is orchestrate the horse in such a way that he doesn't lose it when we get on his back. After all, in riding what we are trying to do is get horses to do natural acts that they already do but with humans on their backs.

With impulsion in the physical sense, "Go equals whoa, and whoa equals go." That means if you have snappy departures, you should have equally graceful, downward transitions? With most horses, it takes less than 4 ounces of effort to make them have snappy departures, but 400 pounds to make downward transitions. In other words, it takes very little to make them move forward, but lots to make them stop.

With other horses, it requires an effort to make them go, but very little suggestion to make them slow down or stop. This is the other extreme I call non-responsive. Impulsion is getting "go" and "whoa" balanced where both are equal. It should take only 4 ounces to get a horse to go full tilt, and it should takes only 4 ounces to get him to come down to a halt and a back-up.

3/ Flexion

To be physically flexible, the horse first must have mental flexibility, and he has that by having a human who is flexible, one who is able to adjust to fit whatever situation arises. If the human is flexible, the horse can be flexible, too. Non-flexibility can be seen in a horse who is sluggish away from the barn, but yet he jigs back to the barn; or when on a trail ride, he wants to be ridden only when things are quiet. If things get a little raucous, he gets nervous and lets his surroundings bother him. There are many other ways to see lack of mental flexibility in horses.

If your horse is having trouble with mental flexibility, go back to getting his

Vertical flexion is more than just getting a horse's nose in and down.

respect before you ask for impulsion and the physical aspects of flexion.

In regard to the physical aspects of flexion, there are two types: lateral flexion and vertical flexion. Lateral flexion is for control of the horse, and vertical flexion is for communication with the horse.

With respect to lateral flexion, think of the horse as an arrow. The straighter he is, the faster, the stronger, the farther he can go. The more bent he is, the less chance he has of going somewhere. For example, if you pull the left rein on a horse who is running and take the life out of the left side of the horse's body, the right side cannot run any faster than the left side. So if the left side is in a complete arc, the right side will be in an arc as well, and vice versa. The horse will move in a tight circle. You'll have control of the horse's body and, therefore, the horse.

Vertical flexion is more than just getting a horse's nose in and down. Think of a horse's body as a buggy whip. The base of the whip, which is the thickest part, is compared to the horse's hindquarters. The lash or thin end is like his head and neck. Bend the whip and bring the lash end of the whip in (like the horse's neck when his head is on the vertical). As the whip bends, it gets strong over its top end, and it puts the power to the base (or hindquarters). This is what happens when you engage the horse's hindquarters.

This is good as long as the horse has the right attitude. Remember, a horse is an attitude with four feet. If he is scared or mad or disrespectful and you use vertical flexion, you've just engaged his hindquarters and caused him to be more powerful and possibly more dangerous. It's like letting the clutch out. It's common to see horses with their noses tucked to their chests running off. In order for a horse to rear, prance, run off, or any of these things, he needs to have power to his hindquarters. Therefore, using vertical flexion is a great way of getting your horse to do what you don't want him to do in a magnified way.

On the other hand, using one rein for lateral flexion takes the power away from the horse because it causes him to cross his hind legs under each other. This puts him in a base-narrow stance and disengages his hindquarters. A quick way for you to feel this is for you to stand with your left heel to your right toe. Left foot in front, right foot behind. See how powerless your stance is? Whereas if you spread your legs in a wide stance, your body would be in a powerful position; i.e. engaged. By being disengaged, a horse doesn't have the power to run, rear, prance, etc.

Dynamics of Horse Movement

To be an effective horseman, you should know how a horse moves, how his feet work to make him perform. Knowing where a horse's feet are at all times and where his weight should be helps you to know how to help him do what you want him to do with a natural balance.

Horses have five natural gaits: walk, trot, canter, gallop, and back up. Of course, gaited horses, such as Tennessee Walkers and Paso Finos, differ from this norm. For the most part, gaited horses don't trot, but perform a smooth, ambling, four-beat, lateral gait, sometimes referred to as an intermediate or single-foot gait. In most of these lateral gaits, each foot hits the ground separately in a rapid, rhythmic fashion, which produces a smooth ride.

For the purposes of this book, however, I'll refer to the vast majority of riding horses who have the five gaits mentioned above. The horse's footfall patterns are different for every gait, and the number of beats that occur in each stride of each gait varies.

Beats in each gait: 1/ walk—four; 2/ trot—two; 3/ canter—three; 4/ gallop—four; 5/ back-up—two.

When a horse is standing still, such as in a halt, he has all four feet standing at once. Therefore, I like to say that horses have five natural gaits and a place called halt.

The following is a description of each footfall pattern. The photos demonstrate the footfall sequence.

1/ Walk—If you start counting each of the four beats with the front feet, the pattern would be: right front, left hind, left front, right hind. But if you start counting with the hind feet, the pattern would be: right hind, right front, left hind, left front.

2/ Trot—The trot has two beats because the legs work in diagonal pairs: right hind-left front, and left hind-right front. To post to the right, I suggest you rise in the stirrups when the right hind and left front legs lift and vice versa.

3/ Canter or lope—This is a three-beat gait with the horse's legs hitting the ground in the following three-beat manner. For a left lead: right hind foot strikes the ground first, followed by the diagonal left hind and right front, then the left front foot hits last. For a right lead: left hind strikes the ground first, followed by a diagonal right hind and left front, then the right front foot hits last. There is a moment of suspension, when all four feet are off the ground, after the leading front foot hits the ground and before the new stride starts with the hind foot.

Note: One of the three beats is a pair of diagonal legs hitting the ground at the same time. Go back and study the diagonals at the trot to see the correlation.

4/ Gallop—Although the gallop appears to be a faster version of the canter, it is actually a four-beat gait. However, the horse still has a leading leg, just like he did in the canter. For a left lead, the footfall pattern is: right hind, left hind, right front, left front. For a right lead: left hind, right hind, left front, right front. The moment of suspension follows the leading leg as it does in the canter.

5/ Back-Up—The back-up and the trot are both two-beat gaits, thus they are related. When a horse moves backward naturally and without interference, he does it in a two-beat diagonal fashion. Only with normal interference (versus natural guidance) from the rider will the horse switch over and do an awkward four-beat gait.

By their footfall pattern, horses actually trot backward. Their feet move in diagonal pairs as they do in a trot, only backwards: right front moves with the left hind, and left front moves with the right hind.

By now you can probably see the close relationship between the back-up and the trot. You'll find that the only real difference between the two is the fact that in the back-up, the horse's weight is tipped back 51 to 70 percent. The trot is the only gait the horse can do in place because his weight is distributed 50/50. He can literally trot in place.

Because both the trot and the back-up have a diagonal movement, you should understand how often a horse uses his diagonals in his natural movements. For example, in the canter, one of the three beats is a diagonal move. Therefore, by getting good at backing up and trotting, you'll better understand how to coordinate with the horse's hind legs in the canter. For instance, by clueing into the left hind leg in the diagonal movement during the trot (instead of the right front), you can get in rhythm with your horse for a left lead canter.

On their own, horses do not normally move their feet backward or sideways often. However, we use these maneuvers often in riding, and, therefore, the horse needs to be familiar and comfortable with them. The better your horse yields backward, as well as sideways, the better he will do everything else. By this I mean, if you've developed your horse to be light, supple, and responsive enough so that backing up and side-passing are easy for him, he's probably light, supple, and responsive enough for all other maneuvers.

WALK
—four beats

The descriptions of the following gaits refer to the feet the horse has on the ground, with the exception of the walk. To show the walk effectively in a photographic sequence, the foot just about to be put on the ground is the one shown lifted in the photo.

First beat—right front

Second beat—left hind

*Third beat—
left front*

*Fourth beat—
right hind*

TROT
—two beats

First beat—right hind and left front

Second beat—left hind and right front

First beat—right hind and left front

Second beat—left hind and right front

CANTER or LOPE —three beats

This sequence shows a horse on the right lead.

First beat— left hind

Second beat— right hind and left front

*Third beat—
right front*

Suspension

GALLOP —four beats

This sequence shows a horse on the right lead.

First beat—left hind

Second beat—right hind

Third beat—left front

Fourth beat—*a/ Right front*

b/ Pushing off right front

Suspension

BACK UP
—two beats

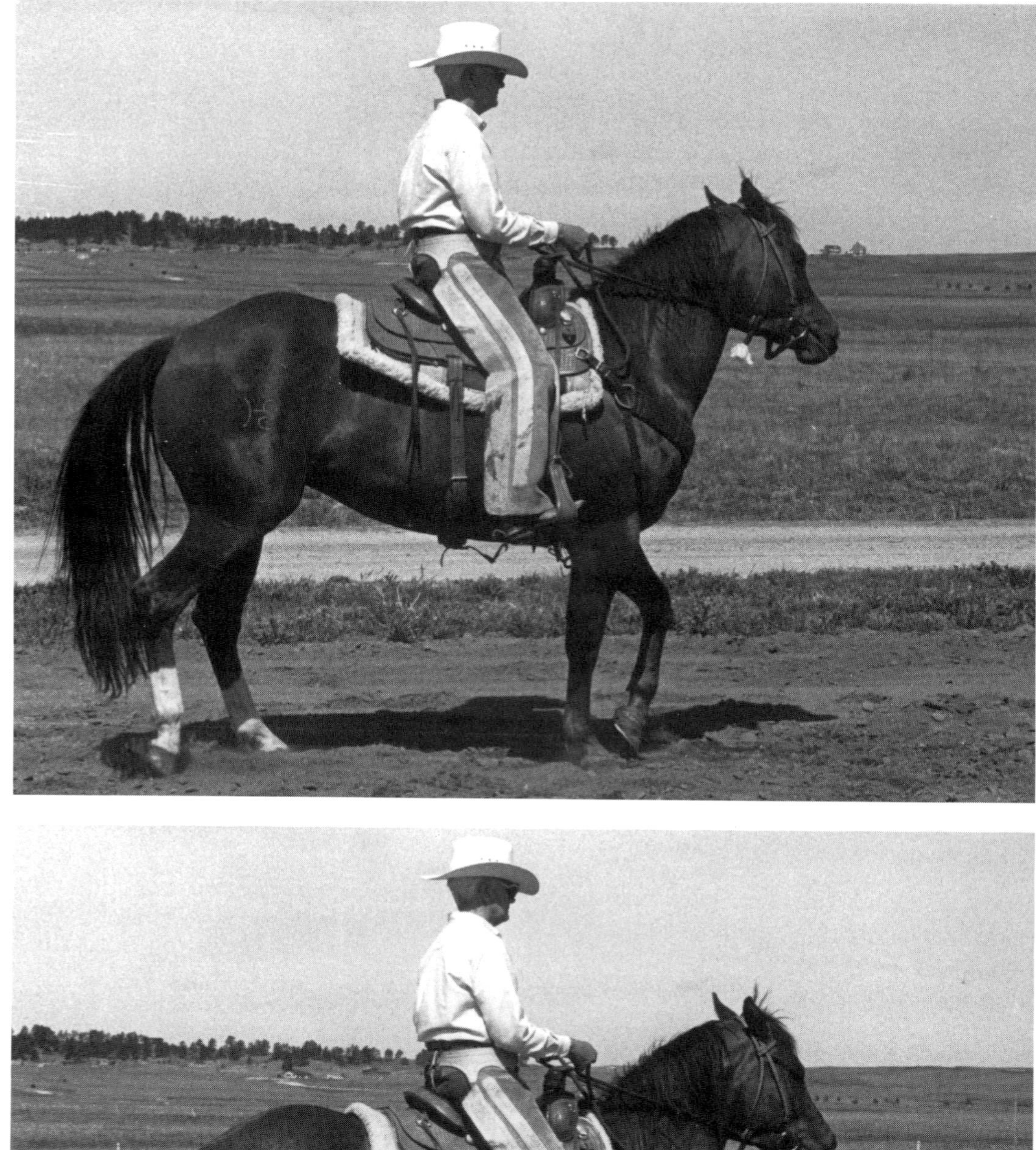

First beat—
right front and
left hind

Second beat—
left front and
right hind

First beat—
right front and
left hind

Second beat—
left front and
right hind

Understand that whatever spirit a horse has is what you've got to deal with, and leave it alone.

Gait Speed

Each gait basically has three speeds: slow, medium, and fast. In some circles, these speeds are referred to as collected (slow), working or regular (medium), and extended (fast). However, extended gaits aren't necessarily extremely fast gaits. Extension is the opposite of collection. In collection, the horse gathers his body and puts it into a tighter frame with a higher stride than he does during his normal or regular working body position. In extended gaits, the horse's body frame lengthens along with his stride.

I need to make one other distinction regarding collection. To me, it's not just the horse's body frame, but his frame of mind. Collection is a combination of respect, impulsion, and flexion naturally combined. It's not just when the horse tucks his nose in and down. That's only vertical flexion.

Horse's Distribution of Body Weight

A horse's body weight is never static. It moves or shifts as he moves and it's different in each of his gaits.

1/ Halt—When standing, a horse has most of his weight on his front end—approximately 60 percent.

2/ Walk—At the walk, a horse carries approximately 60 percent of his weight on his front end.

3/ Trot—While trotting, a horse carries his weight evenly—50 percent on the front end and 50 percent on the hindquarters. The trot is the only gait that a horse can do in place. This is called the piaffe, in dressage lingo.

4/ Canter—When cantering or loping, a horse tips his weight back with approximately 60 percent on the hindquarters and 40 percent on the front.

5/ Gallop—During the gallop, a horse's body weight tips forward between 51 and 70 percent.

6/ Back-Up—In this gait, a horse carries between 51 to 70 percent of his weight on his hindquarters. If it goes over that, the horse would sit down or tip over. If it goes under that percentage, the horse is probably performing a piaffe.

It's good to learn where a horse's weight is naturally at all gaits and do what he does. For example, to get a horse to take a particular lead, don't lean forward, because his weight needs to be tipped to his hindquarters. That's where your weight should be.

Every horse has a drive line (center of balance), which is situated near his withers. To be in natural balance, try to stay behind the drive line. The only time you should stick your nose in front of that drive line is when you're roping, racing, going uphill, jumping, or getting bucked off.

Horse-Analities

Just as important as knowing how a horse moves is knowing how a horse feels about what he is doing. In playing with different horses, I've noticed that all horses have their own "horse-analities," or what we call personalities in people.

A horse-anality is based on three things: 1/ innate characteristics, 2/ learned behavior, and 3/ spirit. Every horse has his own horse-anality because of these three separate ingredients.

Innate characteristics are what the horse is born with, his genetic makeup. I've talked about horses being born cowards, born claustrophobics, and born full-throttle-aholics. To what degree was the horse born with these characteristics? How much of a coward is he? Some horses are born as gentle as dogs, and others snort at everything the day after they are born. These are innate characteristics. The horse hasn't had time to learn about anything else yet.

Horses get their learned behavior first from their mothers, second from the herd, third from their environment, and fourth from us. Humans can be involved in the learned behavior in different stages, such as foal imprinting and critical learning

Horses get their learned behavior from their mothers, the herd, the environment, and from humans. People can have a great impact on foals during critical early learning periods right after birth. This foal learns to lead with just a progress string around his body.

periods. We have to realize that part of the horse's horse-anality today is based on his learned behavior. A horse can actually change his horse-anality or modify it through learned behavior.

Spirit is part of a horse's innate package, but has to do with the amount of life or energy he puts into things. Spirit is the multiplying factor. For example, horses are born with the innate characteristic to be sensitive and aware of things. If a horse doesn't have a lot of spirit, he is not going to put a whole lot of energy into his sensitivity or awareness. But a horse with a lot of spirit is going to really react to something another horse would practically ignore. Some horses are born spooky, but they don't have a lot of spirit. But one that is born spooky and spirited is a lot of horse to deal with.

When selecting a horse, you should select one with the innate characteristics you like and those that fit your personality, whether it is mental attributes, disposition, or spirit. Be careful to pick the spirit that fits you. A lot of people tend to pick their poison and often are out-spirited by their horses. Then, they try to subdue the horses through mechanical or physical means. After they get frustrated or afraid, they sell those horses and then go out and buy other horses with exactly the same innate characteristics and spirit. Don't pick your poison!

Understand that whatever spirit a horse has is what you've got to deal with, and leave it alone. If you don't, you'll destroy the horse's spirit, and that's a mortal sin to a Natural Horse-Man.

Learn how horse-analities are made up and become a good "pick" or selector of horse-analities that fit your personality. Pick the type of horse-anality that you're able to deal with effectively. The part that you can modify or change or shape up the way you like is through learned behavior. So by becoming a good pick of horse-analities, you're making sure that your personality and your horse's horse-anality profiles match. It's important to understand at what level of Natural Horse-Man-Ship you are so you can pick a horse to fit your particular situation.

Horse Talents

Horses have six, basic, natural talents: 1/ running; 2/ jumping, 3/ bucking, 4/ herding, 5/ playing, and 6/ pulling.

We use these talents, or a combination of these talents, for the various sports we play with horses. A natural horseman should learn to become a good judge of a horse's potential through aptitude testing.

I have found that the best way to find a horse's aptitude for any of these six talents is to watch a horse, particularly a young horse, when he is at play or when he is scared. A horse will never be more athletic than at those two times. A horse who is fast will jump out in front of the others. One who is apt to jump or buck well, will at that time. One who is bold enough for herding will show that by herding his pasture mates. Horses who are apt to do a lot of turning and spinning, prancing, dancing, and all the natural maneuvers we ask horses to do in dressage or reining will do so if they are innately strong on frolicking or playing.

Throughout history, humans have observed horses and made sport of the different talents their horses have. For example, one day someone might have said, "My horse is faster than your horse," and the person he was talking to disbelieved him. They wagered on a race between the two horses.

When two people wanted to see whose horse could jump the highest, they created the contest of jumping. Then, there always was the horse who couldn't be rode, and the cowboy who couldn't be throwed, and rodeo came into being. It's easy to see how sports involving running, jumping, and bucking evolved.

Herding, playing, and pulling are probably not as self-explanatory as running, jumping, and bucking.

Herding is a natural instinct in horses, derived from an innate trait to keep the herd together, which means safety. It's stronger in some individuals than in others. It stems from the herd hierarchy and structure. In today's world, the naturalness some horses have to herd and to dominate has been genetically coded and bred into them. We call these horses "cow horses," or we say that such a horse has a lot of "cow." There are various forms of cow horses, from roping horses to cutting horses. I've noticed that most cutting horses are also very dominant horses within the herd.

Watching horses at play has always been a favorite pastime for humans. And I'm sure that people have long dreamed of being able to duplicate the natural acts that horses perform when they frolic while they are on the horses' backs. I think this has helped develop the sports of dressage and reining, which are English and western counterparts to each other. In them, the rider basically asks his horse to more or less frolic and do the other athletic maneuvers.

Pulling has always been the hallmark of the strong horse. Throughout history, big, strong horses have pulled plows, wagons, and carriages as part of their work. Today, we also enjoy pulling and driving for recreation and contest.

What's important in all this is to remember that while we try to genetically code our horses and breed them for specific things, this does not always work. Often, horses who are bred for something specific are not good at that particular activity. On the other hand, there are others who weren't bred for a certain activity, yet they fool their owners and become great. They had talent no one knew they had.

If we'll be more objective in our analyzation of a horse's aptitudes, there might be a gem in the rough waiting to be discovered. When you're disappointed that your race horse does not show speed, maybe he has other talents, such as jumping or running barrels.

For example, Doc Bar was bred to be a race horse, yet he was a halter horse, and later became the all-time sire of great cutting horses. Some of his sons, daughters, and grandget have made their names known among reining and pleasure horse circles as well.

I had a personal example some years ago. A girl brought a horse to me to be trained. She had raised the horse and wanted to use him as a trail horse. This horse, an Appaloosa, was somewhat spirited and a real natural at stopping and turning around. The owner had no interest in having the horse for any other purpose than trail riding. The horse would have been okay at trail riding, but he was great at reining. The solution that we came up with was to sell him to somebody who was looking for exactly that type of horse. With the money she received, she bought herself a horse who better fit her needs. Everybody, including the horses, came out on top.

So, pay attention to your horse's talents, traits, and characteristics. If he is a real bossy individual, he might be exhibiting some talents as a cutting horse. If he constantly jumps out of his pasture or pen, he might be your next jumping champion.

Eight Responsibilities

In the partnership of horse and human, each has responsibilites.

Four Responsibilities of the Human

Most people tend to do the wrong things at the right time because they haven't upheld their four responsibilities in the partnership.

1/ Act like a partner, not like a predator.

To not act like a predator, the human must be mentally, emotionally, and physically fit. Mental fitness means to learn the natural knowledge about horses; emotional fitness means to be stable to deliver good leadership; and physical fitness means to be able to ride the horse and stay out of his way.

2/ Have an independent seat.

An independent seat starts with being mentally, emotionally, and physically fit.

An independent seat means that you do not use the reins for balance; you do not squeeze below your knees for grip; and you do not use two reins in an "Oh, no" situation. When the horse starts acting like a prey animal, the human shouldn't act like a predator by pulling back on the reins and squeezing him in the belly at the same time. Instead, the human should reach down one rein and bend the horse, using lateral flexion.

3/ Think like a horse.

The next thing is learning to think like a horse, rather than a human. That's what this whole section on knowledge is about. It's a responsibility of the human to learn to think laterally, which means to look at a situation as a horse would. Instead of immediately reacting to a situation like a human, try to see it from the horse's point of view.

For example, you should know that horses do not have great depth perception, but humans do. Knowing that a horse has bilateral vision and is color blind helps you to walk a minute or a mile in the horse's horseshoes. If you can do that, you have one of the ingredients in becoming a Natural Horse-Man.

It takes time to study horses to see what motivates them. One good way is to watch horses in a herd situation, where they act and react the way nature programmed them.

4/ Use the natural power of focus.

The human should come to understand and use the natural power of focus. What does focus mean? In every endeavor, sport, or anything we do, whether it is flying an airplane, driving a car, running a hurdle race, or snow skiing, focus and the line of direction are the most important ingredients.

What does this means in relationship to horses? If you look where you're going, your horse will take you where you want to go. Most people look at their horses' heads because of a lack of emotional fitness. Typically, when the horse, a live animal, acts up beneath an emotionally unfit rider, he or she gasps, tightens up, and looks down at the horse.

This is where learning about the natural power of focus comes into play. Pick something in the distance and ride to it. Then pick another point in the distance and ride to it. The horse will learn to follow under you. He will follow your lead.

Here's a concept I'd like for you to consider. There is a place called somewhere; there's a place called nowhere; and there's a place called somewhere else. If you want to go somewhere, say straight ahead, you've got to look there; you've got to focus straight ahead of you. If you want to go somewhere else, you've got to look to your right or left and go somewhere else. If you want to go nowhere, look down at the ground and go nowhere.

Focus has got to be the first thing that happens. Then your body will follow and your horse will follow the suggestions of your body. If you focus on going to the right, your eyes roll to the right and then your head turns to the right, which turns the neck, which turns the spine, which then turns the pelvis; then your hands come. This is what happens before what happens happens, and this is what the horse feels. As you look to the right, your right hand goes off to the right and your left hand comes over to the right. Your right leg opens up, your left leg pushes across. All of these things happen in association with focusing on where you want to go or on what you want to do. This is why it's so important to understand the power of focus.

Four Responsibilities of the Horse

Horses are subject to normality also. The normal thing for horses to become is frightened prey animals. But they can become gentle, ridable animals, too.

In order for a partnership between horse and human to happen, the horse has to have some responsibilities, just like the human.

1/ Act like a partner, not like a prey animal.

First of all, the horse needs to learn, through exposure and experience, how not to act like a prey animal—a born coward, born claustrophobic, and born full-throttle-aholic. One way to do this is to expose the horse in such a way that he becomes more mentally, emotionally, and physically fit.

For example, when you say "whoa," your horse must learn to stop physically, mentally, and emotionally. He must not only come to a complete halt, but mentally shift gears, and emotionally calm down. He has to willingly quit whatever he's doing. He must understand that quitting at your request is one of the ultimate rewards. His new motto becomes: "Don't just do something, stand there." The horse has learned to stop, think about things, and stay gregarious with the human who's on his back.

How do we get a horse to do this? Again, through exposure and experience you can teach a horse not to do something, but just stand there. The best way I know to get a horse to not act like a prey animal is for the human to not act like a predator—neither a scared predator, nor an angry one.

2/ Not change gaits.

The horse needs to learn to maintain his gait by himself. It shouldn't be necessary to continually leg him on or hold him back. It's a frustrating thing when you have to hold a horse back with the bit or to push him on with spurs. If you're walking, he should walk, not jig, trot, canter, or stop.

One of the tests to see if your horse is a dependable horse is to put him on a loose rein and ask him to hold that gait, whether you're traveling alone or in a group. The trot is a good gait to do this in because it's faster than a walk, but not as fast as a canter. There's a potential for the horse to make a mistake either way. He can slow down to the walk or speed up to the canter.

3/ Not change directions.

The horse needs to learn to not change directions. If you rein your horse to go in a certain direction, he should not take off on his own and go the way he wants.

If you left a horse up to his own devices, he might go back to the barn or over to the gate (if you're in an arena). You have to let a horse know that if he does these things, you're going to do something about it. You're going to cause those undesirable things to be difficult, and, he'll learn that it's much easier to do the things you desire.

4/ Watch where he's going.

The horse needs to look where we are asking him to put his feet. This is something that a horse does naturally for himself while he is out in the pasture. But unless the human sets it up and requires the horse to watch where he's going, the horse will leave it up to the human to watch where they're going.

Most humans, when they ride horses, turn them at every corner of the arena they come to, as though the horse would run into the fence. If there were a jump or log on the ground, the human almost invariably looks down at it and picks up on the reins as if to say to the horse, "You're a dumb horse, let me look at it for you."

We have to learn to develop this responsibility in our horses. I'm not saying just turn him loose and hope everything comes out. This is just one of our many goals.

The difference between Natural Horse-Man-Ship and normal horsemanship is that most people are not aware of their responsibilities, and, at the same time, take the horse's responsibilities away from him. The natural horseman gets his horse to accept his four responsibilities while at the same time he accepts his own.

Communication Aids

The communication aids we were born with include hands, arms, legs, feet, seat, voice, and even facial expressions. Eighty percent of all communication, whether it is between humans and horses or humans and humans, is non-verbal. It's very easy to give a prey animal a conflicting aid. It would be like looking to the right and saying, "Don't look to the left." These are very easy things to do, especially if the human is not mentally, emotionally, and physically fit, does not have an independent seat, thinks like a person instead of a horse, and does not know the natural power of focus.

In communicating to the horse, you should cause the undesirable thing to be difficult and allow the desirable thing to be easy.

Almost every undesirable thing a horse does can be based on the fact that most horses are overfed and underexercised. Feeding means protein and nutrient intake, and exercise means mental and emotional, as well as physical output.

The natural horse usually runs in a herd on the open range with plenty of land to roam. The horses in the herd get all the mental, emotional, and physical exercise they need. They travel up to 30 miles a day, playing dominance games about who is going to drink out of the water hole first, and watching out for predators. By the time the day is done, they've all balanced themselves with the amount of nutritional intake they need as well as mental, emotional, and physical exercise.

Very few stabled horses get that. Most are overfed and underexercised because very few riders offer horses much more than just adequate physical exercise. The object is to give the horse the mental and emotional exercise he needs along with physical exercise. Be a provocative horse owner. If the horse is supposed to be recreation for you, can you be recreation for your horse?

Positive and Negative Reinforcement Versus Punishment and Reward

Punishment and reward is something you do after the fact. Positive and negative reinforcement is something that happens at the fact. For example, when a horse puts his nose on an electric fence, he gets a negative reinforcement immediately.

An example of positive reinforcement: You ask the horse to yield sideways with steady leg pressure and at his slightest try, you release the pressure. You let him know how to get away the pressure.

An example of reward: One of your employees did a good deed and you never said anything, but you rewarded him with a $50 bonus in his paycheck a week later. He'd appreciate that, but in the interim, he might have thought that you didn't even notice. He might have cussed you for not giving praise and recognition at the moment of his good deed. Positive reinforcement would have been to praise the employee immediately.

Positive and/or negative reinforcement is doing less sooner, instead of more later. This is what a "causer" does. He causes all of his ideas to become the horse's ideas, but he understands the horse's ideas first. At the slightest try, he gives positive reinforcement.

There is a difference between what motivates prey animals and predators. Predators need praise, recognition, and money in that order. What motivates prey animals, however, is being comfortable—moving toward comfort areas, and moving away from discomfort areas. This is a completely different psychology. Petting your dog is an example of praise and recognition of one predator to another.

Prey animals are comfort seekers. It's not what you do. It's when you quit doing what you're doing that gives the horse his comfort zone. First, he is comfortable because he's either doing nothing or his own thing, and he enjoys it. Then you stimulate him to do something, and he's uncomfortable because now he has to work and probably doesn't really want to. When he tries to respond to you, even slightly, you stop stimulating him immediately and leave him alone. Then he's back to his comfort zone again.

Rating System

When it comes to performance of any kind, I rate everything the horse does. The scale goes from a -10 for the worst possible ill response or reaction a horse can have, all the way up to a +10 for the best response.

A horse can have a response, an ill response, or a reaction. A response has thought process, understanding, and respect. An ill response has thought process, understanding, and disrespect. A reaction has no thought process, no understanding, and has fear and/or surprise involved.

The response starts on the positive side of 0. Anything below 0 has to be either an ill response or a reaction. Depending on the severity of the ill response, that's how far down the scale the horse is rated. Every time you ask for one of the six yields or a combination of them, try to rate how well the horse did. If the horse responded to you, rate it anywhere from a 1 on up. If the horse had an ill response or a reaction to you, rate it as a negative from 0 on down. 0 is actually not as bad a score as you think.

The horse is involved with the rating system as well. How would the horse rate you on your communication? Was it soft, obvious, and steady? Or was it hard, confusing, and jerky or jabby? You have to be subjective and do the rating for the horse. You've got to be realistic in how the horse would have viewed the communication that you gave.

Rate everything your horse does, from his riding performance to his manners on the ground. Here Pat asks a horse to climb an embankment as he tails after the animal. What score do you think he would give the horse? The two obviously have their communication system working well.

AN OVERVIEW

TOOLS

"You should be able to tell a Natural Horse-Man by the tools he uses and the ones he won't."

IN NATURAL Horse-Man-Ship, we use the bigger brain instead of the bigger bit approach. Wouldn't you like to be able to communicate with your horse with no strings attached, no halters, no lead ropes, no bits, no spurs, no sticks—just you and your horse at liberty with each other? It's possible through Natural Horse-Man-Ship. However, in your journey through Natural Horse-Man-Ship, you must first understand what the four categories of tools are and how to use them naturally.

Every horseman uses tools to communicate with his horse. These tools are aids and there are two kinds: artificial and natural. Natural aids are what you were born with: hands, arms, legs, voice, seat. Artificial aids are anything you are not born with. You weren't born with a stick in your hand, halter, lead rope, and spurs.

There are four categories of artificial aids and all four are used for teaching, controlling, reinforcing, and refining something specific. In later chapters, each will be described in detail.

Four categories of tools: 1/ halters and ropes, jaquimas (hackamores), and mecates—for basic communication, 2/ sticks—as extensions of your arms, 3/ bits—for riding refinement, and 4/ spurs—as extensions of your legs.

With these four categories of tools, you can play with any horse and build a natural foundation between the two of you. The halter and lead rope are to be used to teach, control, reinforce, and refine the six yields (forward, backward, right, left, up, and down) on the ground, as well as on the horse's back. The stick can be used as an extension of your arms to teach, control, reinforce, and refine the six yields while on horse's back or on the ground. The bit is used to teach, control, reinforce, and refine the six yields while on his back. The spur is used as an extension of your legs to teach, control, reinforce, and refine the six yields while on the horse's back.

There are common misconceptions about the use of these tools. One is that halters and lead ropes are for dragging a horse from point A to point B and then tying him to point B. Another is that a stick is used to make a horse go forward, and/or to flog the horse with when the rider is mad or completely frustrated with the horse.

In riding, a bit is usually used as a set of brakes or a steering wheel. In Spanish, the word for bit is "freno." Freno is also brakes for a wagon or a car. However, it's a universally misunderstood concept that a bit is a brake or a lever with which to stop a horse.

Since the snaffle bit gives you all you need to put a foundation on a horse, it is the only bit I will refer to in this book.

Many riders think that spurs are used to make horses go faster. How often do you see jockeys wear spurs? The spur is not to lengthen the horse's stride, but to heighten his stride and/or cause him to move laterally.

These misconceptions are all part of normal horsemanship and not having the natural knowledge about horses, or knowing what the tools are naturally used for.

The object of this book is to show you how to use the keys and principles that I describe. Any technique, tool, or piece of knowledge that I offer you in this book will work for you if you use the natural attitude, feel, timing, balance, savvy, and experience.

You should be able to tell a Natural Horse-Man by the tools he uses. But, you should also be able to tell a Natural Horse-Man by the tools he doesn't use. In other words, the tools he wouldn't use would be regarded as restrictive devices, such as tie-downs, martingales, cavessons, and different types of bits designed as torture devices. There are many things that people use to restrict a horse's movement and/or behavior. These are all what I consider and classify as good excuses for bad hands and not enough knowledge.

There are three major differences between what a Natural Horse-Man does with horses and what most other people do. First, Natural Horse-Men play with horses, rather than work with horses. Second, the tools they use are simplistic, user-friendly, and horse-friendly, and third, the techniques they use are lateral-thinking techniques, described in later chapters.

The tools of a Natural Horse-Man are hackamores (made of natural materials, such as rope, rawhide, or leather), four lengths of rope (6-, 12-, 22-, and 45-foot, for use on the ground), sticks (used as an extension of your arm), plain snaffle bits, some leverage bits, a mild set of spurs (used as an extension of your legs), and the saddle of your choice. Accessories are such things as chaps and gloves.

Every horseman uses tools to communicate with his horse.

I keep my equipment in what I call a "portable round corral," which is much like a sailor's sea bag. I have been able to go around the world and work many different kinds of horses in all types of situations with just these tools.

Most people exercise their horses in arenas, round corrals, or on longe lines. Troy Henry, one of my mentors, once told me that using a round corral or a longe line is the easiest way to develop a relationship with the horse, if used naturally. But if used normally, it's the easiest way to ruin your horse's mind.

Most people who read this book don't own, and never will own, a round corral. Therefore, I haven't listed a conventional round corral as a tool. If the natural attitude, feel, timing, balance, savvy, and experience are applied to the Natural Horse-Man's tools, you can gain the same psychological advantage as though you were in a round corral, without the physical boundaries of the round corral.

AN
OVERVIEW

TECHNIQUES

"It's important to be mentally, emotionally, and physically fit to ride."

THE DYNAMICS of horsemanship have been most often explained with these normal techniques: saddle a horse and get on, kick him to go, and pull him to stop. Often, the person who is doing the explaining will throw in, "Oh yeah, rein him across the neck to get him to turn."

The dynamics and techniques of Natural Horse-Man-Ship are vastly different. Here are some to consider.

Lateral Longeing

For centuries, people have owned, bred, and fed horses to be dynamic and energetic, yet for the same amount of time people have longed horses to get rid of their excess energy. (And often they longe them in mindless circles to the left.) Usually, what happens is the horse gets stronger and stronger physically and weaker and weaker mentally. In other words, when you do this, you exercise the horses's body, but not his mind.

Lateral longeing is a term I use to describe a communication system between human and horse. This communication system is built on the six yields—causing a horse to go forward, backward, right, left, up, or down. The yields are first performed on a 12-foot lead rope, then increasingly longer lengths of rope. Used separately or in combination, the yields turn into a series of maneuvers that exercise the horse's mind along with his body.

This is where lateral longeing differs from normal longeing. In lateral longeing, you exercise the horse's mind, causing the horse to yield to you mentally. When you do this, his body naturally follows.

In normal longeing, the handler exercises the horse's body with no thought to communicating with the horse, just letting him work off the edge so he'll be easier to ride. With normal longeing, if it takes 10 minutes to wear down the horse today, in 2 weeks, it will take 20. Two weeks from then, the horse will be more fit, and it will take 40 minutes. Pretty soon, you and two strong men can't get the horse to settle down.

With lateral longeing, it might take an hour today to get your horse mentally collected, but tomorrow it will only take half an hour. The third day it might only take 15 minutes. The fourth day it might take only 7½ minutes, then 3¼. In time, you can tell which side of the corral your horse got up on within 2 or 3 minutes.

When you use lateral longeing as a ritual, you can get your horse to become mentally collected in an extremely short amount of time. As you go through this book, you'll find that mental collection gives you emotional collection, which gives you the ability to get the horse physically collected. Then, you are on your way to building a lifetime partnership.

Remember that prior and proper preparation is what prevents poor performance. Prior and proper preparation on the ground means getting the horse mentally in tune with the human through lateral longeing. Instead of going in circles, you have the opportunity to get your horse to go backward and sideways. It's been a saying among natural horsemen that the better a horse backs up and goes sideways, the better he does everything else.

There are only six things a horse can do: go forward, backward, right, left, up, and down. He can also do combinations of those six movements. So, if you can get your horse to go forward, backward, and sideways when you want him to, then you're already building in snappy departures, smooth downward transitions, and graceful turns and yields to the side.

Horsemanship throughout history, such as that practiced at the Spanish Riding School, has proven that to get the horse to do all the airs above the ground and all the simple and complex moves horses are expected to do, maneuvers are first taught on the ground. There are those people who would see a videotape of the Lipizzaner horses and say, "Wow, that was great! Let's go out and ride." They took the demonstration they saw to heart, but they didn't take it to mind. They should have said, "I need to get my horse to go forward, backward, right, left, up, and down while I have him on the ground."

Another benefit of lateral longeing is that it gets the horse to accept the human as the alpha member of his society. Equally as important, the human gets to see how many extraordinary things the horse can do.

Let's compare a good horse to a sports car and see where lateral longeing fits in the picture. Realize that horses are full-throttle-aholics by nature. To breed a fast or athletic horse, all you need are individuals with good genetics, and you'll come up with a horse that has a lot of go and/or ability. You've already bred in the motor; now you have to build in the brakes.

By teaching the horse to go backward, you build a good set of brakes to stop him from going forward, since the better a horse backs up, the better he can stop.

When you teach the horse to move sideways, you are essentially putting the steering wheel on him. Therefore, the horse, who already has the nature to go forward, is now taught to stop by backing up, and to steer right and left by going sideways. Moving right or left is a matter of yielding the hindquarters or the forehand, or yielding them both at the same time.

Lateral longeing is going to give you the respect that is needed to collect the horse mentally. From there you'll be able to go to the next step, which is to collect him emotionally.

Realize that everything starts in your mind, goes through your body, and down your legs to your feet.

Riding Dynamics

There are natural dynamics to horsemanship while you are on the horse's back as well as on the ground. In other words, rather than just saddling the horse, kicking him to go, and pulling him to stop, get the horse mentally and emotionally prepared for horsemanship first.

Have you ever seen a jockey kick a horse to make him go faster? Instead of kicking, he uses his whip or spanks him.

Spanking a horse lengthens his stride; kicking a horse heightens his stride.

I'm not advocating that you get after your horse and really whip him. What I want you to realize is that a horse knows what happens before what happens happens. By that I mean, he feels, understands, or comes to associate what you are doing as a preparatory cue for something else.

For example, if you did two or three things in order, and consistently, before you spanked him, he would eventually get to the point where he would respond to those things before the spanking. You would never need to get to the spanking part because the horse would have already responded. He knew what was going to happen before it happened, because he associated the preparatory cues with the act.

Here's an example of preparatory cues to get a horse to move forward. This is what happens before what happens happens. As you're riding, smile with all your cheeks. In other words, start smiling and squeezing with your buttocks. When that doesn't make the horse go forward, turn the smile into a squeeze with your legs down to your ankles and use a kiss, cluck, or smooch sound as a verbal cue.

If that still doesn't work, then give the horse a spank. What you'll quickly find is that just as you bring up the life in yourself (put energy into your actions) by doing all these things, you'll find your horse making the departure to move forward.

Realize that everything starts in your mind, goes through your body, and down your legs to your feet. This is what the horse feels. This is why you should smile with all your cheeks, turn the smile into a squeeze, and then a verbal cue if you like. If that doesn't work, give your horse a spank.

You'll find that the closer to the center of the tail head you spank, the straighter the horse will go. If you spank on the right side, he'll tend to push off to the left, which often produces a left lead. If you spank on the left side, he'll push off to the right on a right lead. All of a sudden, right and left leads and snappy departures are easily explained. This is not something that is difficult for the horse. Later, when the dynamics of the horse's gaits and movements are explained, you'll understand what your body position needs to be.

As for getting a horse to stop, there are four things that people usually do. Some people *let* horses stop. Others *allow* horses to stop. Then there's *causing* a horse to stop, and there's *making* a horse stop.

First of all, letting a horse stop is something I recommend you try not to do. It means you're plodding along and if the horse decides to quit, he does. When this happens, the person thinks, "Oh darn, I wanted to keep going." The horse laughs in his tracks and doesn't go anywhere. Letting a horse stop is different than allowing him to stop.

In allowing a horse to stop, let's say you were cantering in an arena on a loose rein and you're causing a horse to go by keeping up with his energy. Then you put both of your hands on your thighs, relaxed, and looked down at your belly button, or you did nothing. Eventually, the horse will realize or wake up to the fact that you're asleep and he's going to stop. You set this up and allowed him to stop. You did nothing with your reins. You just quit riding.

In causing a horse to stop, you give the horse a preparatory command that you want to stop. For example, you pick up your reins and go from a casual riding position to a concentrated position. Then, you simply hold the reins while you quit riding. The only thing you do is try to make sure the horse stays straight. This causes the horse to stop. He might not stop suddenly or as quickly as you might like, but as long as he comes down to a stop, you're causing and allowing at the same time.

There are two ways I know to make a horse stop, or try to make a horse stop. One is to pull back with both reins. That is the normal way people try to make a horse stop. Probably nine out of ten times it will work. But some horses get wise to this and tuck their noses on their chests and keep going. Others keep flipping their heads in the air and keep going.

If you want to get your horse to stop, bend his neck. If you can stop the right side of your horse with one rein, you can be pretty sure the left side is not going run off by itself.

In normal horsemanship dynamics, there are a couple of syndromes that are caused by riders not having independent seats. There is the classic "go-whoa" syndrome. Here, the rider kicks with his or her legs to giddyup, and pulls back with the reins at the same time. The horse really doesn't know what to do.

Then, there's the antithesis to that called the "whoa-go" syndrome. That's where the rider hauls back on the reins with both arms and, at the same time, squeezes with the legs. This produces a open-mouthed, stiff-kneed, jacked-up, kangaroo stop by the confused horse. In either case, the rider is giving conflicting signals.

Why do people give conflicting signals to their horses? I think it's often a defensive reaction. Even though they want to go, they don't want to go very much. So they inadvertently hold back on the reins at the same time they tell their horses to go.

One day I saw something that reminded me of this syndrome. I saw a pumpkin fall off a harvest wagon and I thought about how hard it would be to keep a pumpkin on top of a horse's back. I came up with the imaginary Mr. Pumpkin trying to ride a horse. After several years, Mr. Pumpkin figured out that if he could hold hard enough with his legs, squeeze below his knees, and use his reins for balance, that he could manage to stay on the horse.

How can you learn not to ride like Mr. Pumpkin? The first step is to become conscious that you have to become mentally fit with horses. Many times, a horse will snort and spook at something and it scares the rider. The horse feels the rider tighten up and thinks, "Oh, it even scared my predator." Something you're going to discover in Natural Horse-Man-Ship is that the better you understand how to play with horses on the ground, through longe line logic and lateral longeing, the better you'll get at mental and emotional fitness and learn to ride naturally, instead of like Mr. Pumpkin.

It's important to be mentally, emotionally, and physically fit to ride. Your horse can only go as far as you can. To put it in a human perspective, Ginger Rogers had Fred Astaire for a dance partner. What if she had had Fred Flintstone?

Which one are you? Fred Astaire or Fred Flintstone? Mental, emotional, and physical unfitness are the major ingredients that keep people from achieving excellence with horses. It's not the horse's fault. Natural Horse-Man-Ship techniques can help make you mentally, emotionally, and physically fit.

TIME

HOW LONG does it take to become a Natural Horse-Man? Well, if you're green, you're growing; if you're ripe, you're rotten. This is a question of time and levels of ability.

"It's what you learn after you know it all that counts." Natural horsemen Tom Dorrance (left) and Pat have put in the time it takes to learn.

Let's talk about time. It usually takes the average rider about 500 hours of applying Natural Horse-Man-Ship to reach the level of ability of a Natural Horse-Man. If a person rode an hour a day 5 days a week, that's 20 hours a month, which makes 240 hours a year. Add a couple of weekends, multiply by 2 years and you're there! I put it into an hour-mode for a logistical reason. If I say it takes around 2 years to reach the level of a Natural Horse-Man, and you only work on Natural Horse-Man-Ship once a month for 2 years, you haven't put in enough time. Measure the time you're putting into Natural Horse-Man-Ship by the hour.

Levels of Natural Horse-Man-Ship

There is a Levels Program incorporated in Natural Horse-Man-Ship. It's a step-ladder of ability or achievement similar to the belt levels attained in martial arts. To progress from one level to the next, you must pass tests designed to identify your abilities with horses. Parelli Natural Horse-Man-Ship Center has developed these tests and can provide them for students of Natural Horse-Man-Ship. Level 1 test is included in the back of this book.

You're either into Natural Horse-Man-Ship or you're not. You could have ridden for 20, 30, or even 40 years, and still not be to the first level in Natural Horse-Man-Ship.

There are 10 levels in the program. First of all, getting to Level 1 means you've been introduced to Natural Horse-

Man-Ship, and you realize there is a difference between the way people normally do things with horses, and the way people naturally do things with horses. However, at this time, horses are just a hobby for you. As you develop in knowledge and skills from Levels 1 to 3, you can be considered a Natural Horse-Man-Ship enthusiast. Everything from Level 3 to 6 is a craft, and everything from Level 6 to 10 is an art.

After you read this book and/or come to one of my horsemanship courses, you should be able to take a Level 1 test and pass it within 20 to 40 hours of perfect practice. If you'll take some time and make the effort to play with your horse using the techniques and theories I describe, you and your horse should be able to get to Level 1 with a reasonable proficiency.

In Level 3, you and your horse should be able to work solidly together. Getting to Level 3 takes the average person around 500 hours or anywhere from 2 to 5 years, depending on how much time he or she puts in. Once you pass this level, you and your horse can be considered partners for life. This is where horsemanship really starts. After you pass Level 3, you can start calling yourself a Natural Horse-Man.

Reaching Level 6, turning your hobby into a craft, is going to take another 2 to 10 years. When someone gets to Level 6, he or she should be able to be a professional in the horse business, to work in all four categories of horse training. These categories are colt starting (everything from the time the horse is born until his 10th ride), the foundation (the colt's 11th ride until 1,100 hours), refinement (finished performance horse), and problem solving (helping horses with hang-ups). A true horseman is complete and can work with any class of horse from foal to finish, as well as the problem horse.

After Level 6, you refine all that you've learned to that point. The following quote applies here, "It's what you learn after you know it all that counts." At this level, you've turned a craft into an art. It's the little things you now know that make all the difference.

The Levels Program in Natural Horse-Man-Ship is a stepladder of ability or achievement, similar to the belt levels attained in martial arts.

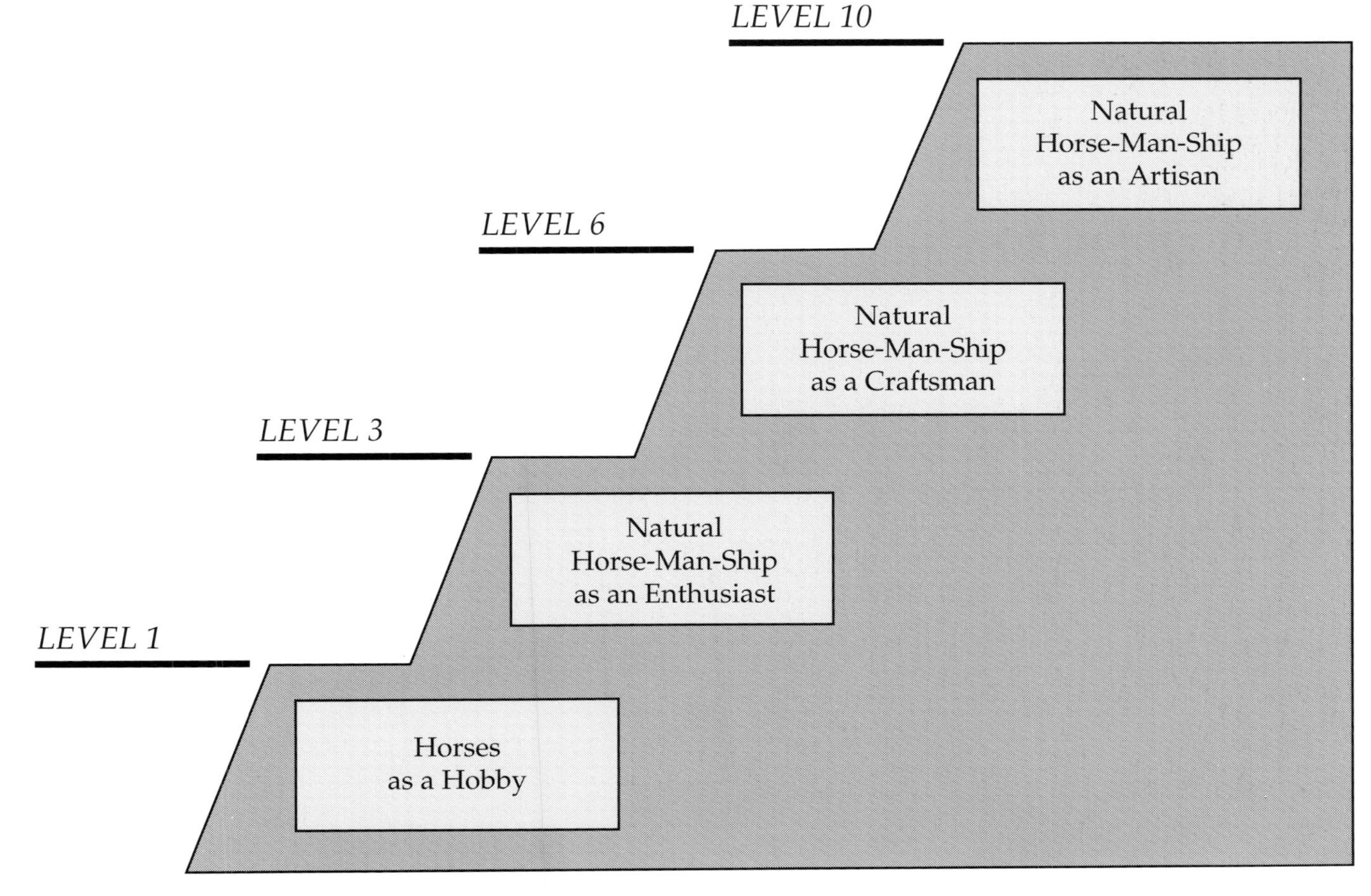

Time for a Horse

Another question that comes up with respect to time is how long does it take for a horse that's never been ridden to become a green horse? And then how much time does it take a green horse to become true blue (a solid riding horse)? Usually it takes about 300 hours for a horse to become totally comfortable with having a human on his back.

You can break this down into blocks of time as I did in the levels. It would take a rider who rides his horse 1 hour every day, excluding weekends, around 300 hours a year to get his horse to the green stage.

In another scenario, let's consider a rider who takes a 2-year-old and starts him with around 10 hours of work, then turns him out and doesn't see him again until the colt is 2½ years old. He plays with him another 20 hours, then turns him out again. He brings the colt back as a 3-year-old and puts another 100 hours on him. Now, the colt has had about 150 hours of education. Then, the rider puts another 150 hours on him when he is a 4-year-old. Now, the colt is almost a 5-year-old, and he finally has 300 hours of riding time.

If a horse had an hour-meter on his withers, you could look down and see how many hours old the horse is on one side and how much riding time he has had on the other. There are 8,766 hours in a year. So if a horse were 4 years old, the meter on one shoulder would read over 35,000 hours old. On the other shoulder, the meter would read how much time he's been ridden. You'd really see a discrepancy in time. On the one side, you'd see that the horse was 35,000 hours old and on the other side that he maybe had less than 400 hours of riding.

If Natural Horse-Man-Ship is applied to horses by a third-level Natural Horse-Man or above, generally speaking it takes about 1,100 hours for the horse to become true-blue—to be a solid, dependable partner.

Then there's the quest to develop your partnership into something that's solid gold. This endeavor takes a lifetime. You never really "finish" a horse, which is a term used in normal horsemanship. In Natural Horse-Man-Ship, you keep refining your partnership.

One of my favorite stories regarding the time it takes to develop horses revolves around the time I was working with Troy Henry. He was asked to do a sliding stop exhibition on a 15-year-old mare he had. That mare slid farther on specially prepared ground than any horse I've seen to date. I asked him about her later and how her age related to the accomplishment.

Troy said that by the time a horse was 7 years old, he should be basically developed and have around 1,500 hours of time on him. Troy's 7-year-old horses were as good as everybody else's 7-year-old horses; but when everybody else's horses were 9, they were washed up. When Troy's horses were 15, they were better than when they were 7. This was in the days before futurities for 2- and 3-year-olds.

Troy told me this in 1978. I took this idea and ran with it. But now, in the days of disposable horses, many horses are washed up at 4. This is a major difference between time in Natural Horse-Man-Ship and developing partners for life, and time in normal horsemanship where you have a kindergarten winner today who might never have a tomorrow.

Time for a Human

The same time question can be asked of riders. How long does it take for a rider to get beyond the green novice stage until he is considered a good rider? I've found that it takes the human about 1,000 hours before he or she is comfortable with being in the saddle. It takes that long before a rider is used to horses and the way they think, act, feel, do, etc. Everything the rider learns after that initial 1,000 hours is what really counts. There is no way a rider can have savvy about horses without riding experience.

When it comes to time, how long should you work with a horse? (Instead of asking how long you can work with a horse, ask how long you can play with a horse.) How long should you laterally longe a horse? Can you overdo anything with a horse? In answer to these questions, as soon as it stops being fun for either one of you, you're not playing any more. Think of it as working on yourself and playing with your horse.

Timing

Timing is probably the one thing about your relationship with your horse that is most important to him. Don't ask when you should do something. Ask when you should quit doing what you are doing. It's not what you do with horses that counts; it's when you quit doing something that counts.

For example, if you stimulate a horse to do something and he tries to do it for you, quit stimulating him. It's your responsibility to recognize that the horse tried, even if it was slight. Then, it's your job to have perfect timing and quit what you're doing after your horse tries. You're more likely to get a positive response that way.

Many people keep stimulating beyond the response. They fail to see that the horse tried. A slight try can be difficult to see, especially if you're can't read the horse's body language. You've got to be able to read your horse like a book. This is one of the things that Natural Horse-Manship is all about—to know if your horse is trying to do what you are asking him to do. Let's say your horse does what you are asking him to do, but he does it with an escapist attitude, and you reward that. You would be rewarding the wrong response and not even know it.

By the same token, if your horse honestly tried to do what you wanted him to do and your timing was slow in rewarding him, the horse would get confused because he thought he tried. When a horse gets no relief after a try, he quits trying. So in timing, how long you do something is not as important as when you quit doing it. That's as important to the technique as the technique itself.

AN OVERVIEW

IMAGINATION

ADULT HUMAN beings are inclined to look for answers logically. They look for rules, regulations, dogmatic answers, and want to apply them to horses. Children, on the other hand, use their imaginations vividly in most everything they do. Usually, humans are regarded as children until they are about 12. After that, they turn into teenagers, at which time they succumb more and more to peer pressure. This is where I believe imagination ends and rules, regulations, and doing what everybody else does begins.

Out of all the key ingredients in Natural Horse-Man-Ship—attitude, knowledge, tools, techniques, time, and imagination—the two most complex to grasp are attitude and imagination. Attitude, at least in the beginning, is hard, but once the person comprehends it, it easily leads to the understanding of knowledge, tools, techniques, and putting in the time.

I've found that the most difficult thing for people to do is to use their imaginations. I've seen many people go a long way with Natural Horse-Man-Ship, and then get stuck at the imagination part. This is the part where people should work on themselves and play with their horses. They need to allow their imaginations to come through in their dealings with horses. It would be good if they were almost childlike with respect to imagination.

Challenges

When I think of imagination, I think of challenges. We need to challenge ourselves and our horses as to what we and they can do. A lot of people are satisfied

"We need to challenge ourselves and our horses as to what we and they can do."

Use your imagination in challenging yourself and your horse to see what you can do. It's difficult enough riding bareback, but bareback, bridleless, and through a stream is even more challenging.

with mediocre results. How many times have you seen a person stuff his horse into a horse trailer anyway he can, then hurry up and shut the door? And he's happy with that.

I'd like to challenge such a person and ask him or her to take a Level 2 horsemanship test by sitting on the fender of the trailer and loading the horse. A Level 3 test would be even harder. He would have to be able to load his horse 45 feet away from the trailer. A Level 6 test requires loading a horse 45 feet or more from the trailer at liberty. Now that is a challenge!

See if you can challenge yourself and your horse. There are only six things a horse can do—forward, backward, right, left, up, and down—but there are a million challenges for each one. That means there are at least 6 million things you can do with your horse.

For example, getting your horse to back is not a big challenge, but maybe you can challenge yourself and your horse by getting him to back into a trailer. I've got horses that can back into a step-up horse trailer. That's not a Level 1 challenge, but it certainly is a challenge.

Next time you go on a trail ride, look for all the challenges. A lot of people think it's a heck of a challenge just to get a horse to cross a creek. But once he does it, it's no longer a challenge. To make it interesting, see if you can get your horse to back or side-pass through the creek. You could even step off your horse, use your mecate-style reins and send the horse across the creek. These are challenges where you use your imagination.

Adjusting To Fit the Situation

Adjusting to fit the situation is all part of using your imagination. This is the difficult part of Natural Horse-Man-Ship. Instead of having a book full of rules that govern all situations, there are no rules in Natural Horse-Man-Ship. There are only goals and principles and adjustments to fit situations. It's just that simple.

Once you have the right attitude toward horses, natural knowledge about them, tools and techniques that work naturally with them, you then put in the time it takes to be successful. Now you have to use your imagination to come up with the proper adjustment to fit whatever situation you find yourself in with your horse. Ask yourself what is going to work naturally? Rather than following the same old rules and saying, "Always do this" and "Never do that," throw out the rules. Give yourself the opportunity to use your imagination to find the necessary adjustment to fit the situation.

The only constant thing in life is change, and things can change rapidly when you're dealing with horses. So rather than training horses to put up with your inadequacies, use the six keys—attitude, knowledge, tools, techniques, time, and imagination—to adjust to the constantly changing situations.

The only constant thing in life is change, and things can change rapidly when you're dealing with horses.

NATURAL HORSE-MAN-SHIP

ON THE GROUND

ATTITUDE

ON THE GROUND

THERE ARE normal attitudes and natural attitudes when it comes to dealing with horses on the ground. One of the most common normal attitudes is that the human thinks he is going to work with his horse on the ground. Working means something like longeing the horse around and around in mindless circles or putting on a set of driving lines and driving him around like he is a plow horse.

"Play with your horse to see where he is mentally and emotionally. When you do, this also gives the horse an opportunity to know where you are."

Through lateral longeing you can determine a lot about your horse's attitude before you step in the saddle.

The natural attitude you could take with your horse on the ground is to play with him and work on yourself. Learn to get in tune with the horse's attitude. You can physically check a horse when you pull him out of the stall to see if he is limping. But you can also check to see if he is lame in the brain. It's easy to see the physical part of a horse. But do you know whether or not that horse is mentally or emotionally fit?

Play with your horse to see where he is mentally and emotionally. When you do, this also gives the horse an opportunity to know where you are.

During this play time, prove to your horse that you are assuming a leadership attitude; you are the alpha member of his society. But being on the ground can be frustrating. You find out quickly that the horse is stronger than you are and probably thinks a lot quicker than you do. He has to—he's a prey animal and it's his job to out-think you. This is where learning the meaning of "polite and passive persistence in the proper position" comes in handy. (This phrase is further defined in Techniques—On the Ground.)

Lateral Longeing

Through lateral longeing, you try to find out where the horse is with respect to his attitude by a series of pre-flight checks. These are similar to what you would do with an airplane. People should take their endeavors with horses as seriously as they would if they were going to fly an airplane. You certainly wouldn't get into an airplane, pull back on the throttle, and go. You'd want to prepare yourself and make sure the airplane was in good shape before you took off.

These pre-flight checks are little tests to see if both the horse and the human are ride-worthy, like an airplane should be airworthy or a ship should be seaworthy. Ideally, the horse and the human would pass all these tests. If they didn't, the human should prepare both of them first.

During lateral longeing, it should be easy to see who the leader is. He's the one who is not moving his feet. I'm not giving you a rule that says, "Don't ever move your feet." I'm giving you an objective and saying, "Try not to move your feet and get your horse to move his feet where you want them."

I know that it can get really frustrating. You're trying to play with your horse and he doesn't want to play with you; or he is playing with you, only he is playing with your mind. Sometimes, you can lose your patience. What you can do to help yourself get through the frustration is to whistle. It's difficult to whistle and frown at the same time. So when you're playing with horses and things get a little frustrating, think of a little tune and start whistling. It can help your attitude.

Principles, Purpose, and Time

The key ingredients in having the right attitude are principles, purpose, and time. The idea is to teach your horse principles, such as the six yields, while you are on the ground. Then you are going to add purpose to it. For example, loading your horse into a horse trailer is a purpose after he has learned the principles of yielding.

Then, take the time it takes so it takes less time. In other words, don't hurry your horse when teaching him principles and giving him purposes or challenges. Take your time and make sure he understands the lesson. Take the time now and go slowly. When you take time on principles and take time on purpose, the next thing you know, in no time, you'll have that horse you wouldn't take a million dollars for.

KNOWLEDGE

WHAT DO you need to know about your horse while you're on the ground? What does on the ground mean? It means everything you do when you're not in the saddle. Your relationship with your horse is going on constantly whether you're riding him or not. Most people think they affect horses only when they are on their backs. Realistically, it's every moment of time you're with your horse, whether you have a halter and lead rope on him, or he's free and you're going to catch him, or when you groom him, etc.

Your horse is thinking of you whenever you're near him. He's probably trying to figure you out, trying to see where you're at, what kind of look you have on your face, what kind of mood you're in, and so

"Your relationship with your horse is going on constantly, whether you're riding him or not."

Through the six yields you can build a communication system with your horse. Here, Pat asks a horse to come forward into the round pen.

The horse's full attention is on Pat.

on. Even when you don't think you're affecting the horse, you probably are in some way or another.

The following three concepts are important to understand about your horse while you're on the ground.

Six Yields

It's up to you to build a polite society with your horse by building in the six yields (forward, backward, right, left, up, and down). You need to know that a horse

Pat asks the horse to back out of the round pen with just a signal down the lead rope, which he continues through any resistance.

Pat sends the horse to the right.

Generally, however, horses have a tendency to go forward rather than backward, go left rather than right, and up rather than down.

can go backward as easily as he can go forward. He can to go the right as easily as he can go to the left, and he can go down as easily as he can go up.

Generally, however, horses have a tendency to go forward rather than backward, go left rather than right, and up rather than down. But they need to do all six directions equally well. If you could measure "equally," how much would it weigh? How much effort does it take to cause your horse to do something?

I call a minimal effort a "yield," and it cannot weigh more than 4 ounces. A horse is not yielding if his response to what you ask requires more than 4 ounces of effort. For example, if you use pressure from your hand or fingers to ask your horse to move out of your way as you pass by, and it takes more than 4 ounces of your effort to get him to move over, he did not yield. The horse resisted, even if slightly, and you have to use more energy to accomplish your task.

Your horse needs to do all six yields equally. You'll probably find that if you'll work on going backward, to the right, and down more than you work on forward, to the left, and up, you'll have a lot more success helping your horse find his balance with all of the six yields.

Pat stops the horse and sends him in the opposite direction.

Liberty

As far as horses are concerned, there are two types of liberty. In one, you've put him in a situation, say a 50-foot round corral, where you can cause him to yield to you in the six ways. Mentally, he is under your supervision. In the second type of liberty, the horse is in a 40-acre pasture, where he's truly at liberty.

In the first scenario, you probably have intentions of playing games with the horse, but possibly in the second scenario, the horse has intentions of playing games with you.

You need to know how to approach your horse and to cause him to do what you want. It might be the attitude you take in walking toward him in that 40-acre pasture that either builds the relationship between the two of you, or destroys it.

One of the most amazing things I've ever seen was in a circus in Lucerne, Switzerland. I saw the great horse trainer

This horse is at liberty in a round pen with extremely low rails. He could easily jump out and truly be at liberty whenever he wanted. Instead, he is under Pat's total control. When Pat asks him to stop running and come to him, the horse does so willingly.

For survival, horses have to be conscious of a predator's distance to them, and the approach he is taking.

Freddie Knei have eight white Arabian stallions come into the ring circling to the right at a trot. He introduced eight more black ones trotting to the left. The ring was 50 feet in diameter, with a wall only 1 ½ feet high. He had them interweave each other at the trot.

After this display, he had four Friesian stallions come in and he played with them at liberty. Then, by signalling verbally to them, he asked all four to lie down simultaneously. After that, he clucked and asked them to sit up. Then he signalled them again, and they all laid back down. He had those horses yielding to him in all ways. It took less than 4 ounces to cause those four horses to lie down simultaneously. Even though the horses were at liberty, they were under Kneigh's supervision mentally and physically.

When you have a halter and lead rope on your horse, he is considered "in hand." He is no longer at liberty or is he? Like liberty, in hand on the ground can also mean two things. One, you've got everything under control; or two, your horse has everything under control and he has you in hand. Many times it's a matter of who's leading whom. Even though you've got a halter and lead rope on a horse and you think you're going to accomplish something on the ground, your horse might have a different idea. And the reverse is also true. It doesn't mean the horse is in control just because he is at liberty. For example, when you play with your horse in a round pen, causing him to yield to you in the six ways, you are still in control of the situation, even if you don't have a halter and lead rope.

Distances and Approaches

Being prey animals, horses are great judges of distance and approach. For survival, horses have to be conscious of a predator's distance to them, and the approach he is taking. This is why straight-line approaches really tend to bother horses. Also, something or someone too abrupt, too clumsy, too unrhythmic, too fast, etc., bothers them.

What a horse understands and accepts most is "approach and retreat." If you approach, stop, then retreat a moment, this gives the horse time to figure you out and see what your intentions are. It's almost like waving a white flag to prove you're no threat.

Whether your horse is out in the pasture or attached to a lead rope, there seem to be some distance markers that the horse recognizes. When you're about 90 feet away, he usually knows what your plans are, and he starts making plans of his own. He considers whether or not to wait for you or to leave. He really starts making some kind of plan when you're about 45 feet away, or half the distance. As you keep chopping that distance in half, it makes more difference to the horse.

Some horses are extremely sensitive to distance while others aren't. With some, if you were 90 feet away and decided to scratch your ear, they'd fly off and run through a fence to get away from you. With others, you might be 4 feet from them and scratch your ear, and they'd only move their heads a bit. A lot of it depends on the particular horse and his horse-anality.

The next distance that seems to make a big difference to the horse is about 22 feet away. After that, it's about half that or 12 feet away. At this point, the horse is asking himself, "What should I do now?" Some horses would have thought at 45

Longeing a horse with a 22-foot rope is more difficult than with a 12-foot rope. Here, Pat is laterally longeing this horse on uneven terrain, purposely challenging the horse.

feet, "Ah, that's all right, you can catch me." You learn to read this in a horse and watch his head and body movements.

At 22 feet, some horses would say, "Darn, I should've done something. Now it's too late." But other horses would say, "Aha, I've still got 22 feet to get away. I've got room to run." Each horse is different. This is where you have to make a judgment about the horse and the situation. Figuring out what a horse can tolerate and what he can't is called learning to read a horse.

The next distance is 12 feet, then 6 feet. At 0 feet, you should be able to catch the horse, who has allowed you to approach him. But I've seen people at 0 feet make the wrong move at the right time, and the horse blows his cork and runs off. Even if the horse accepts your approach, if your body movements are too fast or abrupt, you can still scare the horse. He'll lose confidence in you catching him and make a fast exit.

You might note that 45, 22, 12, and 6 are the distances that make a difference to the horse, and they're also the lengths of rope that I mentioned in Tools—An Overview. You can use all of them to your advantage. For example, let's say you had a 12-foot line and with it you did your lateral longeing exercises and caused your horse to want to go into a horse trailer. Now, can you expand that and play the same game from 22 feet? Your horse might respect you from 12 feet, but not at twice the distance. If you accomplished the feat at 22 feet, could you repeat it at 45 feet?

Distances and approaches and how they affect horses are something to consider when you're with your horse on the ground.

TOOLS

"This type of halter is thin enough to discourage the horse from leaning on it and soft enough to feel comfortable when he yields to his own pressure."

I CATEGORIZE tools into two groups. There are natural tools to use in playing with horses on the ground, and there are normal tools to use in working with horses on the ground. When we are talking about "on the ground," we are talking about everything—exercising, training, longeing, shoeing, doctoring, catching, etc.

Natural tools: 1/ Rope halter or hackamore, 2/ Four different lengths and types of rope (diameters indicated): 6-foot (¼-inch), 12-foot (½-inch), 22-foot (½-inch), and 45-foot (⅜-inch), 3/ Stick (carrot stick), 4/ Plastic bag.

Normal tools: 1/ Nylon web halter, 2/ 25-foot nylon web longe line, 3/ Longeing whip, 4/ Longeing cavesson, 5/ Stallion or stud chain, 6/ Side reins, 7/ Surcingle, 8/ Twitches, 9/ Breeding hobbles, 10/ Regular hobbles, 11/ Hot walker.

Halter and Ropes

I have a rope halter (which in Spanish is *jaquima*) and four lengths of rope so I can play with a horse at short, medium, and long ranges. I have a 6-foot "progress string" (¼-inch), a 12-foot lead line (½-inch), a 22-foot ring rope (½-inch), and a 45-foot nylon rope (⅜-inch), all of which give me several alternatives to fit different situations.

Most people think that a halter and lead rope are used to put on a horse's head to get the horse from point A to point B and then to tie him at point B. I like to think that the natural use of the halter and lead rope is to communicate to the horse's feet to do something or go somewhere. The six directions I teach my horses to go at my request are the six yields: forward, backward, right or left, up and down while I'm on the ground, and from four distances: 6 feet, 12 feet, 22 feet, 45 feet. It's the start of communication. The ultimate goal is to do the same while the horse is at liberty, and later, of course, while you're on his back.

I prefer to use handtied rope halters as opposed to wide, nylon web halters. Because of the latter's construction, horses lean on them instead of respecting them and responding to them. When your horse leans against his halter, he is not listening to what you want, but instead is objecting to what you are asking. This is counterproductive to positive communication between you and your horse.

A rope halter or hackamore made of ¼-inch diameter rope with knots instead of hardware is softer than the normal halter and more effective since it is smaller in diameter. When the horse leans on it, he puts more pressure on himself. Therefore, he learns to yield to and from his own pressure naturally. This type of halter works on pressure points on the nose and poll and teaches the horse to yield to his own pressure—naturally.

I like to use a 12-foot lead rope. I've found that length to be optimum for handling a horse from a distance. Most lead ropes are only 6 to 9 feet long, too short for controlling a horse effectively from a distance. I recommend lateral longeing a horse before a rider ever gets on, and the 12-foot lead rope is ideal for this purpose.

Also, with respect to the size of the lead rope, I like to use a ½-inch diameter rope made out of soft, marine or yacht braid, the same type found on sailboats. This size and this material give the handler the "live feel" necessary to send subtle messages to his horse via the rope. It's like a telegraph wire between you and your horse. You actually talk to him with this kind of halter and lead rope. Also, the material isn't apt to burn your hands, if it runs through your hands, as so many other lead ropes do.

I have four lengths of rope because horses are very good at judging distances and approaches. As explained earlier, horses have different "horse-analities," which are made up of innate characteristics, learned behavior, and spirit. With my tools, I want the ability to make a series of adjustments to fit different situa-

A ¼-inch handtied Natural Horse-Man-Ship rope halter and a 12-foot lead rope made out of ½-inch yacht braid.

The 6-foot progress string has many uses, such as riding with one rein. The 22-foot ring rope is the next step up from the 12-foot lead rope in lateral longeing at longer distances.

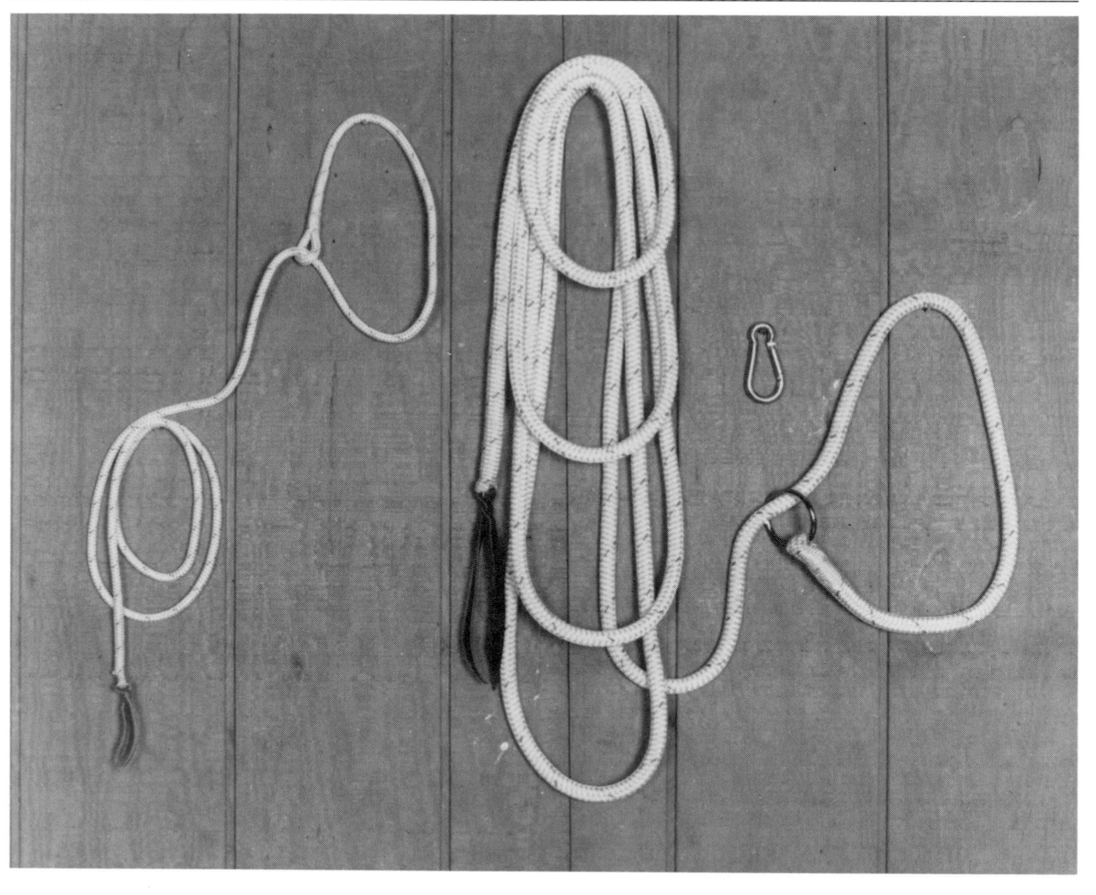

tions when distinct horse-analities pop up. For example, a 6- to 9-foot lead rope is what most people use to drag a horse around with. If you try to load a horse in a trailer or use some of the lateral longeing techniques, you'll find that rope is too short. A 12-foot rope would be more appropriate. But then there are times when you want to ride the horse with just one rein. A 12-foot rope is too long, but a 6-foot rope is perfect. These different types and lengths of rope make things easy for both horse and human.

Some horses are very sensitive and need to be able to drift. That means a horse needs to establish some breathing room between himself and the human. While lateral longeing, you allow him to drift away from you, but you also need to be able to bring him back. So having the ability to allow a horse to drift, but not completely escape, is necessary. If you had a 22-foot rope that did not burn your hands when it ran through them, you could allow the horse to drift away from you, and before he completely escaped, you could set your feet and cause the horse to teeter back to you, which means face you.

If you use this tool (22-foot rope) and the drift and teeter back techniques, even a sensitive horse will learn to give you his respect at a distance. I discovered this tool in my travels in Australia when learning about the Jeffery method of handling horses. There, the Jeffery rope is made of rawhide. I feel I've improved the tool (making it of yacht braid), and I call it the 22-foot ring rope.

If your rope is too short, you can't allow your horse to drift for fear that he'll escape. When he hits the end of the short rope and you cause him to teeter, he thinks you're pouncing on him. Therefore, a short rope makes your horse more fearful, more claustrophobic, and more of a full-throttle-aholic. This is the opposite effect of what you're after.

Some horses need even more drift than the amount they can have with a 22-foot rope. Also, you might want to test your horse's responses at a greater distance. This is where a 45-foot rope comes in handy.

Sticks

Using a stick as an extension of your arm is an interesting proposition. Throughout history, all forms of livestock handlers, including shepherds, swine handlers, cattlemen, and horse owners, have used different lengths and types of sticks in order to teach, control, reinforce, and refine communication with livestock. I have found that in most cases the sticks available were too floppy, had too much lash on them, or were too severe.

I also found that people approached horses with two types or extremes of attitude: the stick approach and the carrot approach. In the stick approach, the human forces or threatens the horse to do something, and in the carrot approach, the human begs the horse to do something.

When it comes to sticks, I came up with something in the middle of these two approaches—the carrot stick. The carrot stick is a tool made to adjust to fit different situations. It's a fiberglass rod about 5 feet long, and it acts as an extension of your arm. It has a leather popper on the end, which is meant to use with horses who are very sensitive. With horses who are not as sensitive and maybe need to show a little more respect, I attach a plastic grocery bag to the leather popper. With other horses, there's a time when you would want a lash. This is where the 6-foot progress string comes out of your portable round corral and goes on the end of your carrot stick.

While you are on the ground, and with the carrot stick as an extension of your arm, you can get the horse to respond to all six of the yields: forward, backward, right, left, up, and down. The carrot stick is probably one of the most valuable tools in teaching a horse lateral longeing and in teaching the horse to yield from pressure.

Basically, you will find that sticks teach horses to yield away (move away) from pressure, and ropes teach horses to yield to (come to) pressure. This is going to become important in your horse's education, and is an important concept for you to understand.

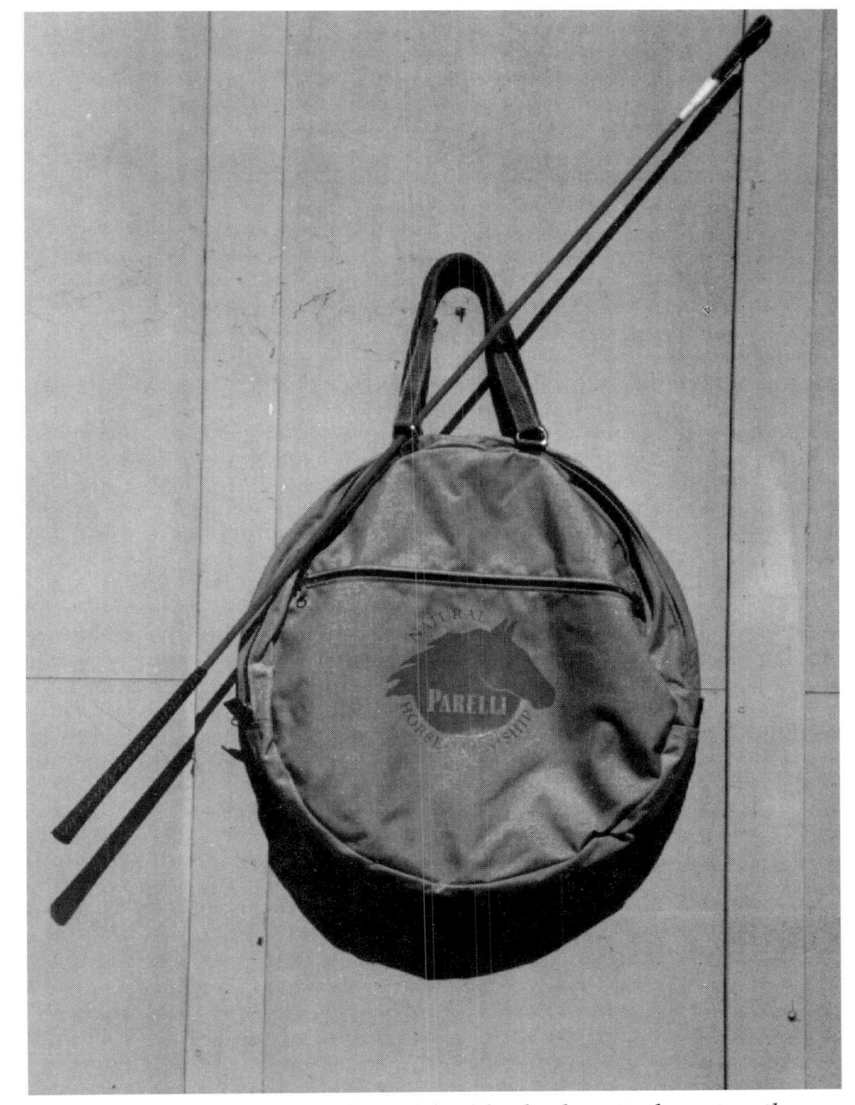

A carrot stick is a 5-foot fiberglass stick with a leather attachment on the end. It's meant to be an extension of your arm, not a whip.

ON THE GROUND

TECHNIQUES

THE TECHNIQUES used in Natural Horse-Man-Ship are built around watching what the horse does naturally, trying to mimic him, and finding ways to cause him do what you want him to do in terms he can understand. Here's a series of techniques to help you deal with your horse on the ground.

Approach and Retreat

One of the most important Natural Horse-Man-Ship techniques to understand is the technique of approach and retreat. As I've said before, there are two categories of animals: prey animals and predators. Predators tend to move in straight lines. Prey animals tend to approach something, and then retreat from it a little bit. They are cautious in their approach, and go up to something only if they perceive it to be harmless.

From a prey animal's point of view, something that walks up to the water hole in a straight line must be a predator. If that something or someone walks toward the water hole, then retreats and looks some more, that must be a prey animal. This is one reason why walking straight up to a horse is sometimes bothersome to him. In his eyes, you are acting like a predator. But, if you approach the horse and retreat, and then approach and retreat again, this gives the horse the confidence that you aren't as bad as he first thought.

"When you are trying to get a horse to yield to you in one of the six ways, position of his eyes is important."

Four-Step Formulas

As you work with different horse-analities, you'll find horses who are skittish, sensitive, or fearful. Then there are those who are disrespectful, domineering, or think they're the alpha member of your society. I have a four-step formula for each of these types of horse-analities and it helps me to understand and deal with them.

For horses who are scared, I use the four steps of confidence, acceptance, understanding, and results. With these horses, I first work to gain their confidence—to get them to accept me and what I'm asking

Pat uses the four-step formula of confidence, acceptance, understanding, and results in teaching this horse to allow his feet to be picked up. Here, Pat approaches the horse in a non-threatening way, then stops and lets the horse approach him. Pat is working on the horse's confidence.

Once your horse has the understanding that you are not going to hurt him, you'll get the results you want.

them to do. Then they start understanding what I want, and from there I can get the results I need.

Horses who have horse-analities that make them disrespectful need to respond with respect. This is where you apply the four-step formula to cause responses. Do this by being polite and passively persistent in a proper position until that horse yields to you. Then, quit what you're doing, but not until he at least tries to respond in a positive way. Do something, even if you have to constantly adjust to fit the situation.

Some horses are like Dr. Jekyll and Mr. Hyde. They are both disrespectful and scared at the same time. They are the most difficult and dangerous horses to work with. This is where you have to be both a psychoanalyst and diagnostician. On the one hand, you've got to work to get their confidence and, on the other hand, work to get their respect. But you should be able to accomplish both if you understand the four-step formula. It has always worked for me.

An example of how to use the four-step formula of confidence, acceptance, understanding, and results might be with a horse who has never had his legs picked up. There's an old cowboy saying, "He's wild and wooly; he's full of fleas; he's never been curried below the knees." I believe horses are more sensitive below the knees because that's where their most vulnerable tendons are, which are crucial to soundness and the ability to flee.

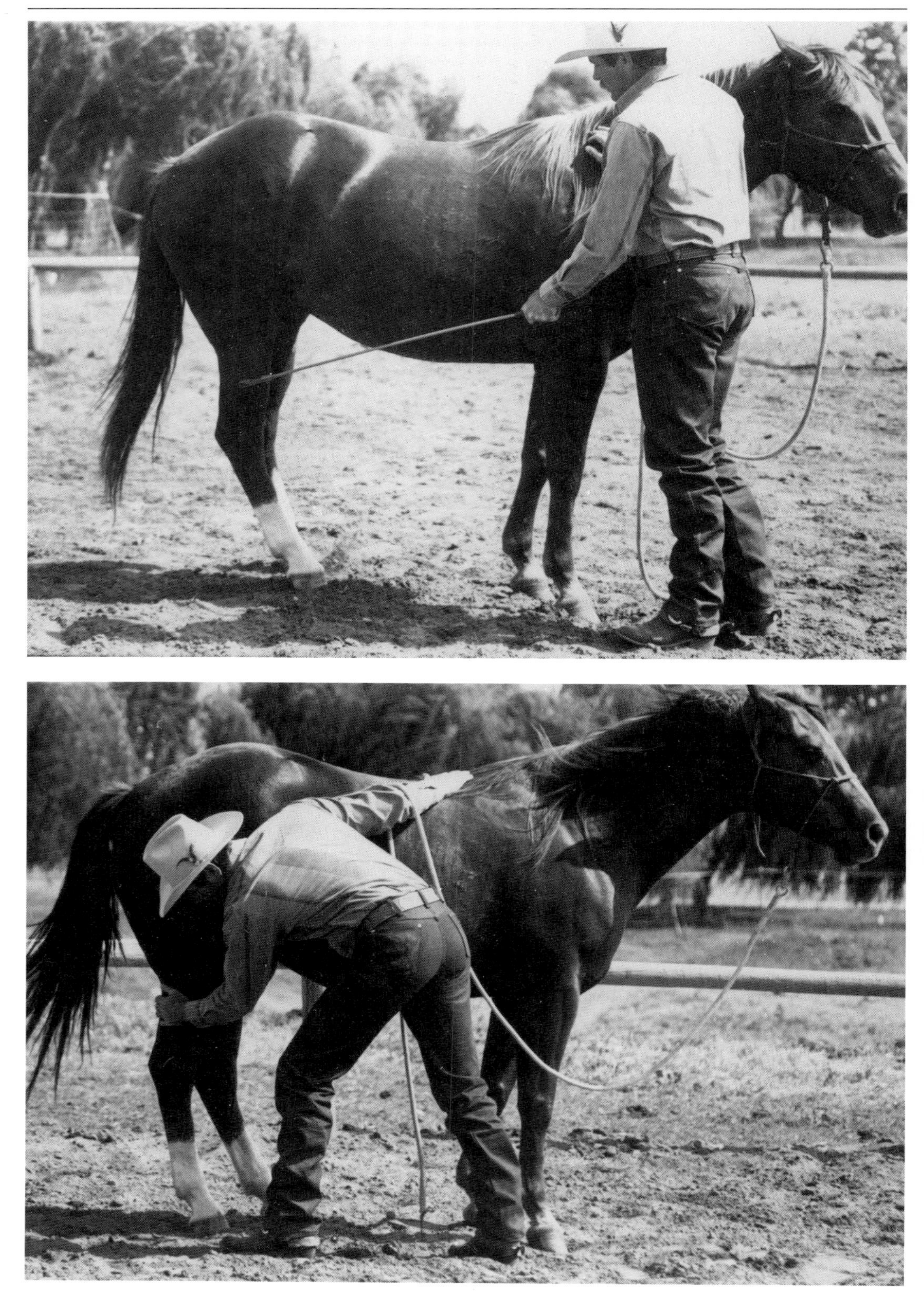

With a carrot stick, Pat rubs the horse all over, including the legs, until the horse accepts being touched.

Next, Pat replaces the carrot stick with his hand and rubs the horse all over again, especially massaging the legs.

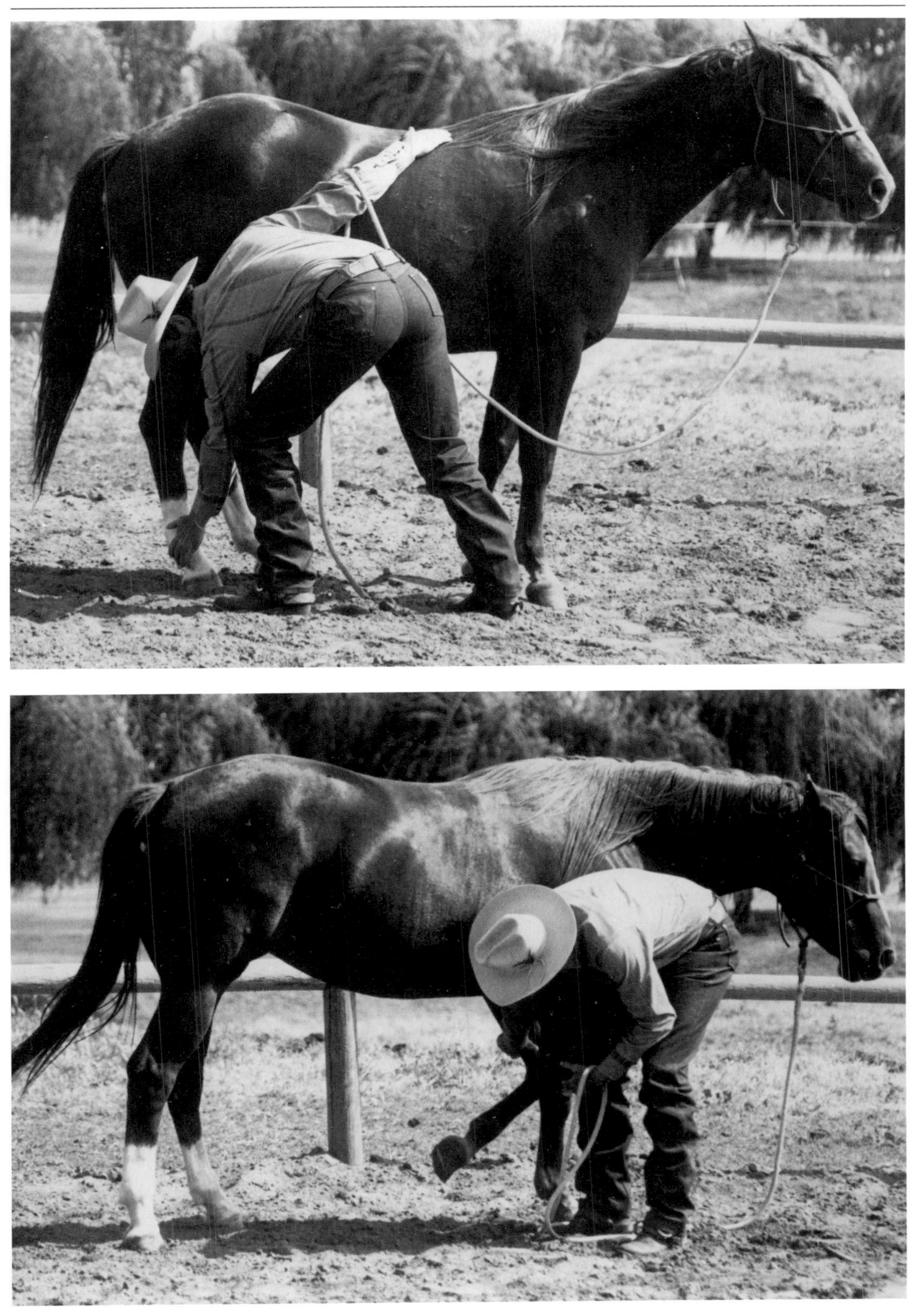

The horse now understands that Pat means no harm.

Pat gets the results he wants—to be able to pick up the horse's feet.

A direct-line approach, rather than using the four-step formula of confidence, acceptance, understanding, and results, would be to try to pick up the horse's feet (one at a time) any way you can, tie them up, and try to get them trimmed or shod, without any preparation or thought of the horse's point of view. Using this direct-line approach, the horse is already scared and doesn't understand. Yet the "normal" human being wants results.

Instead, try the four-step formula. First, get the horse's confidence. A lot of that has to do with the way you catch him. Use approach and retreat techniques and cause the horse to think he is not in a dangerous position when you are around him. When you do have him caught, rub him all over with something like a carrot stick, which is an extension of your arm.

At this point, you want your body as far away from him as you can. That's not only safer for you, but it makes the horse feel less threatened. Rub him everywhere, including the legs all the way down to the hoofs. When he no longer feels threatened or the need to move away, then replace the carrot stick with your own arm. When he is relaxed with that, massage the legs.

Don't pick up the feet up. Just massage his legs for one to ten sessions until he is confident that when you approach his feet, all you are going to do is be nice to him. Once he tolerates this, he learns to accept what is being done to him. The more confidence he has, the more acceptance he'll have.

The understanding comes in when you actually do something with the leg, like pick it up. Don't try to do much at once, such as put shoes on a horse who is just getting used to having his feet picked up. Go slowly and build his confidence and acceptance. Once your horse has the understanding that you are not going to hurt him, you'll get the results you want.

Sensitizing and Desensitizing

There are sensitizing and desensitizing techniques that can help you deal with your horse effectively.

A sensitizing technique is one to which the horse responds by moving away from the pressure of what you are doing. If you want to sensitize a horse, stimulate him until you get a *try* response, and then quit stimulating. It's not what you do, it's when you quit doing what you are doing that causes the horse to become sensitive to what you want.

An example is using spurs. The horse is sensitive to the feeling of the spur and moves away from it. As soon as he does, you should remove the pressure of the spur from his side.

If you want to desensitize a horse, you rhythmically overdo what you are doing. The constant repetition of a stimulus makes the horse relaxed about what you are doing. For example, if you have a horse who is scared of saddle pads and you want to put one on his back, you desensitize him to the actual blanket and to the act of putting it on his back.

In a rhythmical fashion, put it on his back more times than it seems necessary or logical. You rhythmically swing the pad onto the horse's back, then remove it, and swing it up there again and again until the horse becomes used to your motions and the weight on the pad on his back. The horse finally realizes that he can tolerate the pad, and it won't hurt him.

This follows the four-step formula. You get the horse's confidence during the swinging and placement of the pad, and he learns to accept what is going on. Now, he understands that you want him to stand still when you put the pad on his back. Because of the first three steps of the formula, you get the results you want—being able to put a pad on your horse.

Rhythm is something a lot of people have difficulty with. They're just not rhythmical, or tend to do things with little or no rhythm. But horses are rhythmical creatures; they have four beats when they walk or gallop, two when they trot and back up, and three when they canter. A horse is an animal who bases almost everything he does on rhythm. If you're not rhythmical, too, you might appear to be clumsy and/or threatening to him, and the things you want to do with him might not work out. Therefore, practicing to be more rhythmical will come in handy in your dealings with horses.

Right- and Left-Handedness

Another technique is to be conscious of right- and left-handedness in yourself and in your horse. Most horses have left-sided tendencies since most of what humans do with them is on their left sides. A horse can become frightened when something a human does takes place on his right side because he is not used to seeing humans on that side. The point here is to do as many things on the horse's right side as you do on his left. For example, become proficient in mounting on the right, leading your horse from the right, loading your horse in the trailer from the right, etc.

Voice Cues

Learning to be quiet around horses is another technique. Being loud around horses or growling at them when they do something wrong is a common habit many people have. They think they are using voice cues, but what they are really doing is communicating to the horse, via their voices, that they are still predators. Often, people don't even realize how much they are growling or barking at their horses. And horses are not fond of loud noises or abrasive people. I suggest that when you feel like growling or barking or things get frustrating, start whistling. It's hard to growl when you're whistling, and it will give you something to do to help you cool down.

I'm not suggesting that you never use voice cues, just that you become conscious of the number of times you use your voice when you're frustrated or mad.

A voice cue is a technique. To me, the word "cue" is short for communication. A voice cue, or any kind of a cue you use, is a replacement stimulus. It replaces a true stimulus. Tapping the horse lightly on the hindquarters is a stimulus to cause him to go forward. Squeezing your legs replaces the tapping. Making clucking, smooching, or kissing noises replaces the squeezing. Soon these vocal cues replace the tapping cue.

If you use voice cues, be consistent with them. Frankly, most people are not consistent. I suggest that you wait until Level 3 in Natural Horse-Man-Ship before you start using voice cues. By that time, you should be mentally, emotionally, and physically fit enough to use them naturally.

Preparatory Commands

Preparatory commands play a large part in communication with the horse. They are similar to what a drill sergeant in the Army would say when he wants to get his squad to march forward. He would say "Company, forward, march." To the soldiers, the word "company" means to pay attention, "forward" tells them what they are going to do, and when the sergeant says "ch" in the word "march," their left feet should be hitting the pavement.

With respect to preparatory commands, horses really key into what happens before what happens happens. This means they are keenly aware of what is going on right before something happens. A horse can become highly sensitive to your body movement. Before the spur actually touches his side, he can feel the muscles in your calves tense up, and the movement of your leg backward or inward. He knows what's about to happen even before it happens. He might even learn to respond when he feels the calf muscles tighten, and spurs will be unnecessary.

Position to the Eye

When you're on the ground, most everything you do relates to position of the eye—the horse's eye, that is. A lot of people have been kicked because they weren't paying attention to their position in relation to a horse's eyes. They weren't

Pat stays within this wild horse's field of vision. Note the horse's left eye is trained on Pat and his left ear is cocked toward him.

Pat wants this mustang to look at him with both eyes. That way he has his full attention.

aware that the horse wasn't aware of their presence.

For example, if you walk into a horse's limited field of vision behind and startle him, there's a good chance you could get kicked. If you had been conscious of whether that horse cocked an ear in your direction and picked you up in his eye, you could be fairly sure he wouldn't kick because he saw you. He might kick you because he doesn't like you, but not because he didn't see you.

When you are trying to get a horse to yield to or from you in one of the six ways, position of his eyes is important. For example, if you want a horse to stop and face you, the horse should look at you with both eyes. If you want a horse to back, he needs to face you and keep focusing both his eyes on you while he's backing. If the horse wants to go the right instead of backward, he will usually quit looking at you with both eyes, and look to his right. In this way, he prepares to change directions, but he usually looks in the direction first.

If you pay attention to where you are in relationship with horses' eyes, you can learn to read horses, and get a feel for what they're thinking and about to do.

Lateral Thinking

In whatever you do with horses, make sure you don't use direct-line thinking as a predator would. For example, don't walk into the pasture only when you want to catch your horse. Go in there for a variety of reasons. Give your horse treats some days. Or catch him, put a halter and lead rope on him, and continue to let him graze. Then take off the halter and leave the pasture. Your horse won't associate getting caught with always being taken to the barn to be ridden.

As another example, don't touch your horses lips only moments before you put a chain on his upper lip to twitch him. Touch him on the lips at other times, just to desensitize him to that action. Don't fall into patterns of actions he will view as negative.

A prime example of lateral thinking would be to take a syringe full of an applesauce and cinnamon mixture and give this dose to your horse for several days. Do this in preparation for deworming day. After you do this, say 10 days in a row, your horse will meet you at the gate, open his mouth, and say, "Please, squirt it in." On the 11th day, when you decide to deworm him, you won't have a problem getting the paste deworming medicine down his throat. Then, give him the applesauce concoction for 10 more days. He's more apt to forgive you and cooperate in the future if you treat him this way than if the only time you open his mouth is to give him some awful-tasting stuff.

Techniques Horses Use on Humans

Because they are usually overfed and underexercised (mentally, emotionally, as well as physically), horses will play games with people as a part of their mental stimulus. They are bored and looking for something to do. They especially like to play games with gunsels, a name for inept or unknowledgeable people.

Since horses are so brilliant with lateral thinking and humans so adept at direct-line thinking, humans are easy for horses to trick. Some of the games are: playing hard to catch, being difficult to load, dragging humans by the lead rope, stepping on toes, being hard to bridle, and the list goes on and on.

Lateral Longeing

Lateral longeing techniques are the surest and quickest ways to get your horse to understand you, respect you, and respond to you as he would one of his own kind. Lateral longeing is the basis of the six yields (forward, backward, right, left, up, and down) and the way you play with your horse on the ground. But they

Lateral longeing techniques are the surest and quickest ways to get your horse to understand you, respect you, and respond to you as he would one of his own kind.

Lateral longeing techniques are based on the horse's natural movements—things horses do to get other horses to respect and respond to them. One menacing look from the gray horse is enough to make the sorrel horse leave. The sorrel yielded to the gray's authority.

should not be confused with normal longeing procedures.

In normal longeing, the handler asks the horse to go round and round in mindless circles, and most of the time to the left. The horse's body is getting exercised, but his mind is going to pot. What you want to do is work with the horse's mind and let his body follow. In order to do that, you have to set up some form of communication that the horse will understand. Before you teach the horse to longe properly at the end of a long longe line, put him through a lateral longeing school, sort of a kindergarten of communication.

The techniques used in lateral longeing are based on the horse's natural movements, things horses in a herd would do to get other horses to respect them and respond to them.

When you think like a horse and act and react like one, your horse will understand what you want of him almost from the start. Eventually, you can transfer what you teach the horse on the ground to what you want him to do while you're in the saddle. Since the horse and you are talking the same language, communication is easy.

I was watching a W.C. Fields movie once and in it he said, "Horse sense is what horses have that makes them not bet on people." When some horses get too much horse sense, they bet against you. They learn exactly what it is you want them to do and then do the opposite.

What a horse needs in order to be a good partner with man, to feel good with a human, is to have some people sense, an ounce of it compared to the gallon of horse sense people need. People sense is the common sense thing to do in a human environment. Your horse needs to learn to follow your suggestions and realize that you won't give him any suggestions that won't be good for him. He needs to trust your judgment and use his as well. Someday, your life may depend on it.

The more your horse understands you on the ground, the more he can perform for you. This is a valuable concept to understand. And because you're relating to the horse on his level, he respects you immediately. Respect is what you get on the ground or you don't. By that I mean, if your horse doesn't respect you on the ground, he might not respect you in the saddle either. You either have his full attention, or you don't. Most people do not have their horses' attention.

A lot of people can get their horses gentle, but not respectful. They are two different things. A gentle horse is used to the presence of humans and tolerates what is being done to him. A respectful horse is alert to his handler's every movement and knows his place in the pecking order. You first; him second.

You can get a horse gentle, but the first time you become assertive enough to ask the horse to do something, he might come uncorked. A horse needs to be gentle and trusting first, but he also needs to be respectful.

Through lateral longeing and yielding techniques you can get that respect, and develop a communication system with your horse as well.

Let's assume by now that your horse no longer considers you a predator. Now, how do you get him to not think of you as a gunsel, somebody to laugh at? You can accomplish that by perfecting the yields. There are only six things a horse can do, and that's go forward, backward, right, left, up, and down. The idea is to get the horse to yield to you in those six ways with an action that takes 4 ounces of energy or less. Remember that a yield weighs a maximum 4 ounces; anything more than that is not a yield.

If you want to test how much energy is in 4 ounces, clip a lead rope onto a cowboy shirt that has snaps, not buttons. Now wiggle the rope. When the snaps pop open, you've gone beyond 4 ounces of energy.

Equipment

For lateral longeing, you'll need certain equipment to be effective with your horse. As I mentioned in earlier chapters, I like to use hand-tied rope halters that are thinner than most halters. That way the horse doesn't lean on the halter and resist it. However, this type of halter is softer than most halters, so when the horse is not leaning on it, it's even lighter on him than the typical halter. It's almost as if he has no halter on at all.

At first in lateral longeing, you'll also use a 12-foot lead rope that I call a horse-handling rope. It has a popper on one end, which adds a little weight to the rope and makes a whirring sound when you twirl the lead rope. I've found that if you have a rope that is shorter than 12 feet, you won't have much luck. You'll be too close to the horse. And, if you have one longer than 12 feet, you'll get tangled up in it.

Later, you'll learn to play with the horse at longer distances using 22- and 45-foot ropes. The horse learns to pay attention to you no matter how far away you are. When you can handle the horse successfully 45 feet away, you'll know you've commanded his attention and respect.

You'll also use a whip or stick (like a carrot stick) as a pointer. You can put some bright or noisy material (such as a plastic bag) on the end of the stick. The noise the bag (or material) makes and its erratic movement keep the horse alert to it and therefore to you. You can also attach a progress string at the end of the carrot stick and use it as a lash.

Gentle Test

Before you ask for the six yields, see how really gentle your horse is. You do this by asking your horse to pass the gentle test. Make sure there aren't any "can't," "won't," "don't," or "yeah but" spots on your horse's body. Horses have sensitive spots on certain areas of their bodies. Some horses say, "You can touch my forehead, but you can't touch my ears." Others say, "You can touch my nose, but I won't let you touch my mouth." Still others say, "Don't touch my hindquarters or else!"

If the horse is gentle, he will allow you to touch him everywhere. If he isn't gentle, he won't allow it. If he is not, get him to pass these tests before going on to the respect system.

The two most sensitive spots on a horse are his mouth and under his tail. Most horses are not happy about having their tails handled. See if you can gently lift your horse's tail. If he lets you, stop, and back off. If he resists, back off anyway. In a while, repeat this step again, slowly. Keep it up until the horse allows you to lift his tail without trying to clamp it down tight. An advance-and-retreat method is best when working with a wary horse

Touch your horse all over his body to make sure there aren't any overly sensitive spots.

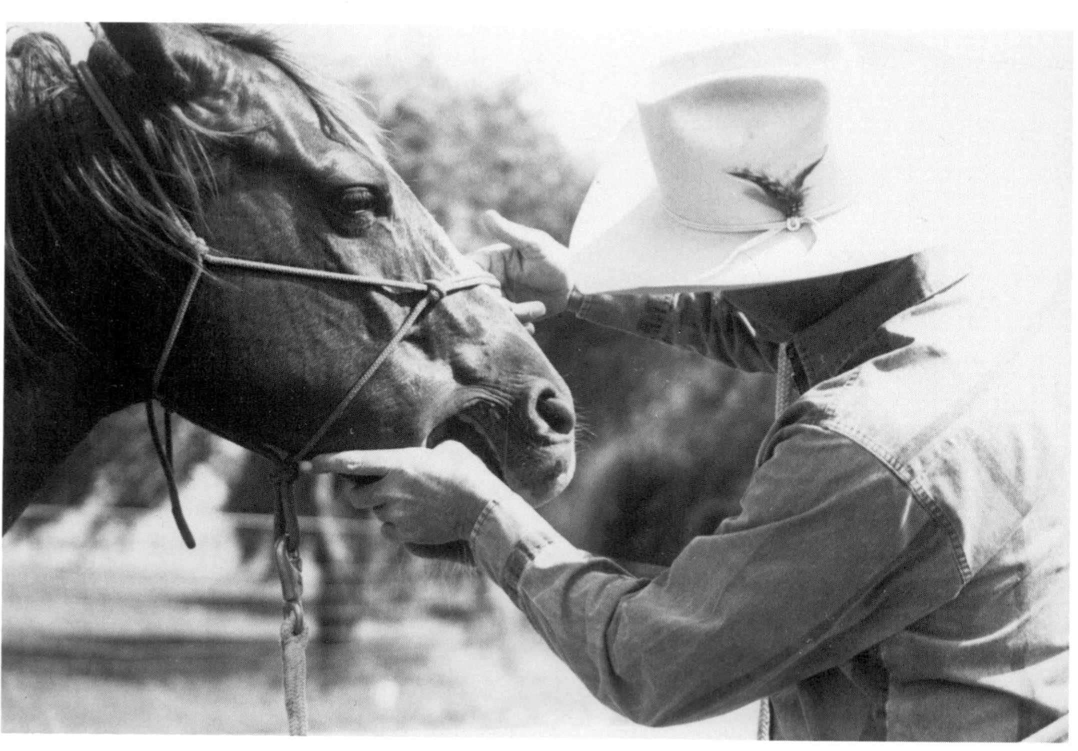

One of the most sensitive spots on a horse is his mouth.

Another sensitive spot is the horse's tail. Keep trying to lift it up until he allows you to without clamping it down.

The drive line differentiates between the horse's forehand and hindquarters, which is important in the yielding techniques.

who is not sure about being handled.

When the horse becomes used to or desensitized to your hand movements, he'll become more visibly relaxed. He'll lick his lips in understanding, or maybe even cock a hind leg. If your horse has sensitive spots, don't go further until you've developed a relationship in which you can touch him everywhere on his body. If you don't, he'll harbor a defense in that area, and it'll show up as a problem somewhere down the line.

Use a carrot stick as an extension of your arm in case your horse is touchy around the flank or other places. This is much safer. Touch him all over and see where he is sensitive. Work on those places until the horse accepts your touch.

Drive Line

Before you begin the yielding techniques, you should understand where a horse's drive line is. Put a progress string around your horse's neck at the base of the neck. This is a focal point for understanding the drive line, which is actually located at mid-point on the withers. The drive line differentiates between the horse's forehand and hindquarters, which is important in the yielding techniques. The area in front of the progress string is the area you touch with your fingers, the lead rope, or carrot stick for moving the horse's front end. Everything behind the progress string is where you touch to cause the hindquarters to move.

Four-Phase Theory

In each of the yields there can be four phases. These phases are things or maneuvers you can do to cause your horse to react in a certain way. If the horse doesn't respond to your request for action in the first phase, go to the second phase, which is a little stronger action than the first phase. If he doesn't respond then, go to phase three, and so on until the horse responds to your requests. And the phases for one yield, say backing, are different from those of side-passing, or coming forward.

In the phases, your actions become progressively stronger to match the horse's level of resistance. If you have to go through all four phases (and sometimes there are even more) in any of the yielding techniques, the secret in each phase is to get progressively faster and firmer, but stay fair and friendly. (The concept of fast, firm, fair, and friendly applies in lateral longeing techniques as well as riding dynamics. See Techniques—In the Saddle.)

In explaining the various yields, I'll go through each phase as it would happen. Going through the phases in order and being faster, firmer, fairer, and friendly when you do, is what the phrase "passive persistence in the proper position" means. You have to learn to get firmer without losing your position. A big mistake a person can make is getting out of the position he was in when he made a request of the horse. The horse ends up dragging him around.

In any of the phases, as soon as the horse responds correctly, quit stimulating him. There's no reason to go to phase four if the horse responded properly after you used phase two. And even if you had to go to phase four to accomplish the task, the next time you ask for the specific movement or maneuver, start over at phase one.

Yields

The logical and natural approach to building a respect system with your horse while you are on the ground is in using the six yields, as I've mentioned before. In using this approach, you'll ask your horse to yield to and from you in the six ways (forward, backward, right, left, up, and down), first at close range and then at greater and greater distances. This system runs the gamut all the way from fingertip yielding to playing with your horse on a 45-foot line.

1/ Fingertip Yielding

Use your fingers to push with energy. This means that your fingers actively press into the horse's body. Use assertiveness to get your point across. Some horses are extremely sensitive and need very little pressure from your fingers. Other horses have been dull for so long, they don't pay much attention to humans. In that case, you'll have to get your horse's attention

To get your horse to back up using fingertip yielding, put your hand on the bridge of the horse's nose and push with the palm of your hand.

Another technique to get your horse to back is to press your fingers into the horse's chest, about where the breast collar would go.

first and use more assertiveness with your finger movements.

a) Backing Up. To cause your horse to back up, put your right hand on the bridge of his nose and push with the palm of your hand, which would be phase one. If he doesn't back, go to phase two—push your thumb and middle finger on the facial nerves alongside the bridge of the nose. In phase three, you'll need to increase the pressure until the horse tucks his nose and then takes a step backward.

As soon as you feel him do either one, quit pressing and start rubbing his nose. Let him know he did good by releasing the pressure and doing something pleasant to the horse. If you need phase four, simply apply more pressure on the horse's nose until he moves backward. Each time you ask him to back, see how little it takes to

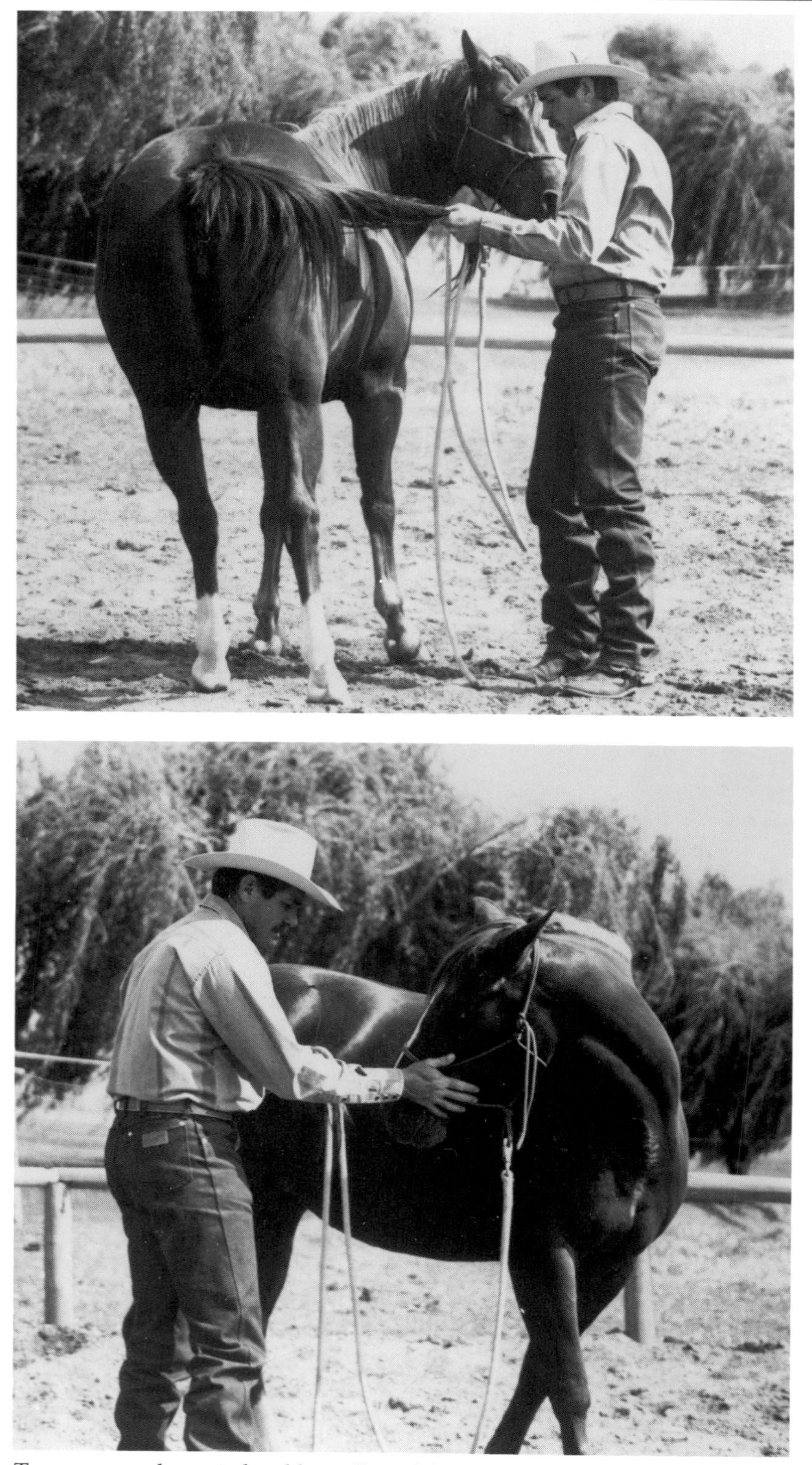

To cause your horse to bend laterally, ask him to smell his tail. Put your left hand on his tail and pull it slowly toward his head as you bring his head around with your right hand.

get him to tuck his nose and take a step backward. In time, maybe a week, you should be able to get him to back up 30 or 40 feet by lightly touching his nose. But right now, be happy with just a step or two.

Another similar technique to get your horse to back is to press both of your hands into the middle of his chest, about where the breast collar would go. Rub him there first (phase one). Then, with your thumbs, press slowly and firmly into his chest until he backs up a step or two (phase two). Then rub him. Keep doing this rubbing-and-pressing technique until he backs easily and quickly. If the horse doesn't step back, phases three and four would constitute increasing the pressure until he does.

b) Lateral Flexion and Moving the Hindquarters. Try to cause your horse to bend laterally by asking him to smell his tail for 10 seconds. Start on the right side first. Put your left hand on the horse's tail and pull it slowly toward his head as you bring his head around with your right hand (phase one). You're suggesting to your horse to bend his neck laterally to smell his tail. When he can do this for 10 seconds without moving his feet, let go of his tail and rub him in the flanks. Now press your fingers slowly into his flanks, without letting go of his head, until his hindquarters drift away from you (phase two). Increase the intensity or stiffness of your fingers, but don't jab (phase three). When he does move his hindquarters, rub him on the head as a reward for moving his rump away enough to face you. Phase four, if you need it, would be to keep increasing the intensity of your fingers.

If the horse does not stand still to smell his tail, start again and ask him more slowly. Hold the tail and bring in his nose inch by inch until he can touch or smell his tail for 10 seconds. Then try the same thing on the other side. This time put your right hand on his tail and your left hand on his head, and ask him to bring his head around to smell his tail. When he does, let go of the tail, rub him in the flanks, and then start pressing his flanks slightly with your fingers, while still holding on to the head. When the horse moves his hindquarters away, rub him on the head again.

At this point, since he is facing you, you might as well back him up. This time try

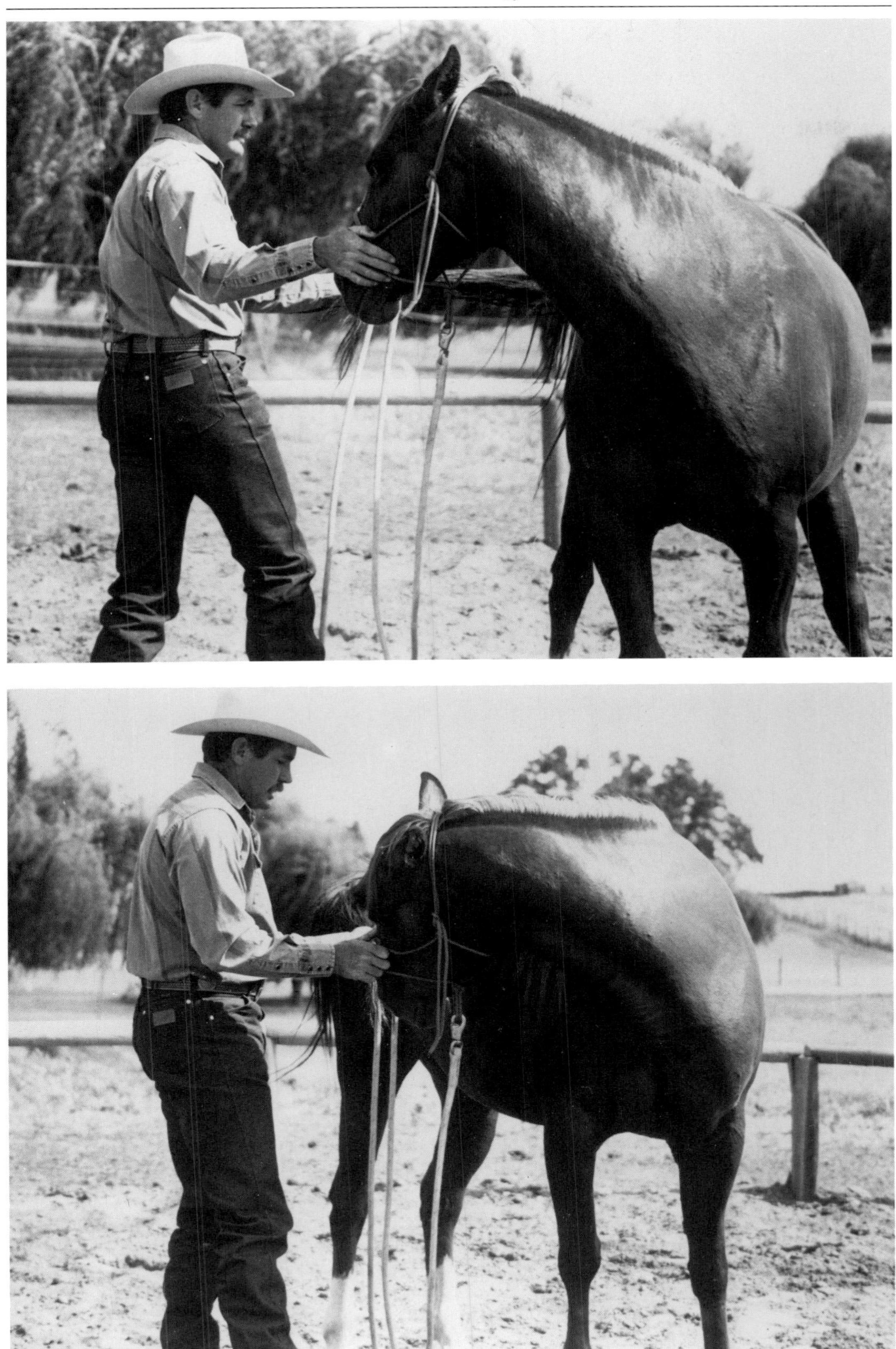

Do this until he can stand still for 10 seconds.

After he bends his neck laterally, cause your horse to move his hindquarters by pressing your fingers into his flanks until he moves his rump away from you.

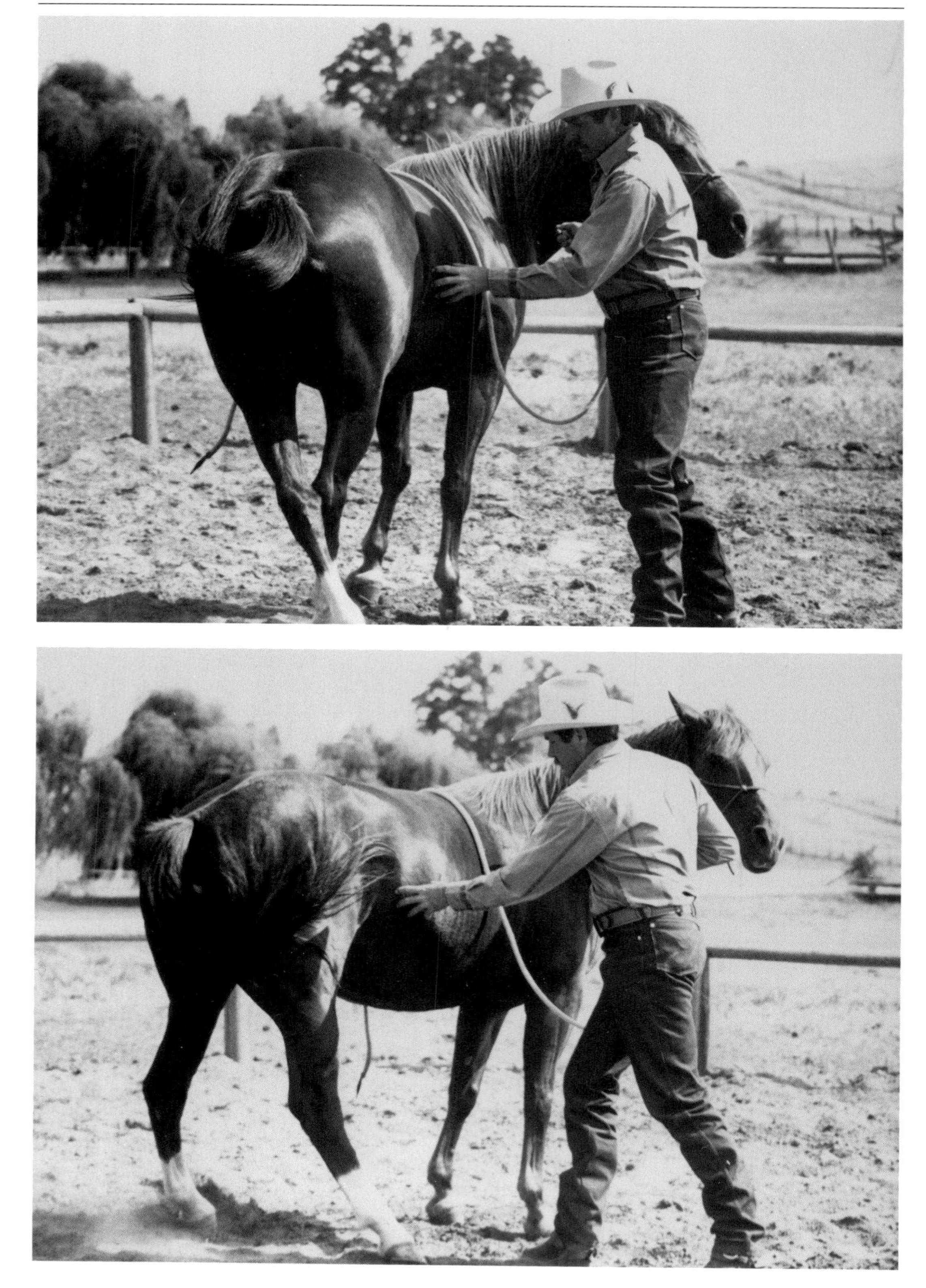

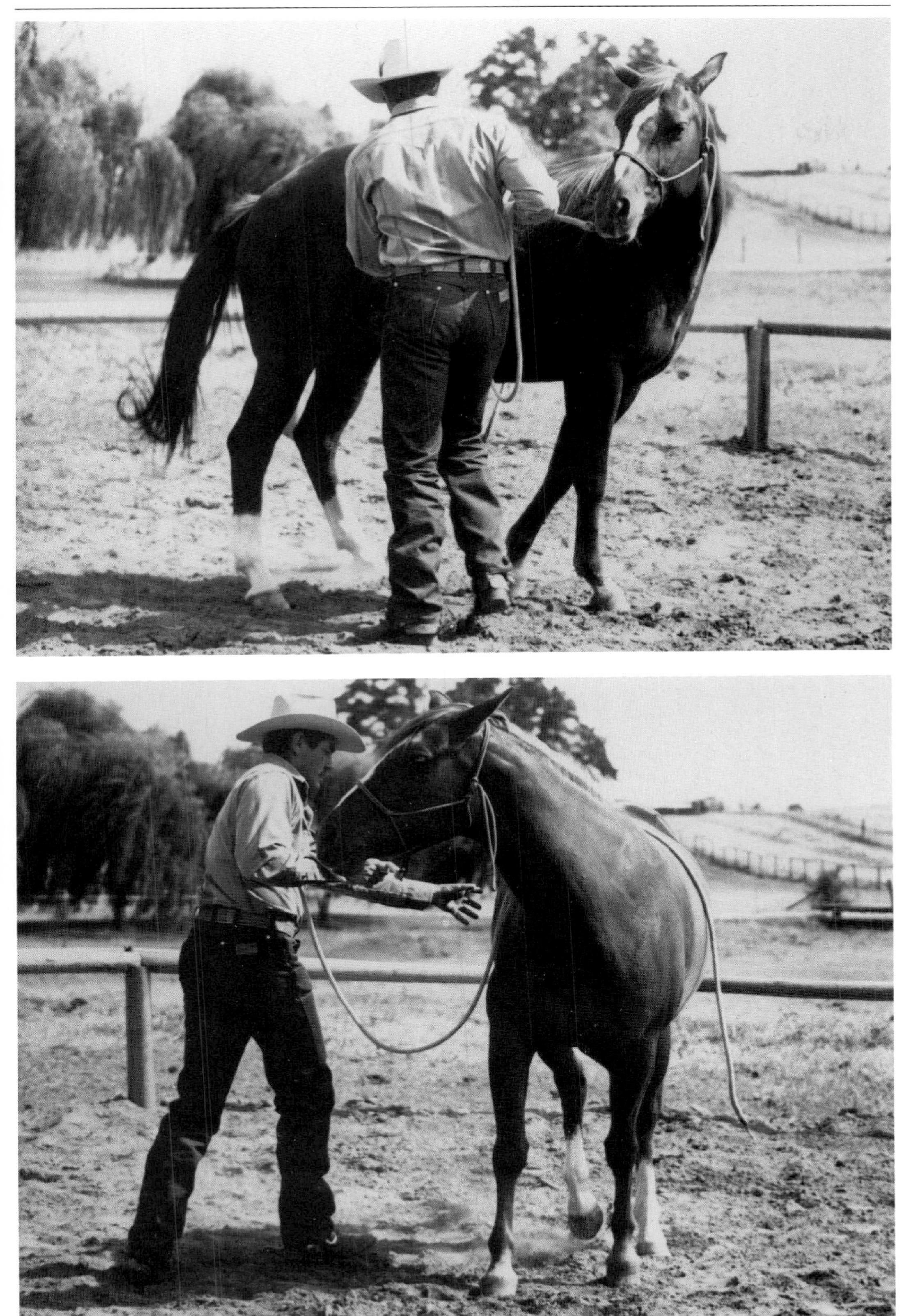

To cause your horse to move his forehand away from you, put your right hand on his jaw and your left hand near the cinch area. Press with your fingers as you walk toward him.

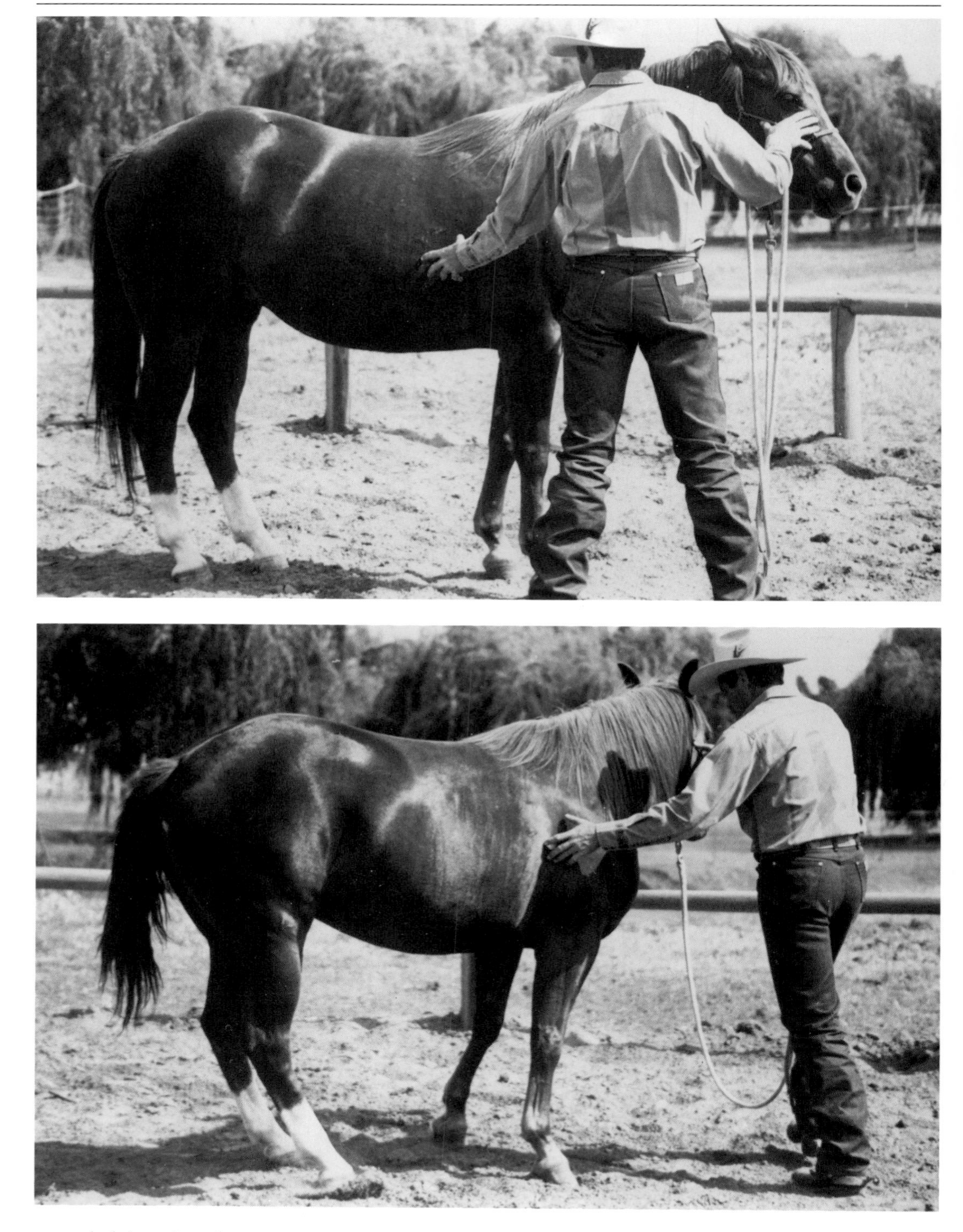

your left hand on his nose.

Remember, the better a horse backs up and also goes sideways, the better he'll do everything else.

c) Moving the Forehand. To cause your horse to move his forehand away from you, stand on his right side first. Put your right hand on his jaw and your left hand near his cinch area. Rub a little first (phase one). Then put pressure on his jaw and cinch area with your fingers (phase two). You'll be walking toward him as you do this, which also encourages him to move out of the way (phase three). Keep walking and increase the intensity of the pressure until he moves his forehand even one step (phase four). To get him to stop, quit stimulating him to move and rub him. Keep walking with him until you've

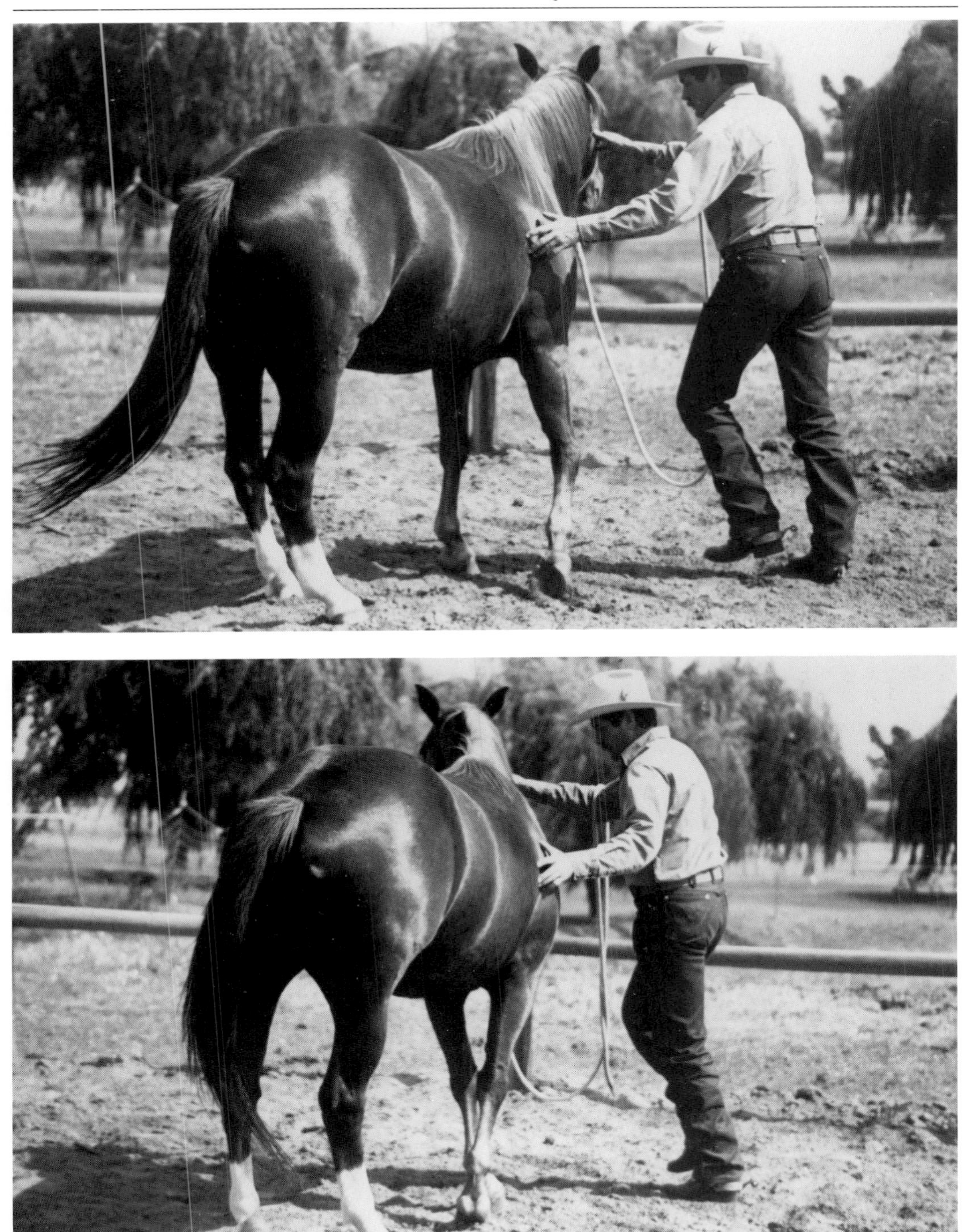

rubbed him to a stop, rather than stopping and letting him walk away from you. This would only teach him to escape from your fingers. Repeat on the other side.

d) Forward. See if you can get your horse to yield forward by either gently pulling his forelock or mane toward you, or putting your hand under his jawbone and encouraging him to move forward with you. Or turn your back on him and see if he will follow you without you touching him at all. In the first two cases, you would use the four-phase theory by just increasing the intensity of your actions, as you did in the other maneuvers.

If you can use your fingers to cause your horse to move forward, back up, bend laterally, move his hindquarters, and move his forehand, you are ready to get him to yield on the different lengths of longe line—12, 22, and 45 feet.

Pat throws energy down the 22-foot rope by wiggling it harder and faster until the horse takes a step backward.

2/ Lead Rope or Longe Line Yielding

Once you're successful in getting your horse to yield to your fingertips, start with a 12-foot lead rope and ask him to yield from you in the following ways. Use the four-phase theory throughout these exercises.

a) Back Up. In phase one, take the tail end of the lead rope by the leather popper and put it in your right hand. Shake your finger at the horse, while holding the lead rope. This is a form of body language that suggests to the horse that you want him to back up. If the horse doesn't move at this suggestion, go to phase two.

In phase two, start wiggling the lead rope or throwing "life" down the lead rope to get his attention and make your point. Although the rope is in action, it's not really affecting the horse directly. It's just moving between you and him. If he still doesn't understand or respond, go to phase three.

In phase three, wiggle the rope faster and firmer so that it will affect the horse directly. The horse should now feel the life of the lead rope and this should be about 4 ounces worth of energy. He feels this life or energy around his head area from the movement of the lead rope, which in turn causes the halter to move. If he is still standing there and not moving, go to phase four.

In phase four, to get your point across, use more energy than the customary 4 ounces in wiggling the lead rope. If you feel you need a fifth phase, continue with even more energy until the horse responds by backing away from you. All this depends on how much the horse resists you.

Most times it's better not to go beyond phase four, with around a pound (16 ounces) of energy. Stay in phase four with that weight or strength of energy and wait for the horse to respond. Look for the slightest try forward or back. Reinforce this behavior by ceasing the action on your part. Remember, some horses are slower than others.

The most common avoidance behavior is for the horse to get himself out of position by taking both his eyes off you and

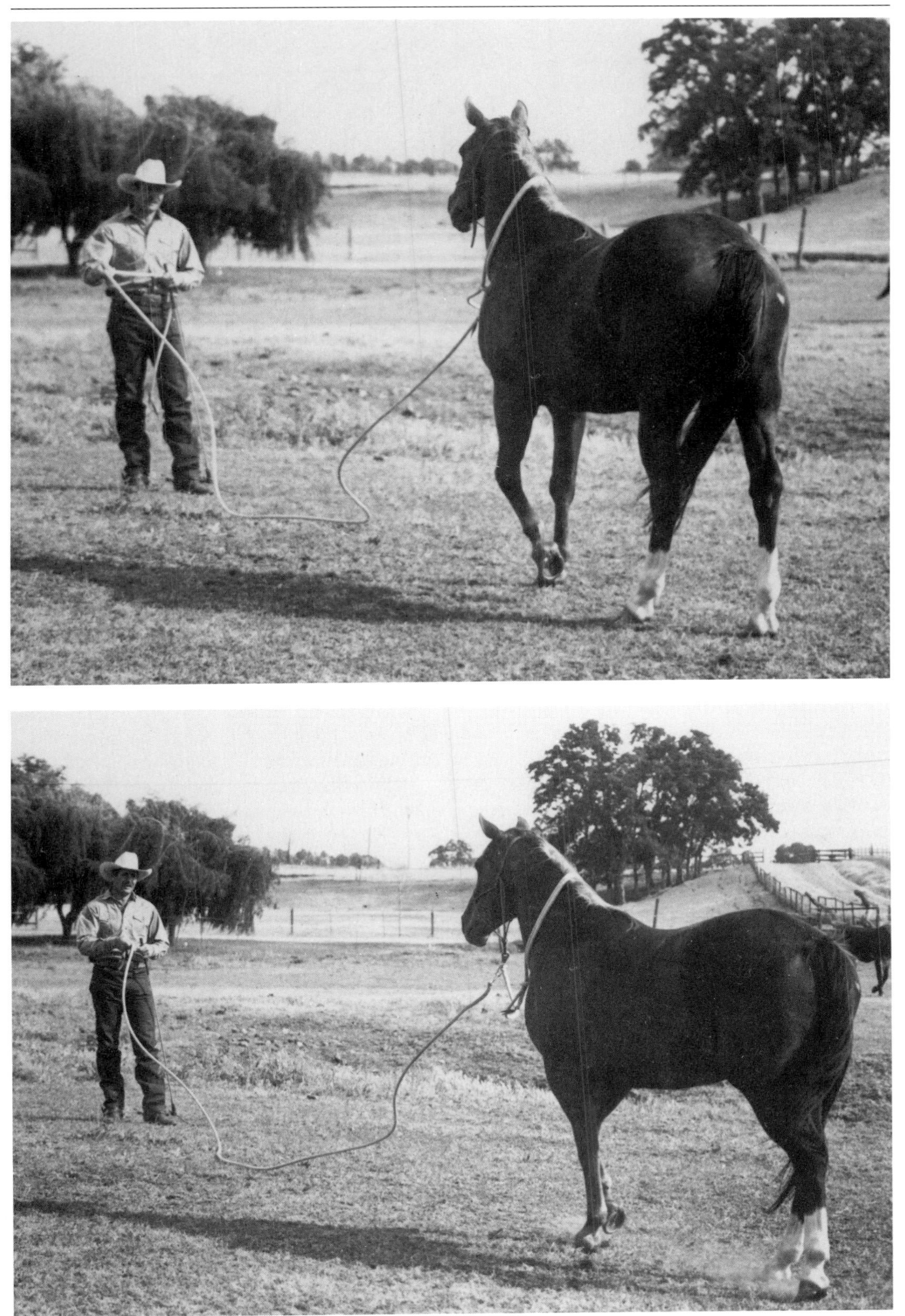

To ask the horse to move in a circle to the right, extend your right hand out to the side and with your left hand swing the tail end of lead rope toward his right nostril. Tell him to quit looking at you with both eyes and go in the direction you're asking. As soon as the horse moves to the right, quit swinging the lead rope at him.

looking at you with only his left eye. This indicates he is thinking of going to his right, rather than straight back.

b) Forward. Here are the four phases of causing a horse to come to you. In phase one, you comb the rope (pull it in hand over hand), asking the horse to come to you. In phase two, your hands are going to close a little more on the rope. In phase three, your hands are going to comb the rope faster, almost to the point where your hands are getting warm. In phase four, your hands lock onto the rope, and as they do, lock your feet and your elbows, and match the horse's resistance. As soon as the horse gives, your hands spring open as if you feel electricity in the rope.

When you do cause the horse to come to you, rub him on the head. Let him stand there, relax, lick his lips, collect his thoughts. Give him 30 seconds to a minute. Then, ask him to back again. Let him settle for 30 seconds, then ask him to come forward. Play this game until you can get him to go backward and come forward by just using phase one and with him keeping both of his eyes on you.

c) Right Circle—Two-Lap Maximum. This is an exercise in which the horse circles around you. You are teaching him to yield his forehand and move out and around you to the right. I suggest you start and end each two laps with the horse facing you with both his eyes front and center. Give him at least a 5-second rest before asking him to yield around you for two more laps.

To get into the proper position for this exercise, think about a pitcher in a baseball game standing on a mound. Draw a little circle around your feet and that's where you should try to stay. That's your mound. For example, in baseball, when a right-handed pitcher throws the ball, he must keep his right foot on the mound until the ball is released. I'd like you to do the same thing.

So, in phase one, ask the horse to move off to the right by straightening your right elbow and stretching your right leg out to the side at the same time. That shows the horse the direction you want him to go. Your left foot is on the imaginary mound.

In phase two, swing the tail of the 12-foot lead rope (which is in your left hand) anywhere from 2 feet in front of his nose to his withers. By swinging the energy in that area, you tell the horse to stop look-

To have the horse move around you in a circle to the left, extend your left hand and with your right hand swing the tail end of the lead rope at the horse's left nostril until he moves to the left.

ing at you with both eyes and go in the direction you're asking. His right eye should be the only one on you and his left eye should be looking in the direction you want him to go.

In phase three, if the horse hasn't moved off, let the swinging of the rope tap the horse anywhere from his nose to his withers with up to 4 ounces of energy. If he doesn't move, go to phase four, which means tap him more than the 4 ounces.

If he still doesn't move, you have to go to phase five. You come off the mound and move toward that horse with authority. Don't shift your line of direction and go behind the horse. Take a line of direction toward the horse's forequarters and keep going until he leaves. When the horse does finally leave, quit swinging. Allow the rope to slide through your hands and go clear to the end. Pass the rope from one hand to the other hand behind your back as the horse moves behind you. Cause the horse to think he's training you to quit swinging that rope.

After he goes two laps, cause him to stop by first going back to phase one, which is to run your right hand down the rope while holding the tail of the rope in the left hand. Stretch your right arm and your right leg.

In phase two, start swinging the rope at the horse's hindquarters, not his neck or withers this time. You're trying to stop the horse now by directing the hindquarters away from you, which causes the horse to stop in his circle and face you.

In phase three, tap him on the hindquarters with the lead rope up to 4 ounces. In phase four, take a shorter hold of the lead rope, getting your right hand closer to the snap so you can swing the lead rope and tap him on the hindquarters more easily. The more he resists, the more you match his resistance.

d) Left Circle—Two-Lap Maximum. In phase one, the right foot stays on the mound. Stretch the left arm and left leg out to the left. In phase two, with the tail end of the lead rope in your right hand start swinging the rope somewhere between 2 feet in front of his nose and his withers or drive line.

In phase three, allow the swinging of the rope to tap the horse up to 4 ounces. If you have to go to phase four, tap him with more than 4 ounces.

In phase five, start moving off your mound toward him and cause him to move off to the left by constantly swinging the rope's end toward his forequarters.

Allow the horse to go no more than two laps. To stop him, once again keep the right foot stationary, and stretch out your left arm and left leg as in phase one.

In phase two, start swinging the rope toward the hindquarters, and in phase three tap him with it. Phase four, choke up on the rope and make it shorter to stop and turn him toward you. If you need to, use phase five and do more than 4 ounces on his hindquarters.

When he stops and looks at you with both his eyes, quit stimulating him. Cause him to come to you and rub him on the

To side-pass your horse to the left, position him with his head facing a wall or fence. Stand on his right side and point your right finger at his eye in a suggestion that the horse move away. This is phase one. Here, the handler didn't have to go to phase two to get the horse to move over. Phase two would be to swing the end of the lead rope, which should be in your left hand, at the horse's body.

head. Let him relax for 30 seconds to a minute or longer if you feel it's necessary. Sometimes, if you give a horse a bit longer to comprehend, he'll catch on sooner. He'll think, rather than react, and end up doing more mentally than physically.

Until you get to Level 2 in Natural Horse-Man-Ship, you really don't want to do more than two laps in this exercise.

e) Side-Pass. Position your horse with his head facing a wall or a fence. Ask him to go to the right first. In phase one, stand to the left of your horse, straighten your left elbow, and point your left finger at his eye in a suggestion that the horse move away.

Phase two, with your left hand pointing toward his left eye, start swinging the rope, which is in your right hand, toward the middle of your horse. In phase three, walk toward the horse and let him run into the swinging rope. In phase four, you keep coming while swinging the rope faster.

Most likely your horse will know to move when you first start swinging the rope because you've taught him what that means in the previous yielding exercises.

To actually get the horse's body moving sideways, alternate swinging the lead rope toward the horse's forehand and hindquarters. Do this back and forth until the horse moves one part of his body, then the next. In time, the horse will move his entire body sideways and you'll only have to swing the rope at the progress string near his withers, not the forehand first, then the hindquarters. He'll make the connection to move his whole body sideways.

Having the horse face the fence takes care of his forward movement, and the swinging rope encourages him to side-pass away from the handler.

One thing to watch while you're doing this exercise is where you hold the lead rope. Don't hold it too close to the snap. Give the horse at least 5 feet. Holding close to the snap won't leave any room to allow the horse to go sideways. Your horse will get confused and maybe angry if, when you ask him to move away from you, you don't allow him enough slack in the lead rope to do that. Now try the same exercise to the left.

f) Come By. This handy exercise will help in teaching your horse to longe over obstacles, cross creeks, go through gates, and enter stalls and horse trailers.

This is a similar technique to the two-lap maximum circling exercise. However, you're going to keep the horse a little

In this come-by exercise, you want your horse to come by you from right to left. Have him positioned 6 to 8 feet to your right as you face a wall or fence.

Horsemanship is nothing more than a series of good habits.

more perpendicular to you and use a fence, wall, or any obstacle as an aid. You want the horse to come between you and that fence, wall, or obstacle. Again, you'll use the four-phase theory.

In positioning yourself and your horse, stand at least 6 to 8 feet away from the obstacle and have your horse 6 to 8 feet away from you, off to the right. If the horse is too close to you, he will not have enough room to build up momentum to come by you.

The first thing you should do is face the fence. In phase one, to get your horse to come by you, going from your right to your left, plant your right foot on the imaginary mound and extend your left arm and leg. Close your left hand on the lead rope and give your horse up to 4 ounces of suggestion, as if to say, "Come by me." When you do this, you'll end up pivoting toward the horse, who is on your right. In phase two, you swing the tail end of the lead rope with your right hand. In phase three, you allow the rope to touch the horse with 4 ounces of energy somewhere in front of the drive line or forward of the progress string around his neck. As the horse comes forward, quit swinging the rope and pivot back into the same position you started as he comes by you. Let enough rope slip through your hands to allow him to go by you at least 6 to 8 feet.

The object is to get the horse to pass by you, but not circle all the way around you. You then want him to turn and face you. When he does, let him stand there for a minute, go up to him, and rub him on the head.

To have your horse come by to the right, put your left foot on the mound, reach out with your right hand and right leg. If he doesn't move, start swinging the rope somewhere in front of the drive line. In phase three, allow the tail of the rope to touch him with 4 ounces of energy. In phase four, allow the rope to touch him more than 4 ounces.

Here is where you might run into a stumbling block. Typically, the horse will start moving backward, not forward. There are several things you can do when this happens. One, give the horse a wider berth. Step farther away from the wall so it will seem similar to the two-lap maximum circling technique. If you need to, move back 10 or 12 feet to give him enough room.

When the horse starts going backward, usually the person stops swinging the rope and lets the horse drag him backward. Let the horse drag you backward, but keep swinging the rope at his front end. Try not to go behind his hips.

Extend your left arm in a suggestion that the horse move to the left, and with your right hand swing the tail end of the lead rope at the horse. He should come through the space you've provided between you and the fence. This exercise comes in handy when you load your horse in a trailer.

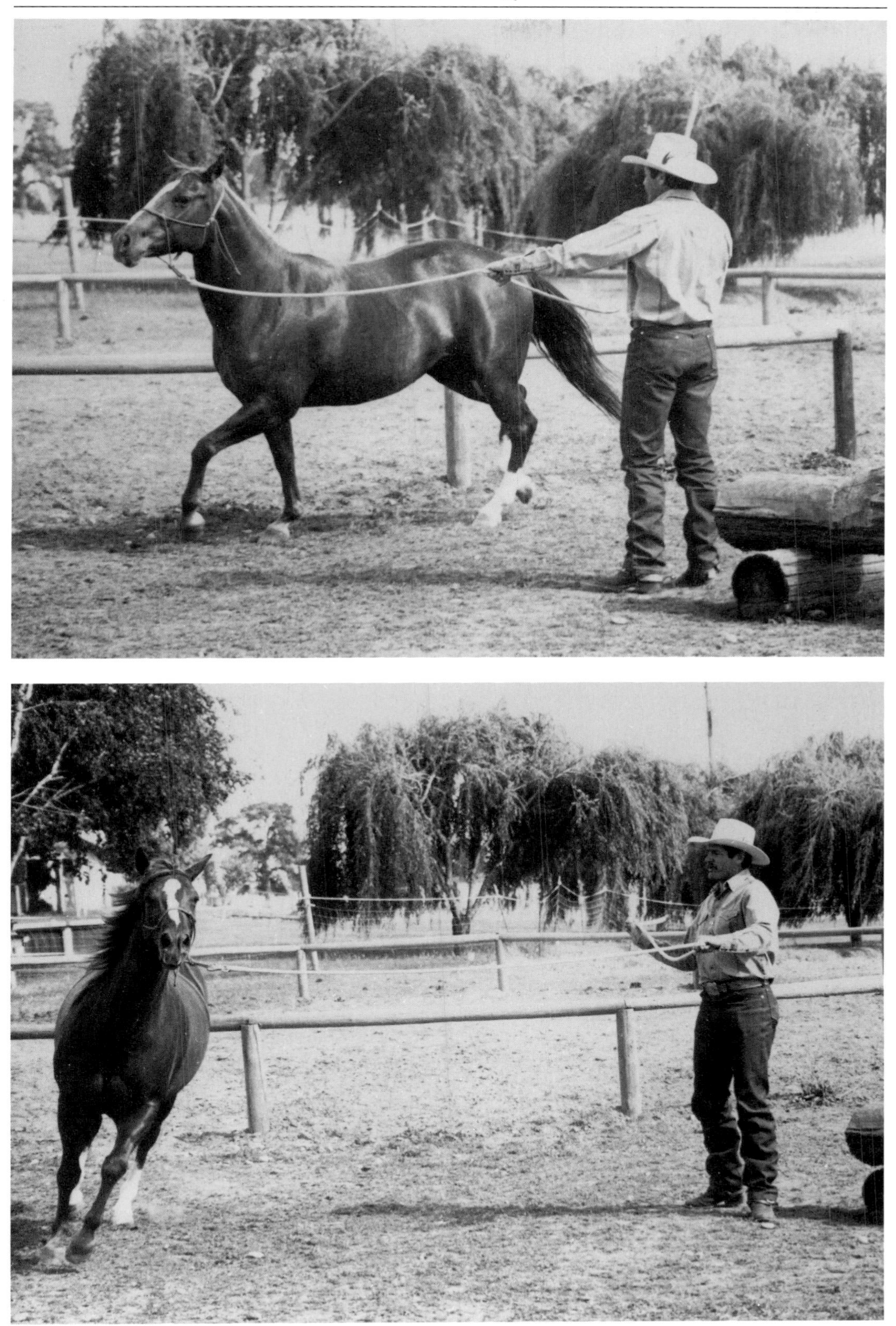

Pat has added an additional challenge to the come-by exercise by asking the horse to continue around and jump a log obstacle.

If this fails, you probably need an extension of your arm as an aid. Pick up your carrot stick and touch him with it. You can use the carrot stick by itself or put a plastic bag or progress string on the end. You shouldn't have to touch him with any more than 4 ounces of energy to get him to come by. If you find you need to use more than 4 ounces, you're probably asking him to go through too narrow a spot at this point in time.

If all fails and you're really having problems, take the 12-foot lead rope off the horse and attach the 22-foot rope. This length rope allows your horse more drift. He doesn't feel as confined as with the 12-foot rope. Some horses really have trouble with this concept, especially since they are born cowards, claustrophobics, and forward-a-holics. Give the horse more time, more space, or more drift.

When you're first trying these techniques with your horse, he might try to outsmart you and cause you to do many defensive things, such as closing your hands on the lead rope too quickly. Remember, hands that close slowly and open quickly are hands that will be effective with horses. Hands that close quickly and openly slowly usually will cause the horse to become heavy

and non-responsive.

Other defensive things he might cause you to do are to quit swinging the rope and to get out of position. If he causes you to do the wrong things at the right time, he wins the game, and that's not what lateral longeing is all about.

Longeing at Longer Distances

When you use a 22-foot rope, use the same procedures to cause your horse to leave the circle and the same techniques to get him to face you that you used with the 12-foot lead rope.

With the longer rope, give your horse a five-lap maximum, instead of a two-lap maximum. Do the five laps in each direction. Use a carrot stick with either a lash string or the plastic bag on the end.

If your horse is on a circle to the right and you want him to increase his speed or go up in gait, follow these phases. In phase one, stretch out your right arm and right leg suggesting that the horse move on faster. At the same time, point the carrot stick 180 degrees out in the other direction, so now your hands are in an outstretched position—the lead rope is in your right

Once you're confident longeing your horse with a 12-foot lead rope, use longer lengths of rope, such as 22 and 45 feet. Put your horse through various challenges. Here, Pat is using a 22-foot rope to longe a horse up and down embankments in a pasture.

hand and the carrot stick or whip in your left. Phase two, spank the carrot stick on the ground about 15 feet behind the horse's tail. This is another suggestion for the horse to move faster. If he doesn't take it, go to phase three, and spank the ground about 7 feet behind the horse's tail. Phase four is around 3 feet. Keep decreasing the distance between you and the horse, until in phase five, you spank directly toward his tail head. Each phase should increase in velocity and tempo.

If you are insistent on getting closer and closer to your horse's tail head with the carrot stick, your horse should increase in speed or go up in gait. That way you can get your horse to go faster at the trot or move up into the canter. Some horses just need more time and more line. But if you've done your work with the 12-foot rope naturally, this should work for you.

There are two commonly made mistakes in this exercise. One, the handler doesn't give his horse a clear suggestion and, two, when he does spank toward the horse, he spanks toward the horse's midsection. From the horse's point of view, this means to yield sideways.

Now, try to get your horse to face you. Your horse is still going to the right. Phase one is to take one giant step with your right leg. Stretch your right arm down the rope to shorten the distance between you and the horse's head. Phase two, start spanking the carrot stick toward the horse's hips. Phase three, take a shorter hold of the rope. Reach down and shorten the rope about 4 to 5 feet while you're spanking your carrot stick toward the horse's hips. Phase four is to reach down one more time until you are close enough to actually touch the horse's hips with the carrot stick or the tail of your rope. It won't take the horse long to realize that if he stops and faces you, he can rest and you'll rub him on the head.

Now you're standing there with the horse near you with both eyes front and center. Repeat the procedure in the other direction. Phase one, ask him to leave. Phase two, raise the stick in the air. If you go to phase three in asking him to leave, make sure you create the energy in front of the drive line.

If all is going well, it's just a matter of increasing the number of laps you want to do. Once you're confident at 22 feet that your horse is listening to you, increase the length of rope to 45 feet.

When you go to the 45-foot line, try playing a game called "Don't change gaits and don't change directions." In this game, if you ask your horse for a trot, say at 22 feet first, he should stay at that gait, even if you feed him more line. He should stay in a circle, not make an oval or take off at an oblique angle to you. If you ask him to canter, he should do the same. He shouldn't change directions or gaits unless you ask him. Whatever length of rope you feed out to him, he should maintain that distance and remain at the same speed he was in before you let out more rope.

When you ask your horse to canter on the line, don't make him keep it up for 20 minutes or more. If you do, you'll create a situation where the horse wants to do less and less. The object is to build the horse's mind, not just exercise his body.

I have three suggestions that you should keep in mind in doing any of these exercises. First, start off going to the right. You might as well get the hard side over with. Most horses do things easier when going to their left.

Second, make sure you can stop your horse on the line as easily as you can get him going. It's just as important to slow down your horse's actions and get him to face you or come to you as it is to get him to follow your requests to move out.

And third, before you go on to the next length of rope, try to challenge yourself and your horse with as many things as you can do at each length. For example, with a 12-foot rope, send a horse over a jump or across a creek, back him into a stall, or load him into a horse trailer. Try these challenges before you go on to a 22-foot rope. This is what longe line logic is all about. The horse learns to meet challenges on short lengths of rope before he graduates to longer ones. One way to increase the challenge is to increase the distance or length of rope. Use your imagination. Plug it in and go.

Application of Concepts and Techniques

Horsemanship is nothing more than a series of good habits. Most horses have bad habits because most people have terrible habits. My goal in this book is to help you form good habits that your horse understands and accepts. With good horse sense habits, developed through the concepts of Natural Horse-Man-Ship, you can communicate effectively with your horse.

I used to think that horsemanship started when you stuck your right leg over the backbone of the horse. I didn't think it had anything to do with what you did before you got on the horse. I, like many other people, fell for the big three lies I mentioned earlier. These lies are told to everyone when they first get on horses: 1/ Just saddle up and get on. 2/ Kick him to make him go. 3/ Pull the reins to make him stop. These three things kept me from getting more than mediocre results. Over many years and through much observation, I've found that the key to real horsemanship is a lot different than saddling, kicking, and pulling. The key is listening to the horse himself and then talking to him on his level.

Here are a series of rituals I call "Pre-Flight Checks" that will make sure two things happen: A/ They will keep you alive. B/ They will put you in a position to have fun with horses. Those are my two aims: Make sure people live through their experiences with horses, and that they have fun. After that, they can excel.

You've learned some longe line logic and lateral longeing techniques. Now, you need to learn how to apply those concepts and that foundation.

Instead of just saddling a horse and getting on like everybody else does, play with your horse every day through lateral longeing and lateral thinking techniques. By giving him the following tests, you can find out what side of the stall or corral he woke up on.

1/ Pre-Flight Checks on the Ground

Rather than just tying up your horse and brushing him off before you saddle, go through some lateral longeing routines. Send him out (with the lead rope) and find out if his hindquarters and forehand will move. Send him forward, and back, move him from side to side. Find out where he is. Do the same thing on both sides.

Offer the saddle (which has been placed in the middle of the pen) to the horse in such a way that he might go to the saddle and find a resting place there. You do this by focusing on the saddle as you send the

Instead of cinching up hard and fast immediately, do it slowly in about three steps.

horse out and around you. When he approaches the saddle, quit longeing him. Let him stop, rest a while, and examine the saddle.

Let's pretend your horse has had only 10 rides in his life. See if your horse will pass a series of these tests. I call them pre-flight checks. In the same way a pilot would check out the airplane before he got in it and took off, you check out your horse before you step foot in the stirrup.

a) Stand by the saddle, which is on the ground, and near the horse's shoulders, but face the horse's hindquarters. Swing the lead rope back and forth over the horse's back. See if you can do this maneuver six times smoothly and with rhythm.

b) See if your horse can handle having the saddle pad put on. Stand on the horse's right side, and put your right foot against the horse's left foot. Reach back, grab the saddle pad, which is on top of the saddle and swing it over to the horse's back.

c) Take the pad and offer it to the horse to smell. Then throw it on his back again.

You do this to make sure the horse can stand your approach and have various things thrown over his back. First throw the rope over, then the pad. Later you'll put the saddle on. Then you can throw your leg over the horse's back. Do everything in a series of small steps that the horse can handle, and from both sides. Try to see the whole process of saddling and mounting from the horse's point of view. If he can get used to these approaches, then you can be polite in saddling and mounting and not abrupt, which is the usual treatment most horses receive from their riders.

2/ Saddling

Most people saddle horses from the horse's left side. From time to time, try saddling from the off side (right side) of the horse. It helps you and your horse become more ambidextrous. Try to become more coordinated; saddling from the off side is one exercise that can help. Besides, you've saved a step. You don't have to walk from the near side to the off side to let down the girth and back cinch.

Now that you're on the right side of the horse, you have to move to the left side to cinch up. Change sides on the horse by standing to one side of his head. Take your hand and ask the horse to move his head to the right and over your head. By doing so, you're now on the left side of the horse's head and have changed sides effectively without moving your feet. You've asked the horse to allow you to change sides. You've asked permission to go through his bilateral vision. Now, you can step to his left shoulder to adjust the cinch.

Many people put themselves in a vulnerable position when saddling by using the right hand and getting a hold of the cinch with the palm up toward the horse's stomach. It bothers some horses, especially sensitive ones. It's like the actions of a predator who gets a hold of the horse's belly.

Instead, keep your toes parallel to the horse, facing his hindquarters, and keep your rope over your elbow so that at any time you can have immediate control if your horse should move. Use the back side of your left hand, allowing it to touch the horse's belly, grab the cinch, and let the cinch replace your left hand. It's a polite way to get a hold of the cinch. Do the same thing with the back cinch; use the backside of your left hand.

Instead of cinching up hard and fast immediately, do it slowly in about three steps. Cinch the saddle firmly enough so that it doesn't slip off, and do a little more lateral longeing before you get on. Ask the horse to pass a few more pre-flight checks, and use the same exercises you've used before.

Cinch up a little more after you play with the horse on the ground. Do this a total of three times before the saddle is secured. Try to time cinching to the breathing of the horse. When he lets out air, cinch up more.

You'll find that if you do lateral longeing first and check your horse out, send your horse over to the saddle, then saddle him politely, pretty soon your horse will be in a more receptive frame of mind to stand still for the saddle. What you're after is respect on the ground because respect later gives you impulsion in the saddle. I don't know if I can stress this enough.

Think of saddling from the horse's point of view. Most people don't really ask their horses for permission. They put them in a situation where they have no choice. The worst scenario for saddling I can think of is cross-tying the horse. At that point, he absolutely has no choice but to succumb.

A lot of people think of themselves as horse lovers, and they do care about horses. They take care of their physical needs by housing them, feeding them, vaccinating, and deworming them, etc. But they don't know how to take care of the mental and emotional states of their horses.

I often saddle my horses while they're untied. I simply put the lead rope over my arm and proceed to saddle the horse. Saddling an untied horse is like asking for permission to put the saddle on, and the horse is granting permission by standing still.

3/ Pre-Flight Checks With Saddle

Here are some pre-flight tests to go through after the horse has been saddled, but before you actually ride. You still have the hand-tied rope halter on the horse's head and the 12-foot lead rope for control. These little tests can be blended together into a nice routine you can put your horse through prior to getting on him.

a) Stand by your horse's side, take the lead rope, and pull the horse's nose to the inside toward you and the saddle. Ask you horse to smell his tail for 10 seconds, then turn loose of the horse's tail and push his flanks away from you with your fingers. This will disengage the horse's hindquarters, and they will move away from you. Now walk in a circle toward the horse's hip. The horse's front end should remain stationary while his rear end moves away from you.

b) Another way to move the hindquarters is to place the rope around the horse's hips. While the horse is standing still, walk behind him with the lead rope. Once you are on the opposite side, pull the rope until the hindquarters disengage, and the horse turns 180 degrees and faces you.

c) Now, when the horse has moved completely around and is facing you, move his forehand away from you. Do this the same way you did in lateral longeing. Raise your hand with the lead rope and move toward the horse's head and

Change sides on a horse by standing to one side of his head. Take your hand and ask your horse to move his head to the right. Now you're on the left side of the horse's head and you've changed sides without moving your feet.

Here's a pre-flight drill to move your horse's hindquarters. Put the lead rope around the horse's hips. Pull the rope until it disengages the hindquarters and the horse moves around 180 degrees to face you.

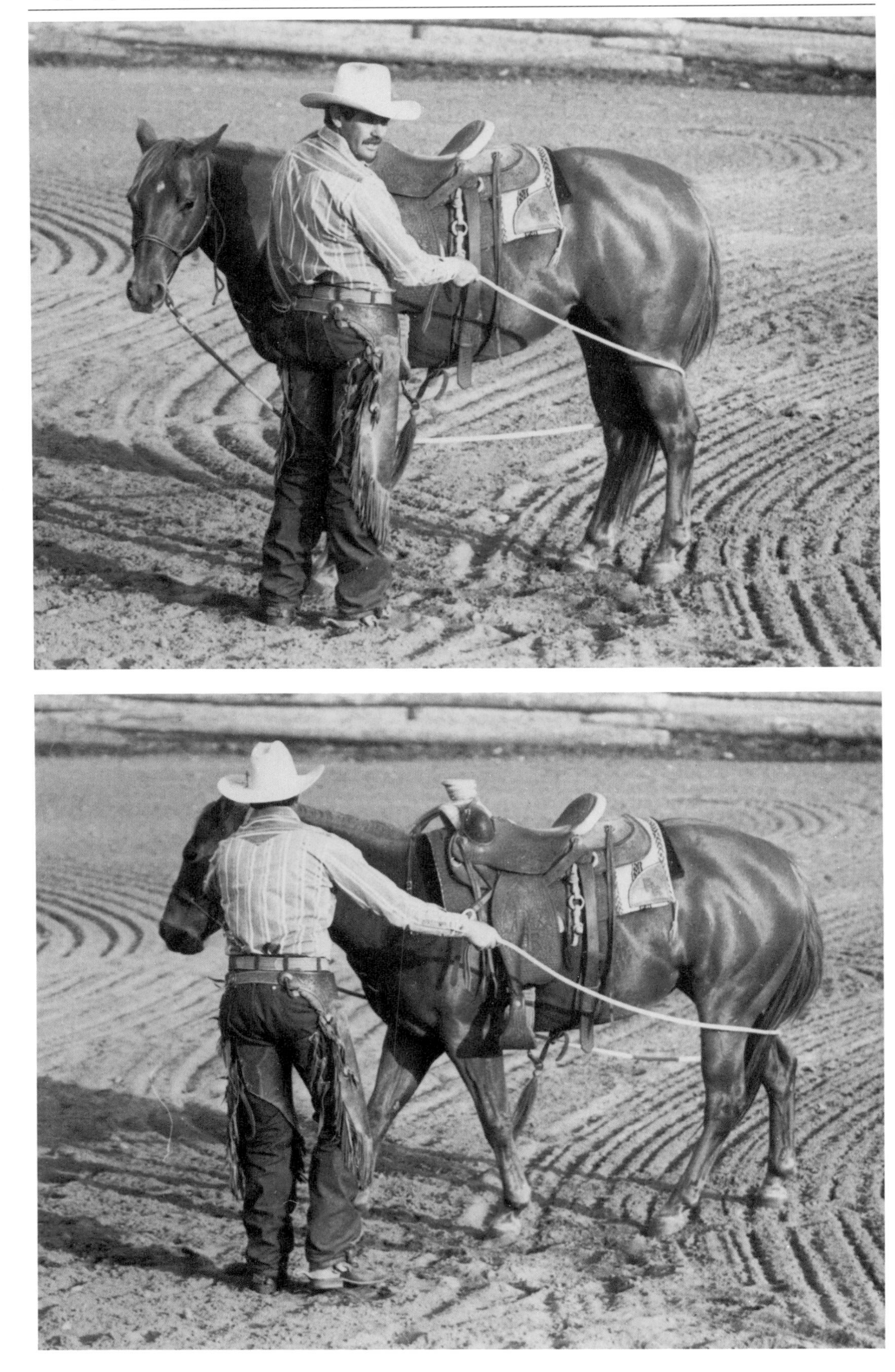

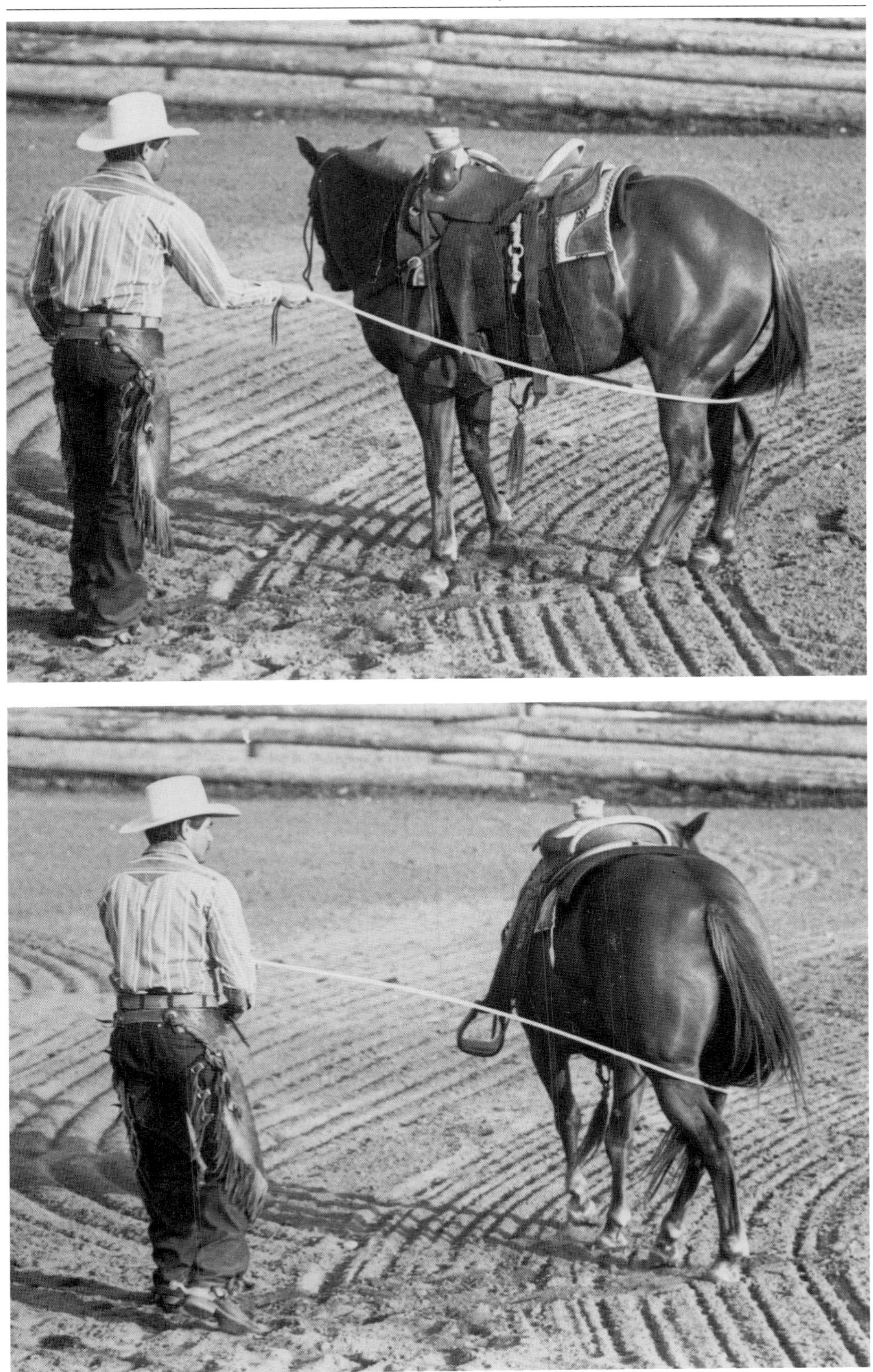

These little tests can be blended together into a nice routine you can put your horse through prior to getting on him.

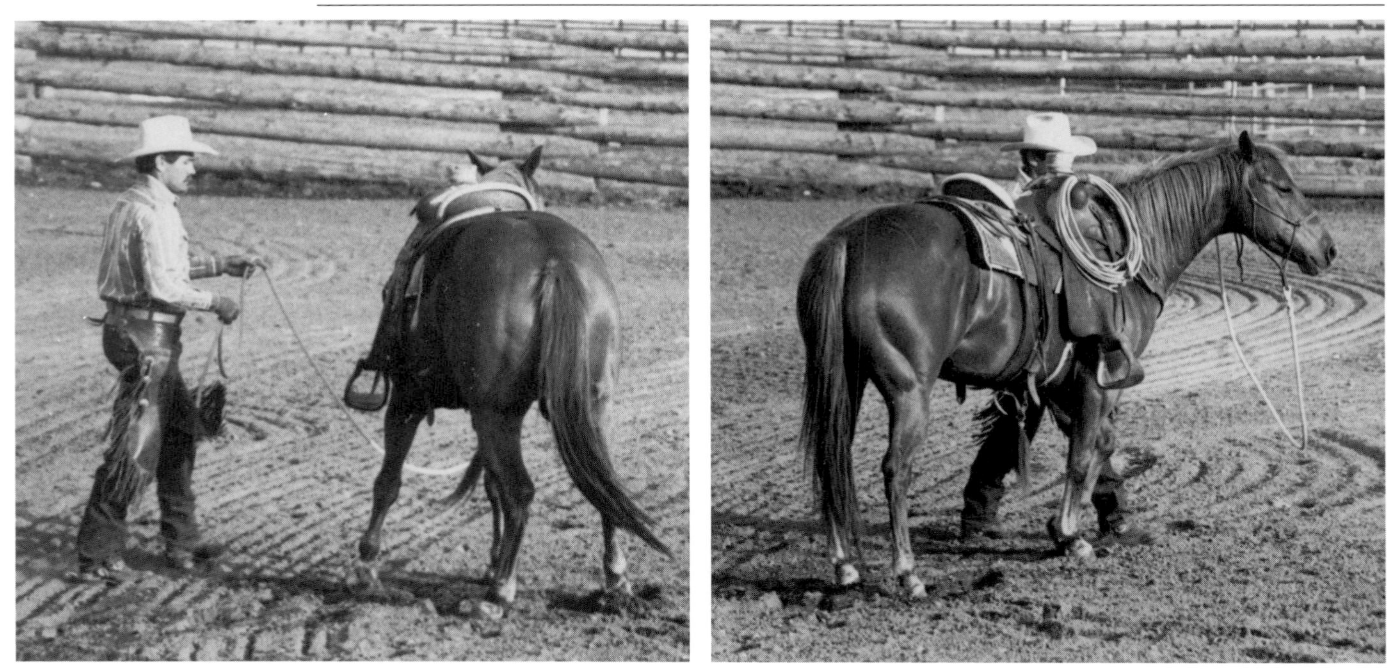

After he is facing you, move his forehand away from you by raising your hand and lead rope and walking toward his head and neck.

neck. If your horse understood his earlier lateral longeing lessons, he should move his front legs over and away from you.

d) When the horse does move away from you, send him out and around, longe him in a circle.

e) Ask him to stop and back up by shaking the lead rope at him as you've done in lateral longeing.

f) Do the above routine on the other side of the horse as well. This way the horse gets used to having you on both sides. He gets to check you out with both eyes.

g) Another drill is to walk slowly toward the horse's right side, put the rope over the horse's poll and around his entire left side, bring it past the saddle, and around the left hip. Take a few steps straight back. When you do, the lead rope pulls the horse's head to his left, and this causes his hindquarters to disengage. Keep pulling until the horse turns all the way around and faces you. Then send him out. This is a fun way to get your horse going out in a circle.

h) Now, do the reverse. Step to the left side of the horse's head and put the lead rope over the head and around the right side of the horse's body. Step straight back and that pulls the horse's head to his right. That disengages his hindquarters, and the horse comes around to his right and finally faces you. Then, let the horse go out and longe around you.

i) Stand by the stirrups and face the horse's head. Swing the lead rope over the head with rhythm. With this little drill, the horse becomes used to things flying over his head. You've done this in earlier exercises, only from a different perspective. You might have occasion someday to have things flying over your horse's head, such as in roping, and want your horse used to this procedure.

j) Quickly walk up to your horse from a few feet away, and position yourself by the stirrup. Put your hand in the horse's mane. Do both sides of the horse. What you are doing is asking the horse for permission to mount. This is a good test for the horse to pass. If he will stand still while you approach him quickly and put your hands on him, he is probably emotionally ready to accept you as the rider.

k) Make sure your horse is standing square on his feet before you get on. See if you can push him off balance by grabbing the saddle horn and moving it back and forth strongly. Do this by putting one hand on the mane and one hand on the saddle horn or pommel. Do both sides.

l) See if the horse will accept you getting on him. Put your foot in the stirrup and get up halfway, but don't mount completely. Rub the other side of the horse's neck with your hand. See if the horse will give you permission to mount by standing still and not fussing. Now, step down. While looking toward the horse's head, back up straight past his hip, and use the lead rope to pull him around to follow you and face you. Again, do both sides. Anybody can get on a horse, but can you get off effectively and in a hurry?

You do these pre-flight checks before you mount because you want to find out where your horse is mentally, and if you can control him with only one rein.

You can easily get into a tricky situation when you first mount a horse. The next thing you know, you're in trouble. I've done it myself. I've saddled up, swung my leg over like John Wayne, and the next thing I knew, uh-oh, the horse is tight and tense and looking at me out of the corner of his eye like "Where did he come from? How did he get there?" I was in trouble then.

Anybody can get on a horse, but can you get off effectively and in a hurry?

4/ Trailer Loading Technique

Don't encourage a horse who's already trying.

Trailer loading is a good example of applying lateral longeing techniques in a real life situation. Remember principles, purpose, and time? Principles is the horse, purpose is the cart, and time is the driver. Lateral longeing provided the principles, trailer loading is the purpose, and time is what you put into it to achieve the desired result.

As I've mentioned many times before, let's first acknowledge that horses are born cowards, born claustrophobics, and born full-throttle-aholics. With that in mind, you're going to use trailer loading to help the horse become braver, less claustrophobic, and less of a full-throttle-aholic. Also, he learns to respect your suggestions.

Horses are programmed by nature to be suspicious of anything like a dark hole or narrow place. No respectable prey animal would ever put himself in such a dangerous position. So consider the horse's point of view before you start out to change his mind. It'll will help you to understand how the horse views the whole procedure.

You'll put a couple of the above-mentioned lateral longeing techniques together and use them in combination all at the same time. The first thing you do is find the proper position to stand and be polite and passively persistent in. Pick a spot to set your stance. Throughout the whole procedure, use rhythm in your movements, and quit stimulating as soon as the horse tries to respond.

First, you ask the horse to pass between you and an obstacle, such as a fence. Make the opening at least 6 feet wide at first. Later you can reduce it to 4 feet, then about 2 ½ feet, which is similar to a trailer's stall width.

To have the horse pass you on the right, place a mark on the ground and put your left foot on it. Put your right foot out in front of your left. Reach out with your right hand on the rope, hold it, and ask the horse to come to you. If the horse resists coming between you and the fence, start swinging the end of the rope (about 2 to 3 feet of it) in your left hand. Match the horse's resistance against the rope with an equal amount of resistance. Keep swinging the rope and don't lose rhythm.

At this point, it doesn't really matter at what you're swinging, but remember position to the eye. So pay attention to what the horse's eye is doing and where it's looking. Where he's looking is where he wants to go.

After the horse resists a little bit, you should feel some kind of a give or yield to your suggestion. At that point, quit swinging, open your right hand and release the slack in the rope, even if the horse didn't pass through the opening between you and the fence.

Repeat the procedure again. And, again, as soon as you feel the horse giving you even the slightest try, quit stimulating him with the swinging rope. Release and let him think about it. Soon, you should have the horse taking your suggestion and moving between you and the fence. After he does come through, you want him to stop and face you and wait for further instructions.

Now, repeat the procedure, but only in reverse. Put your right foot on the spot you've chosen to stand and reach out with your left foot. Also reach out with your left hand on the rope and swing the tail end of the rope with your right hand. As soon as the horse tries to move to the left, quit swinging instantly and open your left hand's hold on the rope. Soon you should have the horse passing between you and the rail.

Now that you have the horse going between you and the fence both directions at about 6 feet away, try the same approach but from a narrower distance, say 4 feet. Remember horses are very perceptive to distances so you must convince your horse that the narrower slot is okay to pass through. Try this until you can get the horse comfortably yielding through the passageway, not escaping or running through quickly out of fear.

Now try this in front of the horse trailer. Place your stance mark to line up exactly in the center of the trailer. If you were facing the trailer, you'd see the divider bar. If you have a tailgate ramp on your trailer, you want your horse to yield over the tailgate, not jump it or refuse it. You want him to move across it with all four feet.

As before, get the horse to pass between you and the trailer at 6 feet away, then decrease that distance until he yields between you and the trailer at 2 ½ feet away. Do both sides until he can pass through equally from right to left.

Before and after shots of Pat loading a reluctant horse into a trailer in front of a group of charros at a clinic in Guadalajara, Mexico.

When your horse passes these tests perfectly, close the space between you and the divider bar. Stand next to it, and as your horse comes around to pass through, ask him to continue on into the trailer and not pass by you. It's that simple.

There are the four things not to do when trailer-loading a horse. These are the four most common mistakes that prove to the horse that you are in fact a predator and not a partner.

1/ Do not wait until you're late for wherever it is you are going—show, rodeo, etc.

2/ Do not lead the horse up to the trailer to see if he won't load.

3/ Do not encourage a horse who is already trying.

4/ Do not holler "Shut the gate," as soon as he gets his hind feet in the trailer the first time.

Instead of making the above mistakes, do the following:

1/ Give yourself plenty of time to practice trailer loading prior to the event. Give yourself all day long if you need to, but it'll probably only take an hour or two the first time. If you give yourself 2 minutes to do a 2-hour job, it'll probably take 2 days.

2/ Don't just lead the horse up to the trailer to see if he won't load. Have your lateral longeing done ahead of time and have your horse responding to all six of the yields before you approach the trailer. Go through the "pass the hole" test as mentioned above.

3/ When I say, "Don't encourage a horse who's already trying," I mean don't keep stimulating him after he's already responded

with a slight try. This is what causes horses to become more claustrophobic. You've probably seen situations in which there are several people involved in trying to load a horse. When the horse gets anywhere near the stall opening, they all start clucking, or they'll clasp their hands together and push him into the trailer. All this does is prove to the horse that you are a predator. This causes him to be more distrustful of you and more claustrophobic.

4/ When the horse finally does put himself in the trailer, hind feet and all, let him come out as soon as he likes. Or wait a couple of minutes and ask him to retreat, then repeat. Cause him to do it several times so it's clear to him what you want, and that it won't hurt to do it.

If you're successful with this, then you have tested to see that your lateral longeing techniques and principles are working. Most other challenges you and your horse engage in should be easy from now on.

TIME

"The secret is to play with your horse, and work on yourself."

HUMANS TEND to be time-oriented, and horses do not. In their natural environment, where they graze all day long, horses are not really concerned with what time it is. But put into the human environment and fed twice a day on time, they can get to know to the minute when it's feeding time.

One of the questions most often asked of me is how long is too long when you work with a horse on the ground, at liberty, and in hand. The answer is 30 seconds. If you work with a horse for 30 seconds, and you realize you are working with him rather than playing with him, that's too long. The secret is to play with your horse, and work on yourself.

How long you should laterally longe a horse is a different question. You should laterally longe a horse until he shows you respect, and you're satisfied that his disposition and energy levels are something you can handle when you get on his back. When I longe a horse and see that he still has a lot of play or buck left in him, I don't mind that, and I like that in my horses. So I wouldn't longe the horse as long as some people would. But what is a thrill for me might be a chill for you. The point is that there are no hard and fast rules when it comes to this question. You adjust to fit your situation. What might fit me, might not fit you, and vice versa. So my suggestion is to laterally longe your horse until you feel your horse's respect system is adequate. Because if you have his respect, you'll have his impulsion. If your horse is very impulsive, then I would do a lot of backward and sideways longeing to diffuse some of that impulsiveness and get him to listen to you and not his oats.

But the most important part of all this is that you are playing with your horse, not working with him. As soon as it isn't play anymore, then 30 seconds later it's too late. Anything after that is work. You should've quit while you were ahead.

Some horses have a lot of play in them. Other horses have a lot of energy and it might not be just play. Read your horse and distinguish the difference between when he is playful and when he is energized.

One way to tell if you've over-exercised your horse in any way is if the horse is sweating over the top of his tailhead. Then, you've probably overdone it. It takes a lot for a horse to work up a complete body sweat and to be sweating over the top of his tailhead.

Another question I get asked often is "What is the longest I've ever seen any particular technique take?" And the answer to that is 2 days. I remember one time I wanted to test my patience in how long a certain technique would take. The technique I was testing was "riding like a passenger." A little mare came to me quite scared to have a human on her back. She was unrealistically frightened. So I set out to see how long it would take, and 48 hours later I was still sitting on her. It took that long for the mare to finally feel she had grown a human on her back. That was a great test of my patience. Today, however, using Natural Horse-Man-Ship techniques and knowing what I know about lateral longeing, I could probably handle this same situation in only 2 hours. In those days, I just saddled up and got on.

Horses are very perceptive to change. A horse might notice the look on your face when you're trying to get him to do something. This is important, but not nearly as important as when you take that look off and quit stimulating. It's not what you do, it's when you quit doing it. Timing is everything.

What is a thrill for me might be a chill for you.

IMAGINATION

USE YOUR imagination in playing with your horse. Learn to see things like a kid again. Think of every new thing or situation as an exciting challenge. Imagine that your horse has had only 10 rides on him. Imagine that you're starting all over again. Imagine that everything is a game.

Work on yourself, but play with your horses. I've mentioned this several times. Use your imagination in the games you dream up. Be provocative. The best way I know how to explain provocative is to explain to you what provocative isn't.

Have you ever had company that wasn't exactly provocative? The kind that makes you yawn and look at your watch. Are you that way for your horse? If your horse is recreation for you, can you be recreation for your horse?

Most horses stand around and are overfed and underexercised, especially mentally and emotionally underexercised in their stalls or paddocks. Horses are very social and playful animals. At every swimming pool I've ever been to, there's a big sign that says "No horseplay." The first

"If your horse is recreation for you, can you be recreation for your horse?"

Use your imagination when you laterally longe your horse. Ask yourself, "What can I get my horse to do?" Here, Pat asks his horse to walk over a tippy bridge, to stand on a mounting block, and to back through a log obstacle.

sign you ought to put up at your stables is "Horseplay done here."

In the courses I've conducted all around the world, I invariably have students come up to me after a morning of lateral longeing, and say to me that they can't believe how good their horses are behaving. They exhibit none of the problems the students came to the clinic to solve, and the students just can't imagine why. I remind them that they just didn't saddle and get on. Remember that prior and proper preparation prevents P-poor performance.

Look around your environment and rather than trying to find the rules about what you are not supposed to do with your horses, think of things you can get your horse to do. Say to yourself, "Can I get my horse to go up that bank or cross that river while I'm standing here or maybe back into his stall? Could I get even more imaginative? Could I get him to back down the aisle of the barn, make a left-hand turn, and back into his stall?

Use your imagination to test your horse to see if he accepts your saddle. Use lateral longeing to send your horse to your saddle, which you've placed out in the arena or pasture. What you want is for your horse to find his comfort zone next to your saddle. After a few days of lateral longeing in which you end the lessons by sending your horse to the saddle, your horse will almost drag you to your saddle. He'll see it

Send your horse to your saddle to inspect it.

When saddling, challenge yourself and your horse. Make it his responsibility to stand still untied, and you try to saddle from the off or right side.

If you're a good leader for your horse, he'll be a good follower.

as his comfort zone, the place where you stop stimulating him. It's almost as if he were saying, "All right, already, get me saddled."

See if you can saddle your horse without him being tied up or anybody holding him. Make it his responsibility to stand still to be saddled. As an additional challenge, saddle your horse from the off side or right side, and see how this one imaginative idea can benefit you and your horse in several ways. 1/ You'll be approaching your horse from his right eye, instead of his left eye which is the typical side. This gets your horse more used to you on his right side and helps balance his left- and right-sidedness. 2/ You'll be using muscles that you don't often use. Therefore, you're practicing more coordination, which helps you to be more physically fit. 3/ If you put your cinches in your keeper, you'll find that you save a full step of walking around the horse to get them down when you saddle your horse.

By using your imagination to challenge your horse, you can help him to become braver, less claustrophobic, and less of a full-throttle-aholic, and he'll learn to respect your ideas and suggestions. For this, your horse will pay you many returns.

Einstein said that imagination is even more valuable than knowledge. I've shared with you some knowledge about how not to just longe a horse around in mindless circles. Now you add in the imagination. Be a good leader for your horse, and he'll be a good follower. Teach him how he can have some people sense. You learn horse sense.

Remember to use your imagination because your horse is using his.

Work on yourself, but play with your horses.

NATURAL HORSE-MAN-SHIP

IN THE SADDLE

ATTITUDE

THERE SEEM to be two major attitudes when it comes to riding horses. One is to approach riding as developing a lifetime partnership. The other is just saddle a horse, get on, and treat the horse like an inanimate object.

I'm going to presume by this time that you are after one thing—to develop a lifetime partnership with your horse. To do this, you really have to develop your attitudes and your mind so that you are a leader, a Natural Horse-Man. You need to be the alpha animal in your horse's society, on the ground and on his back.

If you adhered to the following three things, you would learn very little in 20 years with horses and they would shape your attitudes considerably. 1/ Don't leave your state or your county. 2/ If you ride western, don't watch anybody who rides English. 3/ Don't take up Natural Horse-Man-Ship as a hobby. I guarantee that these are three sure ways not to make much progress in 20 years of owning horses. In the first two, your attitudes toward horses and horsemanship would be shaped by a lack of exposure to other horsemen and types of horsemanship. In the last one, you'd never benefit from all the knowledge that you can learn in Natural Horse-Man-Ship. Your attitudes would remain archaic and you would go nowhere. A good motto here is "Never say 'never.' Don't always say 'always.' Usually say 'usually.'"

To become a Natural Horse-Man, you have to be positive, progressive, and natural. To understand these three things, you have to understand the opposite of each.

The opposite of positive is negative. Instead of using the power of positive thinking, you allow the power of negative thinking to rule you. But if you're in a happy or positive mood while you're riding, you transmit that to your horse and it affects him. If you always do what you've always done, you'll always get what you've always gotten.

At my clinics, I often say, "Smile, whistle, and ride." That's a real powerful state-

"If you're happy or in a positive mood while you're riding, you transmit that to your horse and it affects him." Pat and a student have fun on their horses, and the horses look like they're having fun, too.

You need to be the alpha animal in your horse's society, on the ground and on his back. Note this horse's ears. His full attention is on his rider.

ment because it's hard to frown while you're whistling; but it's easy to whistle while you're smiling.

I know that sometimes the horse can get so good at out-thinking the human that it gets frustrating. Others will advise you to quit riding, get off the horse, and walk away until you are in a better frame of mind. Here's another alternative. Keep riding, but smile and whistle. When you get frustrated, start whistling. You'll bring that smile back.

Allow your horse some freedom to have horseplay, to express himself.

The opposite of progressive is regressive or stuck in the mud. A lot of people get mediocre results with horses and are happy with that. They don't care to pursue new things and to progress.

When it comes to being progressive, a lot of people get horses gentle and handling okay, but really they never go anywhere with them. Unless you and your horse are progressing, you both get stale. You should be challenging your partnership all the time. If you're not going forward, then you're going backward. One encouraging motto is: "Good, better, best, never let it rest. Get your good better and your better best."

The opposite of natural is unnatural. You have to understand the difference between the way nature does things and the way people do things.

As for being natural, horses are horses, let's face it. At thousands of swimming pools across the world I've seen the sign, "No horseplay." I've put up a sign at my ranch that says "Horseplay done around here." Horses love to play, and you have to be natural to allow a horse to play underneath you.

Most people's attitudes change drastically as soon as their horses act up a little and want to play. They yank their mouths to stop them from doing what they're doing. Allow your horse some freedom to have horseplay, to express himself. After all, you are not going to work your horse, you are going to play with him and work on yourself.

Here are some other attitudes to cultivate when it comes to riding your horse.

In the saddle, you need to be assertive, which is somewhere between being aggressive and being a wimp. Then, cause your ideas to become the horse's ideas, but understand his ideas first. "Get your kicks on Route 66, but not on your horse's sides," is a saying I like to use. Not kicking your horse to go is actually an attitude you take when riding.

Hold a conversation with your horse about stopping and yielding back (backing up). You can't pull a conversation, but you can pull a horse. Think of holding a conversation, not pulling your horse.

Our part of the partnership with horses involves four responsibilities and these responsibilities also revolve around attitudes. They are: 1/ Don't act like predator. 2/ Have an independent seat. 3/ Think like

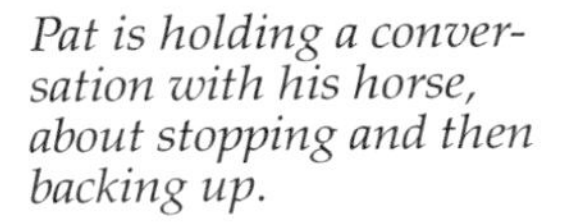

Pat is holding a conversation with his horse, about stopping and then backing up.

a horse. 4/ Use the power of focus.

1/ Don't act like a predator. So many people act like predators when they get scared. They get tight and tense. They also act like predators when they get frustrated or mad. You have to be mentally, emotionally, and physically fit to not act like a predator.

2/ Have an independent seat. It's hard to have an independent seat if you're acting like a predator, either a scared one or a mad one.

3/ Think like a horse. To think like a horse, in this case, a horse-man, is to be half-horse, half-human. We need to have a gallon of horse sense to think like a horse.

4/ Use the power of focus. Using the natural power of focus is a reflection of attitude and is definitely a test of your attitude. You must be strong and fit mentally to ride with a focus. That means you have a picture in your mind of what you want and then you get it. See in your mind where you want to go and cause it to happen. Often, you can tell where a human wants to go by his focus and the look on his face. If, when riding, you look at your horse's head instead of where you're going, you're probably in doubt as to where you're going.

If you can learn to adhere to your responsibilities of the horse-human partnership, you will have the attitude it takes to become a Natural Horse-Man.

If you get your attitude right, anything is possible and four things will come true. 1/ You will be glad that you took up Natural Horse-Man-Ship as a hobby. 2/ You will live through the experience. 3/ You will have fun. 4/ You will obtain excellence.

Watch your thoughts because they become your words. Watch your words because they become your actions. Watch your actions because they become your attitudes. Watch your attitudes because they become your character and you and I are two of life's characters, so watch your thoughts.

This rider is using the natural powers of focus. He is looking where he wants to go, which is to the left. Note the horse's left ear, which is pointed toward the rider. The horse's attention is on the rider and where the rider wants to go.

KNOWLEDGE

RIDING IS nothing more than the mere act of not falling off a horse. A good rider is someone who doesn't fall off a horse almost no matter what the horse does. This also involves knowing when to get out of the horse's way, and not interfering with the horse's movements. You can develop knowledge about riding a horse in the same, natural way you learned about handling a horse on the ground.

Mental, Emotional, and Physical Fitness for the Human

What does mental, emotional, and physical fitness mean? Mental fitness is what this book is all about, natural knowledge. Emotional fitness is something that's within the person. Physical fitness means bodily fit enough to ride well. Usually, the lack of emotional fitness is what keeps most people from achieving true excellence with horses. In other words, a person can become mentally fit by getting the knowledge he needs and become physically fit or coordinated to do what he wants, but he can come emotionally unglued or scattered in a tense or stressful situation. So, emotional fitness is the balancing point between mental and physical fitness.

How do you become mentally, emo-

"A good rider is someone who doesn't fall off a horse almost no matter what the horse does. This involves knowing when to get out of the horse's way and not interfering with the horse's movements."

tionally, and physically fit?

A/ Mental Fitness

To attain mental fitness, you need to seek out knowledge that is going to work naturally. Often, during my trailer loading demonstrations, people ask me, "How can you be so patient?" I look them right in the eye and say, "Because I know it's going to work. Mentally, I'm fit enough to know that the series of adjustments I have to fit this situation will help me make it work. It might not work in 20 seconds or 20 minutes, but it's going to work."

Mental fitness comes from practicing mentally, riding your horse in your mind, or mentally thinking up ways to cause your ideas to be your horse's ideas. It's like playing chess. If you only played chess once every 3 years, you'd never get good at it. But if you mentally played chess every day as you were doing other things and only actually played chess once every 3 years, you still wouldn't be exceptionally good, but at least you'd be a whole lot better at it than if you hadn't practiced mentally at all.

But mental fitness also comes from observing, remembering, and comparing. Know in your mind the things that have worked in the past so you can use that information when the time comes. Observe the behavior and techniques of good horse hands. Remember what worked and what didn't and how it applied to that situation. Compare techniques that fit certain situations and use what works. Many people do something really good with horses by accident and don't know how to duplicate it. They can't re-create the successful solution again because they haven't practiced it in their minds and aren't able to automatically come up with it when needed.

So seek out eagles and fly with them. Search for people who are also mentally fit. Seek out people whose opinions match up with facts. Try to gather a corral full of horsemen.

B/ Emotional Fitness

As I said above, this is something within. Mental fitness is the first thing that is going to help emotional fitness. The stronger you are mentally (and this is attached to the emotional part of yourself), the more sure you are of what you know. Being sure comes with no guarantees, but at least you're sure that you're sure. That might sound a little confusing. But once you understand what "sure" means and how to get sure, you'll develop good judgment. You get good judgment by experiencing and living through your own bad judgment. You learn from that, and then you start learning to get sure. You start taking those pre-flight checks seriously and getting sure that the horse is inviting you on his back, and he is ready to be ridden.

As we get past the age of 35, the kid in us starts leaving. When it does, we try not to exercise the emotional part of us. You'll notice at amusement parks that it's usually the adults who are standing around watching the kids go on thrilling rides. Those thrilling rides exercise an emotional part in us. This is why amusement parks are so popular. It's one of the only ways that we can exercise the emotional part of our bodies and still be sure that we are going to live. There is no guarantee that you are going to live through the ride in the amusement park, but you're pretty sure you will.

Try to be conscious of the above fact and exercise the emotional part of your body. Challenge yourself. What can you handle emotionally? I've seen lots of people really develop intellectually and acquire lots of knowledge about horses, but they don't develop emotionally. And it keeps them from physically ever being able to really achieve their potential.

Open up your mind and become aware of how important your emotions are. Use lateral thinking to find other things you can do to help yourself become more emotionally fit.

Sending your horse to a horse trainer to learn to put up with your inadequacies is only going to last a week at best.

Riding bareback can help you become physically fit for riding. You'll learn to follow your horse's movements and develop an independent seat.

C/ Physical Fitness

If you're going to become a unit with your horse and develop a lifetime partnership with him, you have to become mentally, emotionally, and physically fit as you are trying to get your horse mentally, emotionally, and physically fit. Sending your horse to a horse trainer to learn to put up with your inadequacies is only going to last a week at best. And having the horse get mentally, emotionally, and physically fit and have to carry you (an unfit rider) around is not going to work. So if you want to become a unit, there has to be this parallel. You have to be as fit as your horse.

As part of physical fitness in riding, learn to become a great passenger on your horse. Learn to ride bareback; spend a lot of time riding without a saddle. You'll learn to follow your horse's movements or else you'll fall off. This helps to develop your independent seat.

There are other ways to get more physically fit: bicycling (two-wheel and unicycle), snow skiing, water skiing, swimming, playing on a trampoline, gymnastics, yoga, aerobics, stretching, soccer, dancing, etc. As you get more physically fit, you can be a better leader for your horse.

One of the things that I do personally is ride a unicycle. I believe that the unicycle doesn't just *improve* my balance, it *proves* my balance, and it works on me mentally, emotionally, and physically. Mentally, I have to constantly figure out how to keep my balance and not fall. Emotionally, I have to accept the possibility of falling, and physically all parts of my body have to work to keep me from falling. It's the one "fun-cersize" I've found that improves every aspect it takes to become a great rider.

One of the best ways to help your horse become emotionally fit is to present him with interesting challenges, based on lateral longeing techniques.

Mental, Emotional, and Physical Fitness for the Horse

I've talked about mental, emotional, and physical fitness for the human. Now, let's talk about it for the horse.

A/ Mental Fitness

Mentally, horses tend to use the right side of their brains, the instinctual side, more than the left. Human beings tend to use the left side more. As a goal, you should try to get your horse to exercise the left side of his brain, to become knowledgeable, to get where he can turn loose of Mother Nature, the instinctual side. You want him to be a learn-aholic, to put Mother Nature on the shelf, and want to learn the input you have to offer. Until he puts Mother Nature on the shelf, he won't get mentally fit the way you want.

Some horses get very mentally fit in knowing how to avoid the human or how to cheat him. They play games with humans. What you want is the horse to be mentally fit toward Natural Horse-Man-Ship. Schooling him in lateral longeing is the first step. This helps him to put Mother Nature on the shelf and also helps him want to get in tune with you. Your horse gets interested in what you are doing and takes up Natural Horse-Man-Ship as a hobby. Then you become recreation for your horse.

B/ Emotional Fitness

Emotionally, horses are easily scattered. This is where helping your horse to become braver, less claustrophobic, and less of a full-throttle-aholic comes in handy. Presenting interesting challenges to horses, based on lateral longeing techniques, is one of the best ways to help horses become emotionally fit.

One of the first things we've all been taught, along with saddle up and get on,

Horses key into the emotions of their riders, as well as other horses. On a trail ride this is particularly evident. If all the horses and riders are calm and quiet, they stay that way. But if one horse acts up, the others can be affected.

kick the horse to go, and pull him to stop, is to not let the horse know you're scared. It is a true statement that if you are emotionally distraught, the horse is going to know it. He knows it because horses are programmed to tune in to emotions. They're always aware of the emotions of other horses around them. For example, when you go on a trail ride and one or two horses get hyped up, many of the rest of them come unglued, too.

Because a part of horses' survival mechanism is to stay in tune with the emotions of other animals, they key into our emotions easily. There's no closer kept secret than that between horse and rider. A horse knows when you're shaking in your boots. Take showing horses as an example.

If you've got the show ring jitters, your horse will pick up on it and start to associate your nervousness with competition. Then he becomes scattered, too, which only makes you more nervous because your horse is blowing the class. This is where your emotional fitness is so important. It's something he gets from you. You must be the leader in his environment and control his fears by not giving him any of yours. He'll feel as confident as he can if you'll feel as confident as you can.

C/ Physical Fitness

Physically, horses fly from fear. Get your horse's physical fitness to correlate with his mental and emotional fitness and his flight from fear will turn into impulsion, which you can use in getting him to perform.

You can get your horse physically fit by just riding him, especially trotting. Trot-

Trotting your horse is a good way to help him become physically fit.

When you ride in your mind, you're riding to and from focuses.

ting is the natural gait of the horse, and he can do it longer than he can loping or galloping. When trotting, you should trot each diagonal equally so you develop both sides of the horse and don't wear him out by constantly trotting to only one diagonal. Vary your routine while trotting. Sit the trot and stand the trot. This helps both you and your horse adjust together during the trot.

Other ways to get your horse physically fit are anything involving the six yields. Balance all of them. In other words, try to not just go forward or only do left-hand turns. Instead, practice all six of the yields equally.

It's important to get your horse balanced mentally, emotionally, and physically, and in that order. The same goes for yourself. What you don't want is for your horse to become physically fit and mentally and emotionally scattered. This is a common problem with lots of horses.

Everything in the human starts in the mind, goes through the body down the legs to the feet, and to the horse, which goes into his mind, through his body, down the legs and to his feet. So you can see the correlation between the horse's fitness and yours, between balancing and paralleling the mental, emotional, and physical fitness of both parties for developing a lifetime partnership.

Here, Pat is focusing on spinning to the left. He looks where he wants to go and his body follows. The horse feels Pat's focus and his body movements follow Pat's.

Focus

If riding is nothing more than the mere act of not falling off a horse, then what else is involved in achieving excellence? It's riding in your mind, which means you ride with a focus. You have an overall focus of what you are trying to achieve, and you might have an exact focus on where you want to go.

There are only three places to go as far as I'm concerned and that's to go somewhere, nowhere, or somewhere else. You need to learn the focal points for somewhere, nowhere, and somewhere else. For example, in the dressage arena you have different letters for reference points for going somewhere or somewhere else in a straight line or an arc. The middle of the arena is marked with an "X," the only letter in the arena that can be described as nowhere. It's where you want to start and stop. When you ride from the letters "A" to "C," which are on opposites ends of the arena, you ride from somewhere to somewhere else. When you reach "C," you have to turn and ride somewhere else. You continue to change your focus from somewhere to somewhere else throughout the dressage test. At the end of the test, you decide to stop at "X" and you mentally focus on nowhere. You literally stop riding at "X," which is a physical spot in the dressage arena. But, in time, you learn to carry "X" with you, and it's always under you.

Practice riding somewhere, which is out in front of you. Practice riding nowhere by mentally focusing below yourself. You cause yourself and your horse to come down to nowhere or stop altogether. This is how the horse feels your leadership. When you ride in your mind, you're riding to and from focuses. And what transpires in your mind has an effect on your body, and that, in turn, has an effect on the horse. He actually feels what your body does.

Progressive Steps of Firmness (Ask, Tell, Promise)

Progressive steps of firmness are the steps you take in convincing your horse you want to accomplish what you've focused on doing. Let's say you're riding along a trail; you've got a focus in your mind of where you want to go; you're mentally, emotionally, and physically fit, and your horse is as well. But then your horse doesn't do what you want. He starts to disrespect your leadership decisions. For example, he doesn't want to go forward over a creek. What do you do? You should keep things fun, but start going faster, firmer, and fairer with your encouragement to go forward, while keeping it friendly.

These are the progressive steps of firmness. Another way of saying it is ask, tell, and promise. You are first going to ask your horse to do a specific thing. If he doesn't do it, then you're going to tell him, and finally, you're going to promise him that he is going to do what you want.

Promise is the firmest thing you can do and you need to know what that is. A lot of people think that kicking is the firmest thing you can do to make a horse go. But, as stated earlier, kicking is not the natural dynamic for forward movement—spanking is. So spanking is the firmest thing you can do for going forward. If you got to the point where you had to spank to make your horse go, you'd want to do it faster, firmer, fairer, and friendly without losing the smile on both cheeks and without losing the squeeze below your knees.

What if, instead of not going forward, your horse doesn't want to stop? Pulling back with both hands is the normal technique for stopping a horse. However, the firmest thing to do in Natural Horse-Man-Ship is to reach down and bend the horse with one rein. That is how you would promise a horse that you two are going to stop.

Now, to slow down, stop, and back up without using one rein, you have another conversation with your horse, but this time it's about riding down to a stop and yielding back or backing up. As you're riding along, say at a canter, pick a focus straight in front of you. You're riding away from somewhere. When you want to go nowhere, pick up your reins, hold them in two hands, sit down in your saddle, and relax. Simply quit riding forward. There's a moment of suspension when the horse feels you quit riding forward and instead feels you start riding backward. You take the life out of your body when you quit riding forward. After the horse feels you're not going forward anymore, now you start whatever degree of slow down, stop, and/or back up you want. How far back do you want to go? By that I mean, do you want to slow down from a canter to a trot, or from a canter to a trot to a walk, or from a canter to a trot to a walk to a stop, or from a canter to a trot to a walk to a stop and then to a back up? Your body language tells your horse what you want him to do and how much. This is how the horse feels you. If he doesn't stop at this suggestion, then you go to the next progressive step of firmness.

As you pick up your reins and get the horse's attention, you hold them between your thumbs and your palms. This is about a 4-ounce hold. If the horse didn't stop when you held the reins that way,

Your body language tells your horse what you want him to do and how much. This is how the horse feels you.

*When his owner **asked** him to go into the stream, this horse said "No." When Pat **told** him to cross, he reconsidered his plight before Pat had to **promise** him he'd cross.*

then you could get firmer by closing your index fingers, then even firmer by closing your middle fingers, firmer yet by closing your ring fingers, and firmest by closing your little fingers and, therefore, your entire hands on the reins. You've still not pulled on the reins yet; you're only holding the reins firmly and riding backward.

Now, if all of the above doesn't work, and the horse still hasn't slowed down, reach down with the right or left rein and bend his neck around. Hold his head firmly if you feel you have to get him stopped completely.

This is how you ask, tell, and promise your horse to go forward and backward, and to go from somewhere to nowhere.

TOOLS

TOOLS HAVE to be classified as artificial aids. But there are two distinct types of tools: communication devices and torture devices. You should be able to recognize a Natural Horse-Man by the tools he uses and also by the tools he wouldn't use. The latter are restrictive, non-communication tools of normal horsemanship.

"In Natural Horse-Man-Ship, you learn to ride and develop your skills with only one rein."

The tools I suggest you use for Natural Horse-Man-Ship while riding are:

1/ rope jaquima
2/ progress string
3/ carrot stick
4/ mecate reins
5/ rawhide or leather jaquima (optional)
5/ snaffle bit
6/ bareback pad (optional)
7/ saddle (of your choice)
8/ saddle pad
9/ spurs

These would be all the tools in your tack room you intend to use in developing a foundation on your horse from the 11th ride to 1,100 hours. (From the 11th ride to 1,100 hours is the critical learning period for a horse developing basic riding and handling skills.) With these tools, you would develop your life-long partnership with your horse.

In a normal tack room, you would probably find two to twelve different bits, tie-downs, cavessons (anything from leather to barb wire), running martingales, German martingales, draw reins, different crops and whips, side pulls, spurs, saddles, and saddle pads.

Unfortunately, most humans are direct-line thinkers. They are mechanical in nature, and, therefore, tool-oriented. Most humans look at tools as their progressive steps of firmness. The tools become good excuses for bad hands and not enough knowledge. The intent of this book is to give you natural knowledge—knowledge that works naturally. There are distinct comparisons between Natural Horse-Man-Ship and normal horsemanship.

Natural Horse-Man-Ship is obtained

through communication, understanding, and psychology. Normal horsemanship can be obtained through mechanics, fear, and intimidation. In Natural Horse-Man-Ship, the human is positive, progressive, and believes in the horse's point of view. In normal horsemanship, the human behaves traditionally and believes in his point of view. And instead of adjusting to fit situations, the normal horseman is rule-oriented. Finally, the Natural Horse-Man puts principles in front of goals, while the normal horseman puts goals in front of principles.

Tools a Natural Horse-Man Would Use for Riding

Rope jaquima. The jaquima or hackamore is a tool that has been used for centuries. It can probably be traced back to something that was put on the horse's head to teach him what the human wanted. More than likely, even before bits were invented, man just used something simple like a series of ropes and knots and put it on the horse's head to control him. Later, horsemen used whatever materials were available, such as rawhide or leather.

Hackamores are usually made out of three kinds of material. Rope hackamores are the most gentle, followed by leather, and then rawhide, which is the roughest. None of these hackamores should have any metal parts.

The object of the rope hackamore is to teach the horse what you want, and it's important to use the hackamore one rein at a time. This is why, in Natural Horse-Man-Ship, you learn to ride and develop your skills with only one rein. You can use your 6-foot progress string and attach it to the heel knot of the rope hackamore. You have to use lateral flexion with this type of set-up. You'll soon find out that if you don't have your horse flexing well laterally at the halt or walk, it will get harder and harder to do it at a trot or canter.

So the progress string is your rein at this point, and you're going to try to teach the horse to yield to pressure with the progress string. There are two ways you're going to try to get the horse to yield to pressure: in an indirect rein to move the hindquarters out of the way and a direct rein to lead the front end through. These techniques are detailed later.

Bits. There are two categories of bits: bits without shanks and bits with shanks. There are two types of bits within each one of these categories: communication devices and torture devices.

A bit with no shanks, regardless of the mouthpiece, is called a snaffle. The most common snaffle is the broken mouthpiece snaffle. It's a mistake to think that any bit with a broken mouthpiece is a snaffle. This is not true. If the bit has any kind of shanks or leverage ability, it's not a snaffle.

You could have many different mouthpieces on a snaffle bit, such as a straight bar or a double-jointed mouthpiece, and there are various mouthpiece widths and thicknesses, from thick to thin.

The snaffle bit's basic design has not changed since its invention. It has not really been improved, and it doesn't need to be. The snaffle bit is intended to be used for teaching, controlling, reinforcing, and refining lateral flexion. It is a bit to be used mainly with a sideways pull for lateral flexion. It is not the type of bit you pull on with both hands at the same time.

Whenever you use the hackamore or the snaffle bit, use one active rein at a time, either directly or indirectly, or, use two supporting reins at one time to hold a conversation with your horse about stopping or yielding back (backing up). The latter is a matter of holding the reins, not pulling on them to stop the horse.

There are communication devices and there are torture devices.

Many people get into trouble when they ride their horses in snaffle bits. The usual pattern starts like this: First the rider uses a snaffle bit. He probably uses it improperly and the horse doesn't respond. So he goes to a bit with a broken mouthpiece and short shanks. When he finds that doesn't work, he uses one with longer shanks. Then, he rides the horse with a curb bit and a tie-down, then an even bigger bit. Finally, out of frustration, he sells the horse. This string of normal events happens because most people don't understand that this tool (snaffle) is to be used to teach, control, reinforce, and refine lateral flexion.

This is the type of snaffle bit Pat likes to use. It has 3-inch rings and a 5-inch mouthpiece made of sweet iron inlaid with copper strips to encourage saliva in the horse's mouth.

Bits with shanks were originally intended to be used to teach, control, reinforce, and refine vertical flexion. This becomes a complicated subject, and I'm not going to address shank bits in this book, which only deals with the foundation of Natural Horse-Man-Ship.

As I mentioned before, there are communication devices and there are torture devices. From a Natural Horse-Man-Ship point of view, the following are examples of torture devices: twisted-wire snaffle, gag bit, shanks over 7 ½ inches long, double twisted- wire snaffle, Spanish or Argentine snaffle, long shank snaffle (a common misnomer, especially with bits used for riding western style), slammer bit, Springsteen snaffle, Chileno bit, and mechanical hackamore.

Communication devices are: jaquimas (hackamores made of rope, leather, or rawhide with no metal), plain snaffle bits, and shank bits not intended to be torture devices, such as those used in full bridles.

There is a difference between jaquimas and bits. A jaquima teaches a horse what you want. A bit refines what you mean. So using Natural Horse-Man-Ship logic, you would use a jaquima to teach the horse what you want, and you would use a snaffle bit to refine what you meant in the jaquima. Eventually, you would use bits with shanks (that are not intended as torture devices) to further refine the language you taught him in the snaffle bit.

I use a handmade snaffle bit with 3-inch rings and a 5-inch wide mouthpiece, made of sweet iron with some copper inlays. The mouthpiece is medium-sized, approximately 5/8-inch. Sweet iron rusts and horses like rust, but many people don't. They buy bits made of stainless steel, nickel, or Monel so they don't rust. Rusting metal is going through an oxidation process, and horses enjoy this taste in their mouths.

A little bit of copper adds even more taste and tends to create a little more saliva in the horse's mouth. However, bits with too much copper in them are acidic, and also horses chew on them too much. They actually can cut their mouths on copper mouthpieces that have been chewed and have sharp edges.

Bits that are not made of sweet iron tend to cause a dry mouth. If the horse's mouth is dry, then the bit becomes an irritant, rather than a communication tool.

As far as bits go, though, it's more important that you understand how to use one rather than the technicalities of the bit itself.

Mecate reins. The mecate-style rein is of Spanish heritage. It's pronounced ma-kaw-tae, but some people pronounce it McCarty. Mecate means "hair rope" in Spanish, and traditional mecate reins are made of braided horse hair. I find horse hair, even if it's mane hair, uncomfortable to my hands.

I like to use the same ½-inch yacht braid rope I use in my lead ropes. This really aids me in my communication with the horse. I like this type of rope because it is easier on my hands than leather or horse hair. I also like it because of its unique, live-feel quality and its weight. The weight of the reins causes them to fall away quickly when I release my hold. This quick release then causes the horse to respond faster to my communication. There is not a delayed response. In other words, when the horse gives to pressure

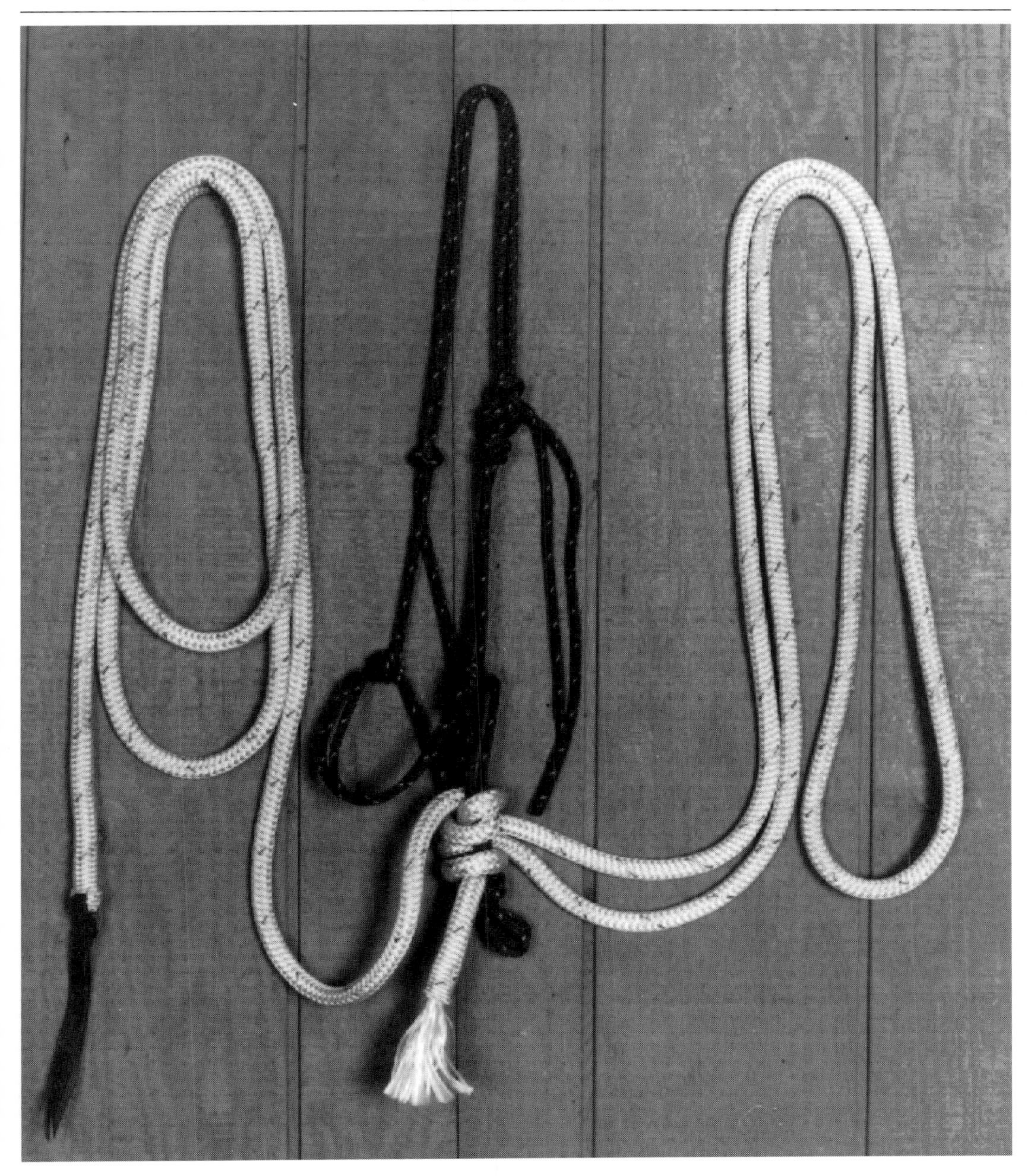

Mecate reins made of ½-inch yacht braid have a "live feel" quality. Here, they are attached to a Natural Horse-Man-Ship rope halter-hackamore.

on the reins, I can instantaneously release my hold on the reins. This gives the horse an instant reward and communication is established immediately.

Most mecates are 22 feet long, with 10 feet devoted to a continuous loop rein, and the remaining 12 feet used as a lead rope. They can be used with either the jaquima or snaffle bit.

The mecate has several advantages. One is that you don't have to worry about dropping a rein as you would a split rein, and if need be, you can use it to tap the horse on the hindquarters for forward movement. Also, when you are off the horse, you can use the 12-foot lead rope for lateral longeing. Another advantage is that if you need to tie your horse up, you can secure the horse in such a way that he will not break your headstall. You shouldn't tie up a horse with any bit, but with mecate reins you can.

Bring the single, continuous loop rein, which is around the horse's neck, out to

This sequence shows the steps in making a safe tie rope out of a set of mecate reins.

Bring the single continous rein, which is around the horse's neck, out to the side.

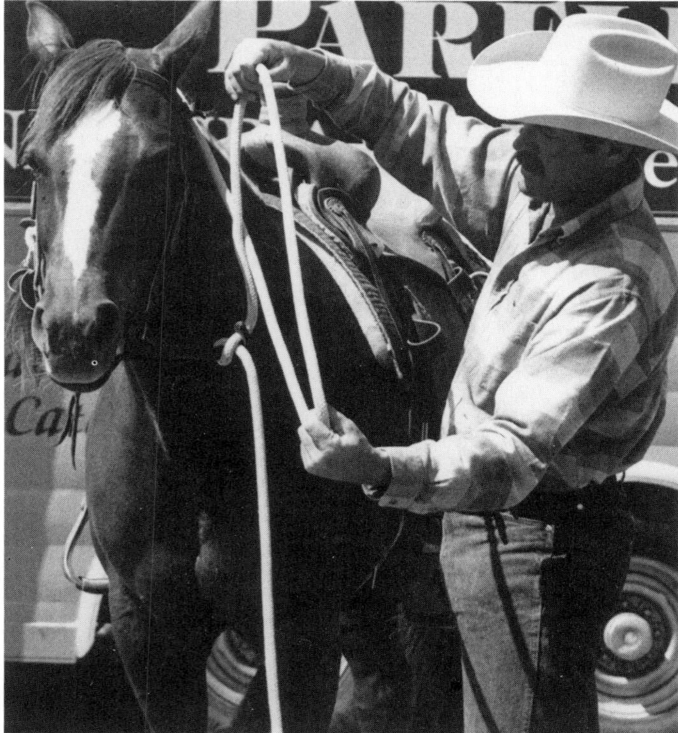

Give it one twist (cross it over itself once).

Put the rein over the horse's nose . . .

. . . ears and around his neck.

You now have a doubled rein over the horse's neck.

Hold the slack (lead rope portion of the mecate) in your left hand, and, with your right hand, bring the popper end of the lead rope under the horse's neck and over the reins.

Pull the popper end through the lead rope to snug it up.

This creates a half-hitch knot. You can now tie your horse up safely. If he pulls back, the rope won't bind on his neck or put any pressure on the bridle.

Mecate reins can be looped around the saddle horn or looped through your belt.

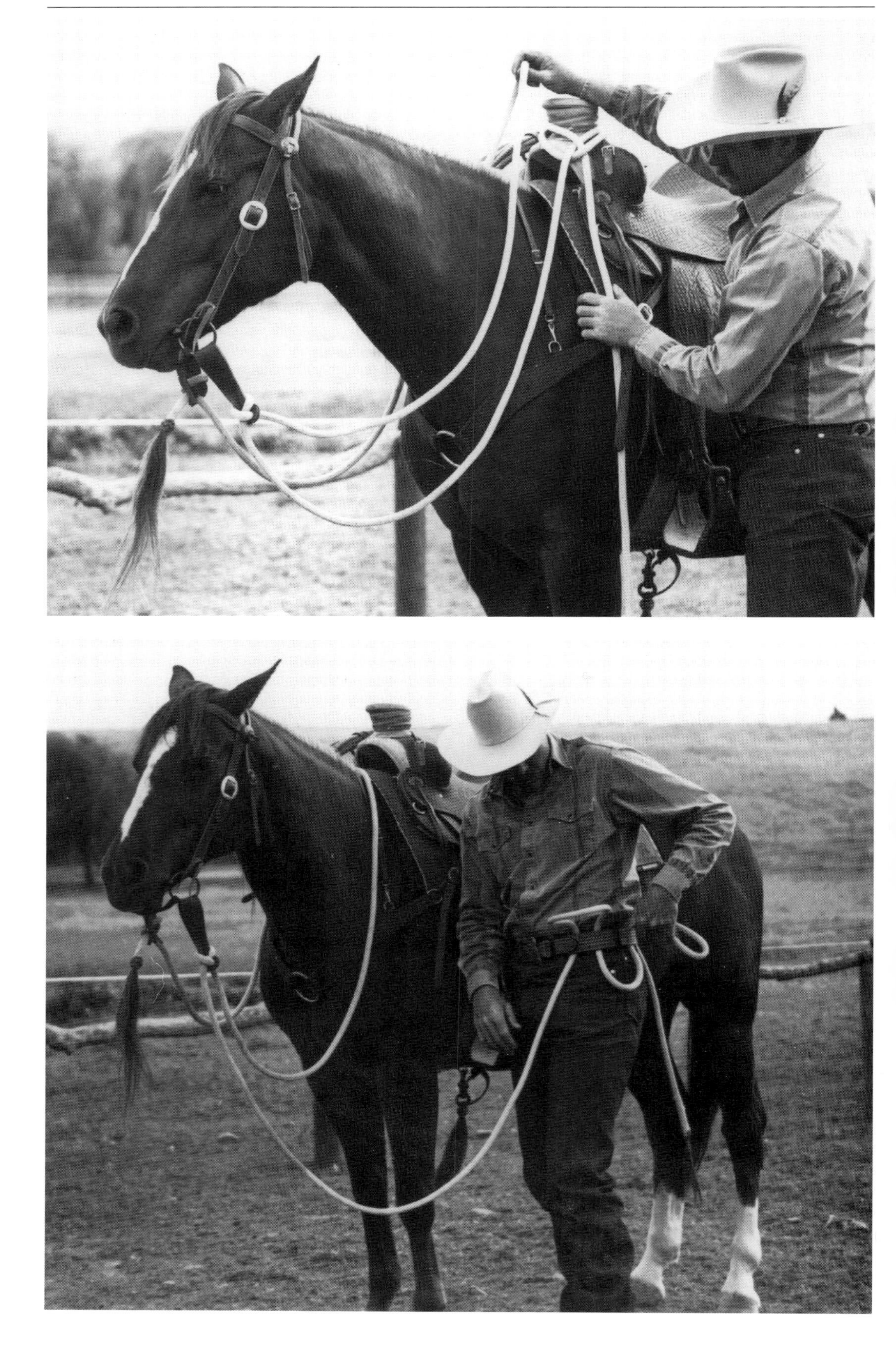

A carrot stick with a plastic bag on the end.

the side and give it one twist (cross it over itself once). This divides your loop rein in half. Then put the rein over the horse's nose, ears, and around his neck. Hold the slack of the lead rope in your left hand and run the popper end of the rope under the horse's neck and over the reins. Then pull the rope through itself and snug it up. This creates a half-hitch knot. This makes a loop around the horse's neck, and that's what holds him. You can tie up the horse with the rope, and it won't bind around the horse's neck if he pulls back. If he does back up, the reins won't put any pressure on the bridle or horse's mouth. You have a safe lead rope to use.

My type of mecate-style reins feels natural to me once I start combining direct, indirect, and supporting reins together. Because of the type of material (yacht braid), it allows the rope to slip through my hands when I want, but I can grip it when I don't want it to slip.

The only advantage I see in using split reins is that you can spank the horse with the ends. Romal reins are similar in that you have something on the end of the rein (the popper) to spank the horse if you need to.

Mecate reins have a tail on them that you can loop around the saddle horn or stick in your belt. The tail, or popper, is available to you at any time you need it. Split reins can drop to the ground, especially when leading the horse and, frequently, the horse steps on the fallen rein. In contrast, mecate reins have their own built-in lead rope, and the continuous-loop rein won't fall on the ground.

Carrot stick. The carrot stick is a 5-foot long orange stick with a handle on one end and a leather keeper on the other. The keeper is there so you can attach other things to the stick, such as a plastic grocery bag or a progress string. You attach the progress string when you want to make the carrot stick longer as an extension of

A close-up of the type of spur Pat likes to use.

your arm. It then looks like a whip, but it doesn't function as something with which to hit the horse.

I suggest starting off with just the leather keeper, depending on your horse's horse-anality and your judgment. You have to know how much encouragement your horse needs, and the grocery bag and progress string are firmer forms of encouragement.

In riding, the object of the carrot stick is to teach the horse to yield from pressure, whereas the progress string attached to the rope hackamore teaches the horse to yield to pressure.

Bareback pad. A bareback pad might be something to consider as an option. However, most bareback pads are made of inexpensive materials and do not cinch up well. They don't offer much for the rider. But there are good ones on the market that are made of leather with felt pad liners, and have latigos and regular mohair cinches.

Saddle pad. When it comes to saddle pads, there are two things to consider. One is that it is made of natural materials (like wool) and two, that it fails the fingernail test. By that I mean, if you can pinch your thumb and index finger together and feel your fingernail, the pad is too thin and not offering enough protection for your horse's back. You'd be surprised how many pads are not made of natural materials and don't pass the fingernail test.

If you are doing a lot of hard riding in a western saddle, a pad and a folded Navajo blanket work well. However, if you are just doing light riding, one good pad is usually sufficient.

Saddle. An appropriate saddle is one of your choice, whether it's English, western, Australian, charro, etc. However, the tree is the most important part. The top of the tree, or seat, is designed for the human; the bars, or bottom of the tree, are designed for your horse. When choosing a saddle, make sure the bars fit your horse's back and the seat is to your liking. For more information on how bars should fit your horse's back, ask a reputable custom saddlemaker.

Spurs. Spurs tend to be a sensitive subject. But I think they are probably one of the most humane tools to use in communication with horses. I'll explain. In early days, horses were ridden and used for transportation or in hunting for food. From a horse's back, a rider was able to shoot an arrow or throw a spear while running full speed ahead. It wasn't necessary for the horse to go forward, backward, right, left, up, and down equally; in other words, perform the six yields. Therefore, spurs were probably not in use in the dawn of horsemanship.

The roots of any type of riding that uses the six yields probably trace back to the early days of Spain and the Spanish custom of working with fighting cattle, especially bulls. And riders probably asked their horses to do these six yields as responses to working fighting cattle or fighting other humans.

The spur was probably invented when the human needed to ask the horse to yield sideways quickly or in a precise way, such as in working wild cattle. The horse was gored by a bull's horns if he didn't move quickly out of harm's way.

Also, when people started using horses as tools on the battlefield, where they had to do hand-to-hand combat, the six yields came into play there as well. I believe that as a consequence of battlefield conditions, spurs were used after many horses had been run through by swords because they did not know to yield from riders' legs. From this point of view the spur was designed as a very humane tool.

There are many kinds of spurs and ways in which they are used: dressage, cutting, roping, reining, rodeo, polo, etc. And there are many attitudes people take with spurs. Some use them as torture devices and punch their horses' sides to make them go forward or to punish them for doing something wrong. Others use them simply as extensions of their legs and gently apply pressure to get a point across.

Spurs are intended to teach, control, reinforce, and refine lateral movement and up and down movement. Use spurs intelligently and effectively and as they are intended. Don't do what normal riders do and use spurs to make horses go faster. In Natural Horse-Man-Ship, we use spurs with the right attitude, feel, timing, balance, savvy, and experience. I'll explain the natural way to use spurs in Techniques—In the Saddle.

It's not necessarily true that the bigger the rowel, the more severe a spur is. What makes a spur severe is the amount of PSI (pounds per square inch) applied to the horse's side. The amount of pain or discomfort the horse feels depends on the size of area the spur rowel covers. The smaller the area, the more painful the spur. Actually, a small rowel that is narrow with just a few points or tines is quite severe because it can produce a lot of force or pounds per square inch. On the other hand, a large, wide rowel with many points has more surface area; therefore, it's less severe. Usually this type of rowel is seen and used for decoration.

Also, the rowel is less severe if it rolls freely. A rowel that does not roll or even a spur without a rowel can be very severe. I have found that a medium shank spur with a rowel that rolls freely is a good type of spur to use.

To summarize the natural knowledge about spurs: 1/ Spurs are not to be used to make horses go faster, but to teach, control, reinforce, and refine lateral and up and down movement, and 2/ Understanding the relationship of form to function in spur design helps the rider know how to pick spurs, and how to use them intelligently as a natural communication tool.

TECHNIQUES

"There are three ways to gain your horse's respect while riding. 1/ Ride with a strong focus. 2/ Ride with one rein. 3/ Ride with an independent seat."

TO THIS point, you've worked to get your horse's respect on the ground. Now you want to transfer that to the saddle. There are three ways to gain your horse's respect while riding: 1/ Ride with a strong focus. 2/ Ride with one rein. 3/ Ride with an independent seat.

Techniques that Natural Horse-Men use for accomplishing these three things are detailed in this chapter. I describe them as assertive techniques because Natural Horse-Men use them with authority and understanding, not aggressiveness, meanness, or timidness.

Riding with a strong focus means concentrating on what you're doing with your horse and where you're going.

Riding with one rein proves how much control you have. In the beginning stages of learning to ride the Natural Horse-Man-Ship way, you still use the same hand-tied halter and 12-foot lead rope you used in the lateral longeing exercises. In essence, this gear gives you a hackamore and one rein. If the horse has gone through lateral longeing first, you actually have more control with this one rein and hackamore than with two reins and two hands. With one rein, you've taught your horse to bend his neck around and disengage his hindquarters. When you disengage a horse's hindquarters, you take away his impulsion or power. Therefore, you truly do have more control than if you had two reins and pulled back on both of them.

Riding with an independent seat means three things: 1/ You don't hang on to the reins for balance. 2/ You don't use both reins for control. 3/ You don't squeeze below the knees for balance. Your horse can't respect you, much less like you, when you're always grabbing and clutching his body for support and security. Gripping the horse's sides and pulling back on the reins at the same time are very confusing signals for the horse. On one hand, you're telling him to move out and, on the other, you're prohibiting him from moving at all.

Here are some assertive techniques that will help you learn to develop a strong focus, to ride with one rein, and acquire an independent seat.

Focus

Focus on where you want to go with your horse and feel down to his feet. Don't look at his ears. They won't fall off. Riding with a focus allows you to move the horse's body wherever you want it to go. Your legs and your hands work together along with your focus.

There's a place called somewhere; it's in front of you. Focus on it and ride forward to it or back away from it. There's a place called somewhere else; it's somewhere else, re-focus and ride forward to it or back up to it. There's a place called nowhere; it's below you. If you want your horse to stop, look on the ground (nowhere). Look down at your stirrup and bend your horse's neck so you can go nowhere. If you want your horse's hindquarters to move, focus on them. If you want to lead the front end through, look up and over. Use the focus so that you get the feel.

Rein Positions and Rein Functions

There are rein positions and rein functions. The three types of rein position are casual, controlled, and concentrated, describing where and how you hold the reins. The three rein functions are indirect, direct, and supporting, describing how you use the reins. These functions can be active or inactive in communicating with your horse.

A/ Casual Rein Position—This is a long, loose rein. Use this rein position when you are using your horse for transportation, standing still, or testing his responsibilities of not changing gaits or directions.

B/ Controlled Rein Position—This is a

Walking on a casual rein.

one-rein procedure. It is used for emergency stopping and, therefore, should be practiced. With a single rein (such as an inactive or active indirect rein, see D/ and E/), run your hand down the rein (or lead rope), ask the horse to bend his neck, and bring his head toward your leg. This causes the horse's hindquarters to disengage, and the horse moves in a tight circle. Remain in this position while focusing on your inside stirrup until the horse will stand still and relax. Reward your horse by releasing the hold on the rein.

This is a little ritual I do if a horse gets nervous or out of control in any way. It's an automatic response on my part to reach down the rein and hold the horse's head around until he relaxes.

You can control your horse's forward movement with just a single rein. Here, Pat uses a progress string as a controlled rein and brings the horse's head toward his leg. When this happens, it causes the horse's hindquarters to disengage.

To move from a casual to a concentrated rein, pick up the reins in one hand, shorten any slack, then take a rein in each hand.

For an inactive indirect rein (neutral or fixed rein), bring the rein to your leg and hold the horse's head. Sit and wait until the horse relaxes.

C/ Concentrated Rein Position—With the concentrated rein, you communicate to your horse that you want to do something specific. Pick up both reins, and put one in each hand. Concentrate the energy in your hands to both reins. This is a fairly short rein, so don't make it any shorter by pulling back too far. Make sure your knuckles don't get behind the saddle horn or pommel, even when you ask your horse to back.

D/ Inactive Indirect Rein Function—The inactive indirect rein completely disengages the horse's hindquarters and stops the horse's movement. Hold one rein in your hand and keep your elbow straight. Place this hand on your thigh. This bends your horse's neck, bringing the head toward your leg. Remain in this position until the horse relaxes. Be passively persistent in the proper position. This can also be a neutral or fixed rein.

E/ Active Indirect Rein Function—An indirect rein moves the horse's hindquarters. Run your hand down the rein. With your elbow bent, bring your hand to your midsection or bellybutton. The difference between this and the inactive indirect rein is the action in your seat and leg and hand positions. With the active indirect rein, you activate the rein by lifting it and bringing it toward your midsection. Use a little leg pressure on the same side to cause the hindquarters to move. Focus on your horse's hindquarters by looking at them. Focus and concentration are all part of getting your horse's body to follow your suggestion.

F/ Direct Rein Function—A direct rein leads the horse's forequarters in the direction you are going. Straighten your elbow and bring your arm out to the side. Moving the rein out to the side directs the horse's front end around.

Focus on where you want to go with your horse and feel down to his feet. Don't look at his ears. They won't fall off.

For an active indirect right rein, bring your right hand to your midsection and lift until the horse gives his head freely and disengages his hindquarters.

For an active indirect left rein, bring your left hand to your midsection and hold until the horse relaxes and disengages his hindquarters.

For a direct right rein, straighten your right elbow and bring your arm up and out to your side. This brings the horse's front end around to the right.

For a direct left rein, straighten your left elbow and bring the horse's front end around to the left. A supporting right rein reinforces the actions of the direct rein.

Practice the indirect and direct rein with the following exercise:

Using the indirect rein, bend the horse's neck and bring his head around, disengaging his hindquarters. Then, straighten out your arm to lead the front end through with the direct rein.

G/ Supporting Rein Function—A supporting rein supports or reinforces the actions of the direct rein. Another way to look at it is that it pushes the front end. For example, in turning to the left, you use the left rein to direct the horse to the left and lay the right rein across the horse's neck to support going to the left. The horse yields to the pressure of the direct rein and away from the pressure of the supporting rein.

Rein Responsibility

The horse has four legs and you have two reins. Each rein controls two of the horse's legs or is responsible for the legs' movement.

A/ Right rein—The right rein is responsible for the right front leg and the left hind leg. If you use a direct rein (move your right arm straight out to the side), it moves the right front leg over. If you bend your right elbow in an indirect rein (as in bringing your hand to your midsection or bellybutton), it causes the left hind leg to move.

B/ Left rein—The left rein is responsible for the left front leg when you use a direct rein to the left. If you use an indirect left rein (pull to the bellybutton), it influences the right hind leg.

Hands and Legs

Your hands and legs work together while you focus on what you want your horse's body to do. In other words, your legs do what your hands do. For example, if you want your horse's hindquarters to move to the left, take the right rein in your right

Your legs and hands should work together. If you want your horse's hindquarters to move to the left, use an indirect right rein. When you bend your right elbow to bring in your right rein, bend your right knee as well.

If you straighten your right elbow to bring your horse's front end around with a direct right rein, straighten out your right knee, too.

In the whole scheme of things in riding, you have to be assertive to ask the horse to yield to and from pressure, but then be agile enough to stay out of this way.

hand, bend your elbow, and bring it to your bellybutton. If your right elbow is bent, so is your right knee. Bring it to your horse's midsection (i.e. his side). Wait until the horse moves away from the pressure of the rein and the leg.

You're doing nothing with your left hand at this time, so do nothing with your left leg either.

If you straighten out your right elbow to bring the horse's front end around, straighten out your right knee as well, thereby taking the pressure off his side. Without your right leg blocking him to the right, your horse can turn to the right more naturally.

Yielding to and From Pressure

Two important assertive techniques are yielding to and from pressure while you're riding. Let's take riding your horse to the left as an example of using assertive rein techniques. You've got a left rein and a right rein, and an inside rein and an outside rein. If you're going to the left, your left rein is your inside rein, and your right rein is your outside rein. You should cause your horse to yield to pressure on the inside rein or left rein, and cause your horse to yield from pressure with your right or outside rein, pushing the horse from right to left.

In riding to the left, you can use your left rein in a direct or indirect fashion, causing your horse to yield to pressure. When you use a direct rein, your left arm leads out to the left, your elbow straightens, and you lead the horse's front end over to the left. In other words, his front legs move over to the left. When using the rein indirectly, you draw it up anywhere from your midsection to your right shoulder, causing the hindquarters to swing away from you. When you activate a rein in this manner, it causes the horse's hindquarters to disengage and move over.

A supporting rein is one that pushes the front end over, and usually you use a bent elbow for this. For example, in going to the left using a direct rein, your left hand would be higher than the right and the left elbow straight out. If you're using a supporting rein on the right, the right arm and elbow would be lower than the left and bent. The right rein would be pushing the horse's neck supporting the direction you are moving, which is from the right to the left.

In everything you do, you're trying to cause the horse to yield to and from the pressure. If you're using your legs and going to the left, your left leg would move off the horse's side, thereby allowing the horse to yield to the pressure. Your right leg would be somewhat bent, pressing on the horse's side, and pushing him from the right to the left, just like the supporting rein. The right leg is causing the horse to yield from the pressure.

Usually, you ask the horse to yield to pressure before yielding from pressure. In other words, you direct the horse before you support him. Yielding to pressure is directing the horse. Yielding from pressure is supporting the horse. This is why these rein techniques are called direct, indirect, and supporting reins.

If you want to go forward, you straighten your elbows out and open up an avenue in the front. You are asking the horse to yield to that pressure. If you squeeze with your legs or spank the horse's rump, you're asking the horse to yield from pressure. But again, it's important that you direct or open up in front before you support from behind. In other words, don't hold the reins tightly while asking the horse for forward motion by squeezing or spanking. He can't go forward unless you open up the way for him. At the very least, he'll be confused and frustrated because you're not allowing him to do what you are asking him to do.

Spurring

Spurring is not intended to lengthen a horse's stride and make him go faster, but is to heighten a horse's stride and/or cause him to move laterally.

To use spurs properly as extensions of your legs, learn to press or squeeze with them. Actually, you press with the spur after you squeeze with your calf. Whatever you do, don't kick or gouge. Cause your horse to yield from your leg at 4 ounces (of pressure). If your horse doesn't respond to your leg, then cause him to yield from your spur by pressing or squeezing harder.

You can learn to be a good passenger by having a friend laterally longe your horse while you are on his back.

The secret to using spurs is pressing in the right spot and then knowing when to quit pressing. This is where focusing comes in. The spur is an extension of your leg. Get your focus, come with your hands and legs, feel for the response, and quit stimulating.

Independent Seat

To be a good rider, you should stay out of your horse's way when he is trying to perform something you've asked him to do. But you need an independent seat to do this. Imagine being a horse and having a rider ask you to jump an obstacle, but then the rider gets in your way when you do. Here's how it would go: After he's asked the horse to jump, the rider loses his balance, leans to one side, pulls on the reins, and squeezes his legs on the horse's barrel to stay on. All these conflicting signals would totally confuse a horse, who is just trying to do his job and jump the jump.

In the whole scheme of things in riding, you have to be assertive to ask the horse to yield to and from pressure, but then be agile enough to stay out of his way. You've got to be able to go with the horse's motion: forward, backward, right, left, up, and down. It's not as simple as just getting on and riding forward.

This is where having an independent seat is so crucial. If you get more than 4 ounces out of kilter (balance) with the horse, you're in the horse's way. In other words, if your weight shift is more than 4 ounces in either direction, your horse probably has to compensate for your mistake by shifting his own weight.

First, a horse learns to carry dead weight, such as a saddle, on his back. Then, he has to learn to carry a passenger, or live weight, on his back.

There's a difference between dead weight and live weight. Let's say you saddle a horse and play with him at liberty or on a longe line, and ask him to do all sorts of things. The horse can calculate what the dead weight of the saddle is going to do. But a horse cannot calculate what live weight is going to do. Yet that live weight tells him what to do and when to do it. Beyond that, someday he must accomplish all of this with vertical flexion. This is why an independent seat is so important in developing a lifetime partnership with a horse. He can't do what you want him to do unless you stay out of his way, and you can't do that unless you develop an independent seat.

How do you get an independent seat? This is probably one of the things that seems like it might take a lifetime to learn. But this ingredient has to be there. It's something you have to achieve.

Some suggestions for developing an independent seat are: 1/ Become mentally, emotionally, and physically fit on the ground first. 2/ Practice lateral longeing techniques, know how to cope with constructive horseplay, and allow a horse to drift and come back to you. Lateral longeing teaches you to be independent of, yet together with, the horse. 3/ When in the saddle, learn to become a great passenger. Go into a small enclosure, such as a round pen, and let go of the reins. Just sit there and try not to disrupt the horse's movement. All you have to do is not fall off and not get out of kilter 4 ounces. You could also have someone else laterally longe your horse while you are on his back, or have someone play with your horse at liberty while you are on his back. 4/ Ride bareback. Spend at least an hour a week riding bareback. 5/ Trot and canter on a loose rein for long distances and periods.

In Natural Horse-Man-Ship, as in everything else, you and your horse must first learn to walk before you can run. The foundation of basic handling you practiced on the ground blends easily into the basics you perform in the saddle. Get solid at these basics first before you try more advanced maneuvers. Don't think of breaking or training a horse, think of preparation, of starting a relationship with your horse, and developing a partnership.

Here are some more basics and techniques for learning them.

Two things you don't often see a horse do on his own are backing up and going sideways. He can do these maneuvers, but he usually prefers to go forward when he has a choice. However, these two movements are important in all riding dynamics.

Introduce these two maneuvers on the ground first, and that makes it easier later in the saddle. To get these concepts across, go back to lateral longeing techniques. Work on pressure points on the horse's body.

Back Up

Ask the horse to back by putting your hand on the bridge of the horse's nose (there are nerves there). Another technique is put your fingers on the tips of his shoulder blades. This is a sensitive area as well. Use "hot fingers" to touch your horse on these pressure points.

Once on the horse, you apply the same principles of pressure and release from pressure when you ask him to back up.

There are nine identifiable steps to a yield back. But prior to the nine steps, there is step 0.

0/ Sit in a casual position in your saddle with no contact with the horse's mouth.

1/ Rise up in the saddle (straighten your back). Lift the reins, which are in one hand, in the air, and make contact with the horse's mouth.

2/ Run your free hand down the reins until you feel you have contact with the horse's mouth.

3/ Now put a rein in each hand, but hold the reins with only with your thumbs. Your fingers should be pointing straight ahead.

4/ Close both of your index fingers at the same time.

5/ Close both of your middle fingers.

6/ Close both of your ring fingers.

7/ Close both of your little fingers.

8/ Bend your elbows.

9/ Sink your back down in the saddle into the backward movement of a back up.

This should cause your horse to feel of you and for you so you can feel together into a yield back.

Hold and when your horse yields to your hands and takes a step back, throw the reins down as if you were surrendering to your horse. Your horse will get the idea that backing up releases the pressure on the reins. In time, he'll back as far and as fast as you want.

If you felt your horse backing crooked, it's probably lack of focus on your part. Focus on "somewhere." Go through the nine steps and whatever corrections you need to make with your hands and legs should come naturally if you focus even stronger.

A good exercise you can do to learn to know where your horse's feet are without

To ask your horse to back, go from a casual rein to a concentrated rein.

Close your fingers on the reins and bring your elbows in to your sides.

When your horse takes a step back, throw the reins down as if you were surrendering to your horse.

looking at them is to walk forward a certain amount of steps, then back a certain amount of steps. Count them as you go. For example, focus on a spot in the distance and walk forward 15 steps to get there. Stop and back up five steps. Try to feel where your horse's feet are when you do this. It'll help you tune into your horse's movements.

Slowing and Stopping

You slow a horse down and stop him the same way you back him. You hold. Here's an exercise to get that concept across.

1/ Pick a focus and ride forward.

2/ Pick up your reins and go from a casual rein to a concentrated rein, closing each finger as you go.

3/ Hold the reins until the horse stops moving and backs away from the pressure.

4/ Release the hold.

5/ Start on these exercises going from a walk down to a back up, a trot down to a back up, and a canter down to a back up.

Here's another little exercise to refine that maneuver. Bring your life up by smiling with all your cheeks or squeezing your legs. That squeeze becomes a squeeze all the way down your legs to your ankles; but it's not a kick. Walk your horse out, pick up the reins, and lift them high above the horse's head to their fullest extent. See if he'll stop at that suggestion. When he backs away from the feeling of pressure on his mouth, release, and put the reins down.

Side-Pass

Use "hot fingers" to move your horse sideways on the ground first before you ask for a side-pass in the saddle. Press your fingers on the horse's head and neck and then his hindquarters in an alternating fashion. In effect, your hot fingers act like spurs. You're teaching the horse to move away from pressure. Do this enough and soon the horse should yield sideways com-

Slow down your horse and stop him with concentrated reins. Hold the reins until the horse stops and backs away from the pressure.

Lift your reins high in the air and see if you can get your horse to stop at the suggestion.

pletely at the suggestion of your hand movements.

When you want to ride sideways, make sure you focus on going in that direction. Also, remember that your legs do what your hands do.

To side-pass to the left, first use the three steps to go from a casual to a concentrated rein. (See first three steps under Back Up.) Focus to the left at about 90 degrees at eye level. Open your left arm and leg. Use a right supporting rein and push from the right side. If you're having trouble, use your progress string in your right hand. And if you're still having trouble, go back to lateral longeing.

Many of these techniques in riding are exaggerated. You exaggerate to teach and refine as you go along. Someday, your horse will listen to your body language and require only slight suggestions to perform.

Pre-Flight Checks in the Saddle With Halter and Lead Rope

There are several pre-flight tests you can to do in the saddle that are built on previous pre-flight checks you did on the ground. These tests are designed to help you see where your horse is mentally, emotionally, and physically before you actually ask him to perform. At this point, you still have the halter and lead rope as head gear.

1/ The first thing you want to do after you've mounted is stand still. Help your horse to learn to stand still. Don't ask him to move the second you throw your leg over the saddle. Sit there for 30 seconds. Teach him patience and to wait for your communication.

2/ Now ask him to pass the test of lateral flexion. Take the slack out of one rein and ask your horse to give you his head. Until he can give you scores of 6s (on the grading scale of +10 to -10), you are not in a good position to go anywhere. If your horse doesn't give you his head well, continue until he relaxes and gives it to you

Get your horse to side-pass on the ground first before you ask him to do it under saddle. Press your fingers on your horse's neck and hindquarters to get him to move sideways away from pressure.

To side-pass to the left, focus to your left, then open up your left arm and leg for the horse, giving the horse room to move to the left as you push with your supporting right rein and leg.

To side-pass to the right, look to the right, open up your right arm and leg, and push with your supporting left rein and leg.

The first pre-flight check you do after you mount is stand still on a loose rein. Teach your horse patience.

willingly and softly. If you can't bend his neck around asking for lateral flexion to disengage the hindquarters, you're in trouble. Go back to the lateral longeing on the ground until you can successfully bend your horse's neck and disengage his hindquarters for control. Don't forget to do both sides.

3/ Bring the front end through by straightening your elbow just as you did in earlier lessons. By bringing the lead rope out to the side, the horse's head must follow as do his front legs. Note: The horse's neck needs to be fairly straight.

4/ From the saddle, throw your lead rope over the horse's head several times. You did this on the ground in earlier lessons, and your horse should be fairly used to it. This test shows that your horse has accepted you on his back, and can tolerate some commotion around him without coming unglued.

If your horse passes the tests of giving you his head, moving the hindquarters, then leading the forehand through, you're ready to go somewhere.

Here are some control drills to help you off to a good start. The drills are all performed with one rein, and should

The second mounted pre-flight check is to ask your horse to pass the test of lateral flexion. If you can't disengage his hind-quarters, you're in trouble and you should go back to lateral longeing exercises on the ground.

Mounted pre-flight check number three is to bring the front end through to see if you have control over the horse's forehand.

The last mounted preflight check is to throw the lead rope over the horse's head several times. Here, Pat is using a progress string. This proves the horse can stand some commotion around him without coming unglued.

Anybody can turn a horse on; can you turn him off?

prove to you the amount of control you have with one rein. If you learn to use one rein naturally, you can combine two reins later and ride effectively.

Control Drills

Here's a handy exercise to use if your horse moves off on his own or gets out of control. Practice this until it becomes an automatic response for you.

As the horse moves forward at a walk (you can do it at any speed), run your hand down the lead rope (almost to the snap) back and forth three or four times as a preparatory command. It looks like you're playing the trombone.

Now, reach down for the rope one more time, bring it to your leg (neutral lateral flexion), and hold it like you've done in previous drills while standing still. Look at your stirrup (as a form of concentration) and bend the horse's neck and hold his head around until he quits moving and stands still. The horse will move, probably in tight little circles. Wait until he stops.

Let go of the horse's head, but be able at any time to run your hand down the rein to bend the neck once more.

Put the rope on other side of the neck. Tap the horse on the rump until you are going forward somewhere. Then, run your hand down two or three times, look to your stirrup, and bend the horse's neck again. While you're looking down at your stirrup and holding your horse's head firmly, relax your body. Hold the horse's head for a long time, around 30 seconds. If you want, you can rub the horse on the head until he relaxes.

Do this drill many times until you get good at it. Get where you can do it with rhythm. Let the horse move anywhere he wants, look to your stirrup, gracefully bend the horse's neck around until he stops and hold on. So many people make the mistake of not holding on. They get the horse bent and stopped, and off they go again. Hold on to that neck; sit and hold the head for 30 seconds. Anybody can turn a horse on; can you turn him off?

Unlike some of the other exercises in lateral flexion that you've used to bend your horse, this bending exercise teaches him that you have total control over his body and his actions. In this exercise, you're asking your horse to make the transition from an active, moving state to a passive, relaxed one in a short amount of time. You're exercising the horse's emotions here. That's why you hold him for around 30 seconds. You change his mind from whatever it was on to your new way of thinking.

Here's an exercise in control going backward. While standing still, raise your lead rope high above your horse's neck. Lift the lead rope up and down (lead rope snap will bump against horse's jaw a little) and the horse should move back away from the pressure. This maneuver is similar to shaking the lead rope at the horse in the lateral longeing exercises you used to get him to back away from you.

If the horse goes crooked, use the lead rope to get in his way by swinging it alongside the horse's neck. For example, if the horse starts to go crooked and turns his head to the right, swing the lead rope on the right side of his neck to straighten out the horse's body.

Another technique with one rein while backing up is to raise the lead rope high above the horse's neck again, but this time push the rope across the horse's neck, much like a supporting rein. You want your horse's front end to move back and over at the same time. The horse ends up backing in a circle. Keep leg pressure off the side you are turning. If your horse is backing in a circle to the right, keep your right leg off the horse, and your left leg on the horse's side. You want to open a door for the horse to go through by keeping your leg off the right side. You can't if both legs are clamped on the horse.

Pick a focus and ride straight to it. See how little effort or squeezing on your part causes your horse to walk, trot, or lope to your focus point.

Here's a drill for snappy departures and graceful transitions. After you depart into a trot for a few steps, make a transition to a walk by running your hand down one rein.

Departures and Transitions

Here are some suggestions for helping your horse to have snappy departures, smooth and graceful downward transi-

To make a transition to the walk, reach down one rein and bring your hand to your thigh.

Hold it there, using neutral lateral flexion, until the horse stops and his emotions are under control.

tions, and handy right and left turns.

Learn to cause your horse to go forward without kicking him by bringing your life up. First, smile with all your cheeks (buttocks). Then squeeze all the way down your legs to your ankles. Give the horse a moment or two and if he doesn't respond, tap or spank him on the rump to cause him to go forward.

In time, your horse will anticipate the spanking, and you won't have to make him go by tapping. He'll start moving before you spank, just by following the smiling (squeezing) cheeks cue.

To help your horse make snappy departures so you don't have to kick him to make him go, pick a focus. Look across the arena or wherever you're riding. Pick an object to ride to, such as a fence. Look at it and aim for it. Without leaning forward, straighten your elbows in the direction of the fence. By just squeezing your legs, see how little it would take to get your horse to either walk, trot, canter, or gallop to that fence. Your job is to stay focused and ride straight. Your horse's job is to respect you enough to keep going straight, watch out where he is going, and stop when you get there.

Squeeze enough with your legs to get your horse going, then hold him straight and relax. Use your focus to keep him straight, and let the fence stop him. When you're stopped, wait there at least 30 seconds or at least until your horse is mentally and emotionally relaxed. Then use an indirect rein and a direct rein and make a half turn. Do the same thing in the opposite direction.

What you want is to be able to look at something, straighten out your elbows, and squeeze, and your horse will know that you want to go somewhere and you want to go straight.

When your horse gets really good at this game, add challenges. Put a small obstacle in the way, such as a low jump, log, or cavalletti. You focus on where you want to go, and let your horse take care of looking at that obstacle. You don't want him to swerve around the obstacle, but to go over it and keep going where your focus told him to go.

Another thing you can do with this technique is to refocus right or left and go somewhere else at the last moment before you get to your original focus point. Get your horse in tune to going somewhere and then somewhere else, and still watch where you have asked him to put his feet. That should be his job, and your job is to maintain the focus.

As you get better at this, you can challenge the focus game. You can use a lone object, such as a tree or telephone pole, to ride to. A lone object is more difficult to ride straight to because the horse could swerve around it at the last moment. You have to focus even harder, maybe on the knothole on the telephone pole. It's also more of a challenge to get the horse stopped at a lone object, unlike the fence.

To make a transition to a slower speed of the gait you're in or to a slower gait, simply quit riding. Instead of being active in the saddle and going with the horse's motions, be still, relax your seat. The horse will feel the difference and change his way of going. From a lope, a horse makes a transition down to a trot, and from a trot, he makes a transition down to a walk.

As a little drill, depart into a trot with a smile. If that doesn't work, spank with your hand. Then, make a transition to a walk by quitting riding. If that doesn't work, bend the horse's neck around until he walks. You can take the life out of your horse by bending him.

When you get all these things going, it's all going to make sense to the horse. If you want your horse to go, don't kick him, bring your life up to bring his life up, smile with all your cheeks or squeeze and tap his rump if you need to. If you want to make a transition, take the life out of your body (quit riding). If you want to stop your horse, use neutral lateral flexion by holding the lead rope on your thigh. Wait until the horse's emotions come back down.

The horse's emotional state plays such an important part in riding. Everybody is concerned about the physical part of the horse. But, to me, it's the mental and emotional part that's really important.

The next two techniques, the Trotting Test and the Cantering Test, are good exercises to work on all the concepts you've learned to this point.

Trotting Test

This is another technique to help you develop an independent seat. It also helps the horse not act like a prey animal and not change gaits or directions. And he has to look where he is going and be careful where he puts his feet.

For the trotting test, pick a trail or the rail of an arena and see if you can get your horse to trot without being held back or without changing directions. You want him to remain trotting on a loose rein. Hold the reins in one hand, but drop your hand on the horse's neck. Don't have any contact with the horse's mouth.

If you're using a trail, see if you can get your horse to stay on the trail and not switch trails, even if you have a horseback friend who goes off in another direction. This is a very tempting situation for a horse. He'll want to follow the horse who left. On the trail, there should be many dips, rises, and small obstacles for your horse to watch where his feet are going. This is an ideal situation.

But if you can't use a trail, use a rail in an arena. In this situation, see if you can get your horse to stay about 3 feet off the rail and go deep into the corners. Also, you don't want the horse to change gaits or directions, cut the corners, cut across the arena, etc.

While doing this, see how independent of the horse you can be by doing one of several things at the trot. Here are some exercises:

1/ Go down the rail with no hands on the reins. Give the horse the responsibility of not changing gaits or directions.

2/ Stand the trot without holding the reins. Try this for 5 minutes.

3/ Post the trot. Most of the time, posting is described as going up and down with the outside front leg. I suggest you do the opposite and go down and up with the right hind leg when going to the right and down and up with the left hind leg when going to the left. Get in tune with the horse's hind legs instead of his front legs because that's where his impulsion begins. Start with the down position and rise up, down, up. But emphasize the "up," not the "down." Cause yourself to go up and allow yourself to go down, rather than let yourself go up and make yourself come down.

4/ Sit the trot. Try feeling the two-beat motion of the horse's back through your torso and follow the rhythm.

5/ Bounce the trot. Raise your knees slightly, take the weight out of your stirrups, and see if you can bounce the trot. Then, put your feet back in the stirrups lightly, and see if you can sit the trot. Then bounce the trot again. Be so in control at the trot that you can bounce on purpose.

6/ Do other things while trotting, like tying a simple knot in a piece of rope, swinging a rope, reading a newspaper, whatever. Focus on doing something else while your body still moves with the trot. The point here is to be able to trot well enough, and still be able to do some secondary function.

Cantering Test

Practice cantering circles on a loose rein until you can do them perfectly. You don't want your horse making egg-shaped circles, or leaning in or out of the circle.

For this technique, place objects on the ground, such as your portable round corral (bag) or some other object, and use that as a center point. Canter about 25 feet away from the bag on a loose rein. Make about three circles to the right, holding the reins only with your right hand. After the third circle, put your rein hand down on the horse's neck and get a hold of the mane. If the horse drifts or leans into the circle, pick up the mane and try to steer him back on track. If that doesn't work, let go of his mane and lift the reins up and re-direct him back to where you want without using two hands. Continue using an up and over motion to get the horse to go where you want him to go, then return your hand to the neutral position on the mane or neck.

If you'll continue this polite and passive persistence and stay in the proper neutral position, your horse will learn how to not change gaits or directions, and to maintain his distance away from the portable round corral that you've used as a center point. In time, you'll be able to do this 40 feet away or more from the bag. Your horse will realize you want to lope a perfect circle, and it's his job to do that.

While cantering the circle, look at the bag in the middle of the arena, and go toward it. See if you can get your horse to stop just before he steps on the bag.

Do the trotting exercise and the cantering exercise long enough that the horse gets into a rhythm. Most people give up too soon. It will take most horses 15 to 30 minutes to find a rhythm. Do both of these exercises until the horse asks you "Can we please quit trotting? Can we please quit cantering? I've had enough." When this happens and you feel your horse wanting to stop, pick up your reins, and try to have a conversation with your horse about coming to a stop and yielding backward. Do this with an effort not exceeding 4 ounces. This is a downward transition from a faster gait to a slower one, then to a stop and back up.

The departures and transitions you've used in all these exercises help set up the horse's leads, as you'll see next.

Leads and Lead Changes

Leads are natural for a horse and so are lead changes. Don't let them be complicated and mystifying for you. When a horse lopes, canters, or gallops, he has a leading set of legs and a trailing set of legs. In the right lead, his right front leg moves in front of his left front leg, and his right hind leg moves in front of his left hind leg. The reverse is true for the left lead.

This next series of trotting and cantering exercises helps you develop leads and lead changes with an approach that is logical for your horse to understand. They are done in the form of a figure eight.

Trotting Exercise

1/ With your rein hand out to the right, ask your horse to start trotting to the right by smiling with all your cheeks. If that doesn't work, use your left hand to spank the horse's hindquarters. Swing a half-circle to the right by bending your elbow and bringing the right rein to your midsection. This puts the horse in a tight circle, and disengages his hindquarters. He should come down to the next slower gait, which is a walk.

2/ When the horse has come down to a walk, turn, and go the other way or left. Change rein hands by putting your reins in the left hand. Move up into a trot by smiling with all your cheeks. If that doesn't work, use your right hand to spank the horse's hindquarters. Turn a half-circle to the left with a bent elbow. You should not only get a half-turn, but you should get a walk. The turn becomes so sharp, the horse naturally makes the transition down to the next slower gait.

3/ Now change your reins to your right hand. You just keep trading rein hands, which comes in handy when you actually do lead changes.

Bring your life up; the horse should trot. Swing a half-circle to the right at the trot by bending the horse. You should get the turn and the transition down to a walk.

4/ Move up into a trot to the left. Swing a half-circle to the left with a bent elbow. This disengages the hindquarters to the right.

Repeat this little exercise until you and your horse become good at changing directions and making transitions in gait.

Disengaging the hindquarters helps set up the horse's body for a lead. Lead changes, done properly, originate from the horse's hindquarters, not his front end. Often, you'll see a horse who picks up his leads in front, but not behind. This horse is cross-cantering or is disunited. This is definitely an incorrect way to move at a lope. Horses should have two leading legs and two trailing legs, and they should be on the same side of the horse while he is moving at a lope or canter.

In the above exercise, you have a leading hand (the one that is stretched out in front and suggests the direction the horse should go) and a trailing hand (the one that spanks the horse's hindquarters). When you are in this position, your body is also in a leading and trailing position and the horse feels it.

For leads and simple lead changes use the same exercise you did above, but do them at the canter or lope. Use the same figure-eight pattern, but be careful not to make the circles too small. Give yourself some room to move in a large circle before you ask your horse to turn and come down to a slower gait.

Cantering Exercise

1/ First ask your horse to go to the right by stretching out your right hand (leading hand) in that direction. Smile with all your cheeks. If that doesn't work, tap the horse on the hindquarters with your left hand (trailing hand). Notice, your right hand and shoulder are leading, which turns your right hip in that direction as well. Your left hand and shoulder are back toward the horse's hindquarters, and so is your left hip. Your body is in the same position as your horse's to obtain the right lead.

The spanking is important here as it encourages the horse to move away from the pressure of the hand on the hindquarters. When the horse moves away, he picks up the lead opposite of the hand that is doing the spanking. In other words, when you spank with your left hand, that encourages the horse to move away from the pressure of your left hand. When he does, he switches leading hind legs, and uses his right hind leg instead of his left hind leg. When he uses his right hind leg, he is striking off into the right lead.

2/ Swing a half-circle to the right by bending your right elbow and bringing your right hand to your midsection, just as you did numerous times at the trot. This sharp turn disengages the horse's hindquarters. You should get a tight half-circle, as well as a transition down to the next slower gait, the trot.

3/ After the sharp turn to the right, turn to the left at the trot and change rein hands. Smile with your cheeks and squeeze to encourage the horse to increase his speed, which should put him in a canter. Spank with the right hand if you don't get an immediate response to go forward and to pick up the left lead. Keep spanking until you get a canter. You can use clucking or kissing noises if that helps speed up your horse.

While in a canter, swing a half-circle to the left by bringing your left hand in to your midsection. The horse's body should bend into the turn, go into a tight circle, then come down to a trot.

4/ The half-circles you are making actually bring you around to change directions. The indirect rein moves the horse's hindquarters a half-turn. A half-circle to the left sets you up to go to the right. Change rein hands and spank with your left hand. You should get a right lead.

This is a drop-to-the-trot, figure-eight exercise in teaching leads and lead changes. It helps you and your horse get handy at picking up leads from the half-turn and the transition. With practice, your horse will learn to follow the suggestions of your body easily and pick up the leads you want at the canter.

Figure Eight Lead Change Sequence

In this sequence the horse completes three lead changes—one to the right and two to the left.

First go to the right by stretching out your right hand indicating the direction you want to go. Spank with your left hand if a squeeze with your legs doesn't cause the horse to move forward.

Notice the right hand and shoulder are leading and the left hand and shoulder are back toward the horse's hindquarters. The rider's body is in the same position as the horse's to obtain the right lead.

Swing a half circle by bending your right elbow and bringing your right hand to your midsection.

This sharp turn disengages the horse's hindquarters. You get a tight half-circle to the right, as well as a transition to the next slower gait, the trot.

At the trot, turn to the left and change rein hands. This time lead with your left hand and spank with your right hand, if necessary.

Keep spanking until you get a canter.

Lope on a left lead for a few strides.

Swing a half-circle to the left.

As you complete the half-circle to the left, you will be in good position to head back to the right.

Drop to the trot as you move around to the right.

Squeeze the horse up into a canter for a few strides. Notice the horse doesn't need to be spanked anymore to move up in gait.

Turn a half-circle to the right. . .

. . . and head back to your left.

Squeeze the horse up into a left-lead canter.

There are only six things a horse can do: go forward, backward, right, left, up, and down, but there are a milllion challenges. That means there are at least 6 million things you can do with a horse.

Cloverleaf Pattern

One of my mentors, Troy Henry, taught me the cloverleaf pattern as a technique to slow down a horse who wants to go too fast, and it also teaches him to stop on a dime.

It works best at a canter and revolves around X, which is the center of the arena. Make four marks or points (A, B, C, and D) equidistant from X on the perimeter of the arena. A, B, C, and D should be mid-points on the arena wall or fence (see illustration). The corners of a square or rectangular arena work nicely, but you can arrange this in an oval arena, too.

First, ride around the arena, making sure the horse goes deep in all the corners. You don't want him to cut off the corners. Make a lap or two until the horse understands he should stay along the rail.

To start, stand in the middle at X. Walk toward A at the end of the arena. At A pick up a right lead, turn right at the corner, and go toward B. When you get to B, turn right and go through X. When you get to D, make a right-hand turn and go to A. At A, turn right and go down the middle of the arena through X toward C. At C, turn right again and head toward D. When you get to D, turn right and go through X to B. When you get to B, turn right, go to the next corner and turn right toward C. Once at C, turn right and head toward X. When you get to X, you have made one complete pattern.

Continue this pattern until your horse is really paying attention to your cues and obviously wants to slow down. The way to test this is when approaching X. Focus across the arena, at the letters A or C, whichever is across from you. Ride toward it. Before you get to X, lift your reins lightly, quit riding, and sink in your saddle. If it only takes 4 ounces to get your horse to halt near X, you were probably accurate in guessing that your horse was asking you to call it quits. This is a good way to build a conversation.

Stop at X, but don't turn at X. X is a stopping place, not a turning place. Only use A, B, C, or D as turning places.

Do this exercise for 15 to 30 minutes to the right, making all right-hand turns. When the horse is relaxed in his canter and doing right-hand turns with only 4 ounces of effort on your part, halt at X. If he halts with only 4 ounces of effort, sit there for 5 minutes, and let the horse catch his breath.

Then walk a straight line from X to A. Start the pattern again, only this time to the left. Repeat the pattern for about the same amount of time. When the horse is once more relaxed, halt again at X. Walk to A again, and start the pattern all over going to the right. When you're finished, do it to the left once more. Note: Remember to teach your horse to go deep into the corners.

If you did this pattern 4 days in a row, it wouldn't take long to teach your horse to come to a graceful and immediate halt. You could just sink in your saddle as you approached X, and your horse would come to a stop. He'd learn to anticipate, and every time you went by X, he'd ask "Are we going to stop?" It would take only a slight suggestion from you to get your horse to stick his tail in the ground and try to find X.

Once he realizes the value of X as being the place to stop and rest, your horse will use you as X. Then, you'll be able to carry X with you, and you can stop anywhere you want. The communication the two of you developed can transfer to other situations as well. This is how horses can get attached to their humans.

Most horses are attached to other prey animals and X is in the middle of the herd, and that is where they want to be. This is why a lot of race horses, when they come out of a starting gate, run to the middle of the herd. They are running scared at that point and look for the security of the herd. Mother Nature tells them to run to the middle of the pack and survive. The horses in the front, back, or outside are the ones who are probably going to get eaten by the predators first.

The cloverleaf pattern is a simple technique with several benefits. It helps you get an independent seat. It teaches the horse to follow your suggestions, slow down, and stop on your suggestion. It helps the horse learn to not change gaits or directions, but to do so only when asked and with only 4 ounces of effort. This particular technique has given me millions of returns.

Challenges

There are only six things a horse can do: go forward, backward, right, left, up, and down, but there are a million challenges. That means there are at least 6 million things you can do with a horse.

The above techniques and patterns, when used consistently, will help you teach a horse what you want him to do. Consistency is a good teacher, but variety is the spice of life. Remember, though, too much variety lacks consistency, and too much consistency is dull and boring.

Vary the patterns and use your imagination by adding challenges, which are obstacles you put in the way of the patterns. For example, you can put two cavallettis near the round corral bag and ask your horse to jump them as you canter in a circle. An additional challenge would be doing a flying lead change over the cavalletti.

You can vary the cloverleaf pattern by trying it in a pasture with a creek in it as an extra challenge. Or, if you're in the arena, don't stop at X, but stop 20 feet past X, or 20 feet before X. Instead of turning at A and C, turn halfway between B and the corner, etc. There are all kinds of things you can do. You can go in a circle around X, spiral in, and teach your horse to spin. Soon, your horse should get the idea that it pays to have a conversation with you.

The normal routine with riders is that

CLOVERLEAF PATTERN

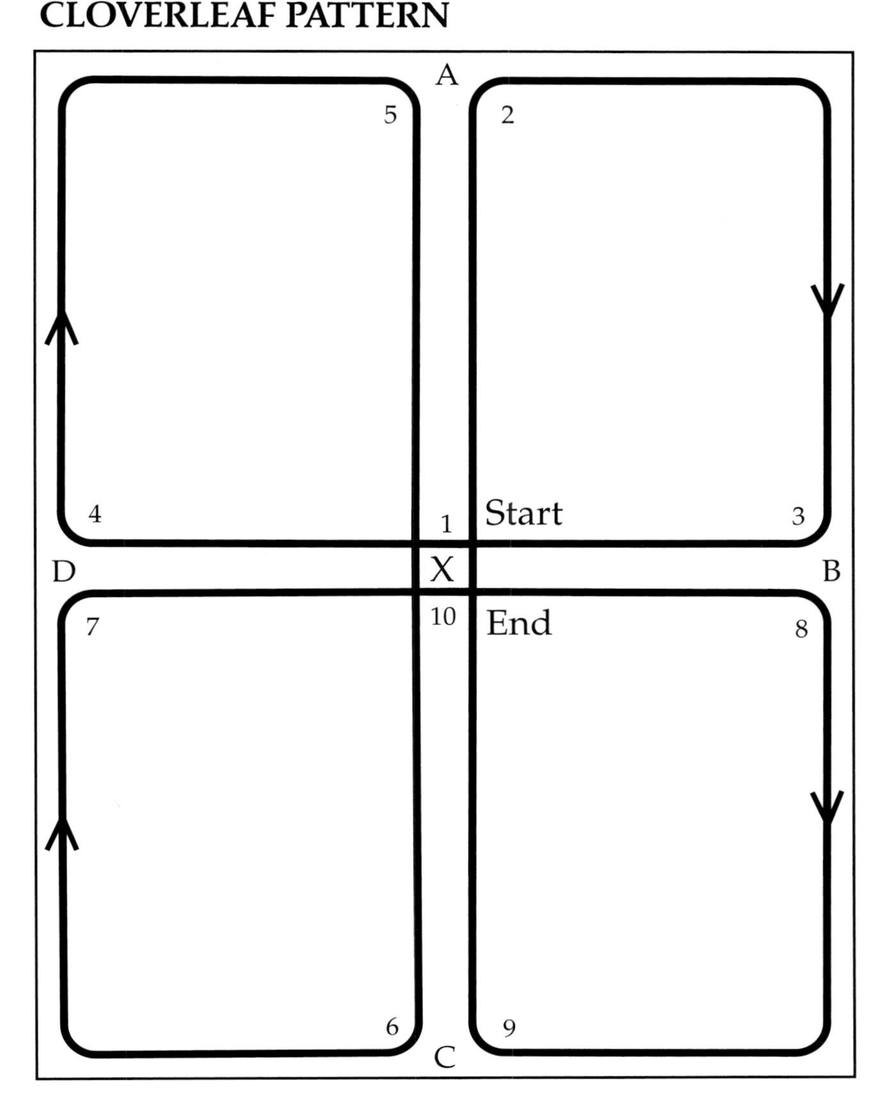

This is a good exercise for many things: teaching a horse to go straight, getting him to stop, preparing him for lead changes, as well as slowing down a horse who wants to go too fast.

In an arena, designate four points that are midway on the wall or fence as A, B, C, and D. These points should be equidistant from X, which is the middle of the arena.

1/ Start in the middle at X. Walk toward A at the end of the arena.
2/ At A, pick up a right lead, turn right at the corner and go toward B.
3/ At B, turn right and go through X to D.
4/ At D, turn right and go to A.
5/ At A, turn right and go through X toward C.
6/ At C, turn right and head toward D.
7/ At D, turn right and go through X toward B.
8/ At B, turn right and go to C.
9/ At C, turn right and go to X.
10/ Stop at X.

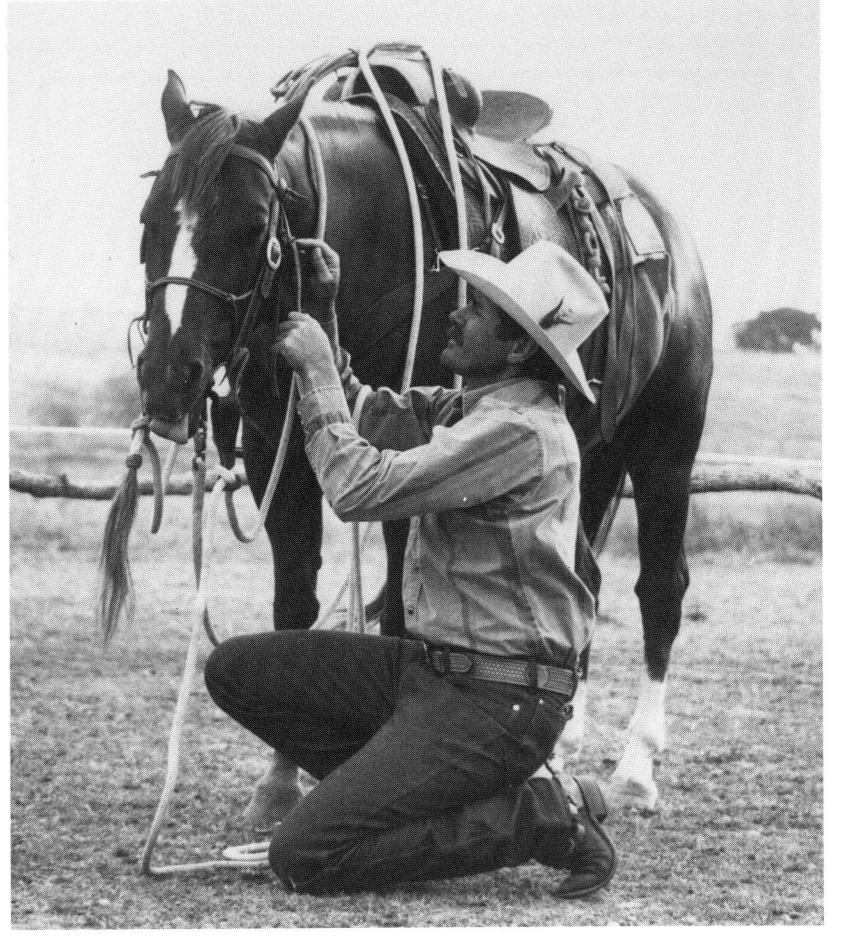

"I think there ought to be a law that says that no human being is allowed to ride a horse with a piece of metal in his mouth until he can get on his bent knee and ask that horse to accept the bit. You have to prove that you have the right attitude, feel, timing, balance, savvy, and experience with a piece of metal in your horse's mouth."

they let their horses go forward, and then try to make them stop. In Natural Horse-Man-Ship, you cause your horse to go forward and allow him to stop, which is completely the opposite.

Pre-Flight Checks With Snaffle Bit and Mecate Reins

I think there ought to be a law that says that no human being is allowed to ride a horse with a piece of metal in his mouth until he can get on his bent knee and ask that the horse accept the bit. I think you have to prove that you have the right attitude, feel, timing, balance, savvy, and experience with a piece of metal in your horse's mouth.

We've been working on all of these qualities in this book and, by this time, you should be able to apply them and Natural Horse-Man-Ship concepts and principles in your relationship with your horse.

You should know, through all of the lateral longeing and pre-flight tests you've done with your horse, that you can communicate and control your horse with nothing in his mouth and with the use of only one rein. Now it's time for a bit and two reins.

With the snaffle bit and mecate reins, repeat the pre-flight checks you performed earlier with the halter and lead rope.

First, secure your mecate lead rope. Make two half hitches around the saddle horn to hold it out of the way. If you're riding an English or Australian saddle which has no horn, then put the lead rope around the horse's neck or tuck it in your belt.

Step up in the stirrup, but don't swing your leg all the way over the saddle. Rub your horse on the other side of his neck, then mount, and sit for 30 seconds or more before checking out the horse's lateral flexion.

Bend his neck with one of your reins as you did with the lead rope. See if he bends as well with the snaffle bit as he did with

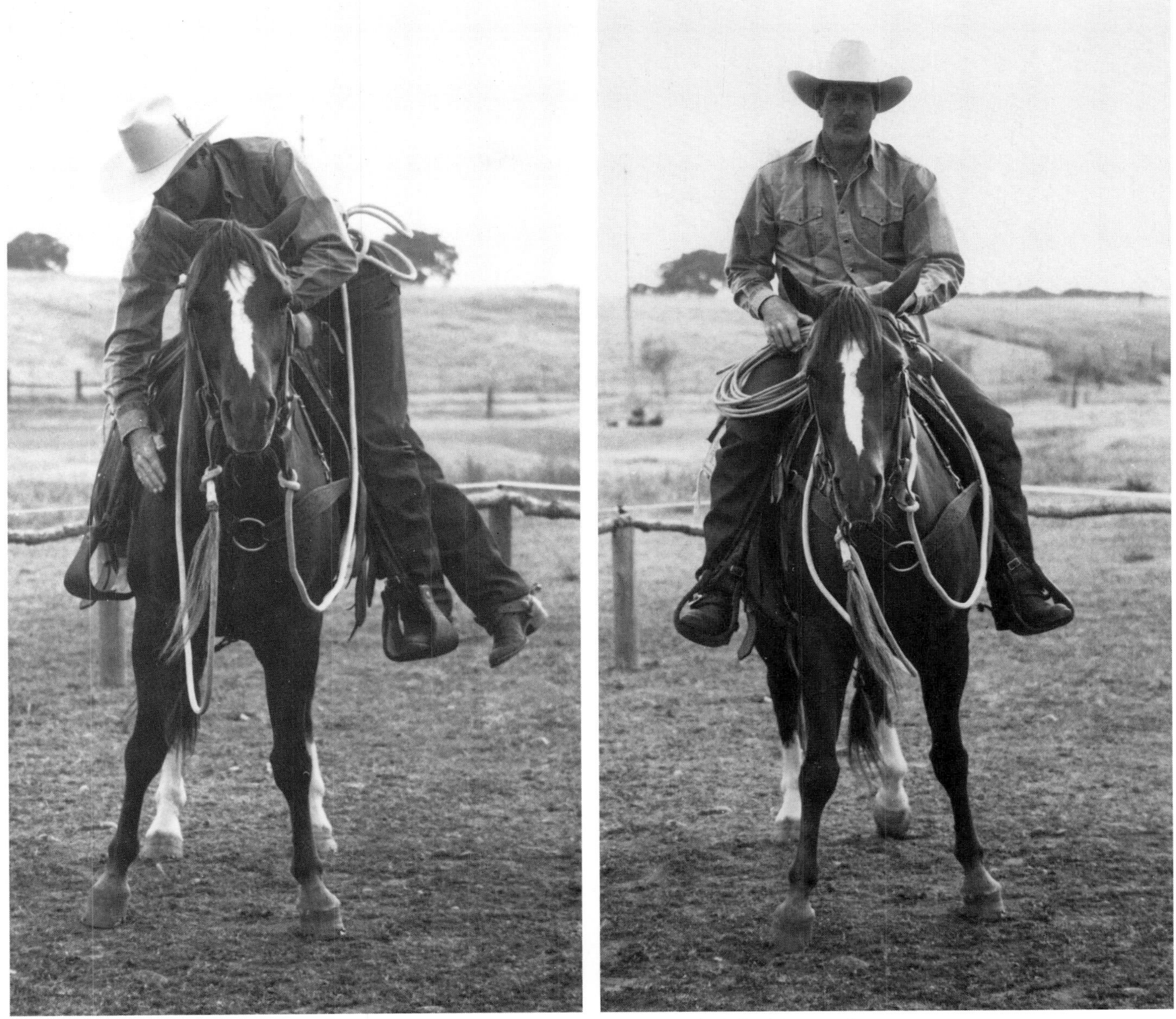

To begin your pre-flight check, step up in the stirrup, but don't swing your leg all the way over the saddle. Rub your horse on the other side of his neck.

Mount and sit for 30 seconds.

Check for lateral flexion of the horse's neck and disengagement of his hindquarters.

Then lead the front end through.

the halter, bosal, or hackamore. As you did before, grade everything your horse does on the scale of -10 to +10. What you're looking for are passing grades, not necessarily perfect scores. Passing would be 6s. You just want to make sure that your horse has a reasonable understanding of what you're asking, that he yields to the bit, not fights it. Later you can refine and perfect each maneuver.

Next, run your hand down the rein, bring it to your belly button or midsection with an indirect rein and move the hindquarters. With all of the prior and proper preparation you've done with your horse, he should be able to make the transition from the halter and lead rope to the snaffle easily. Now, straighten your elbow and lead the front end through and around.

Your horse should just walk right out of this and go forward. Then, reach down, pick up the opposite rein, and bring it to your knee in a neutral rein for lateral flexion. Hold it there and wait. Your horse should move in a tight circle, then eventually stop. When he relaxes, let him walk off again.

Then, pick up the rein and bring it to your midsection again with an indirect rein. That disengages the hindquarters and moves them over. Straighten your elbow and bring the front end through.

Collection

More than 95 percent of this book has been devoted to the foundation of riding—the basics—the concepts and principles of Natural Horse-Man-Ship. However, collection is an advanced concept, and I promise you that if you haven't properly prepared your horse and yourself for this or any other advanced maneuver, you'll never be able to achieve it totally.

Collection is not when the horse brings his nose in and down. That's only vertical flexion. Collection is a combination of respect, impulsion, and flexion totally combined.

True collection is having the horse calm, cool, and collected. And he should have respect for the human and human environment. He doesn't listen to Mother Nature anymore. After you've gained the horse's respect, you can go about gaining his

Before you think about refining vertical flexion, put a lightweight string, such as a progress string, around the base of your horse's neck and see if you can make him do the following with nothing in his mouth or around his nose.

Trot.

Lope.

Stop.

Back up.

Lead the front end through.

Side-pass.

impulsion, which is controlled forward energy that comes from behind. Most of the riding exercises and drills you've done to this point have helped develop your horse's impulsion.

Another aspect of impulsion is that it is the opposite of flight from fear, which is impulsiveness. When you use Natural Horse-Man-Ship techniques, your horse learns to respect and trust you, not fear you.

Once you've established impulsion in the horse, you can then develop flexion. You start off with lateral flexion, which is bending the horse's neck left and right, and getting the horse's body to yield sideways. Only when your horse is flexible from side to side, do you ask him to bring his nose in and down. This is vertical flexion.

When you sacrifice quality for quantity, you won't have anything but quantity—a bunch of junk.

Before you attempt vertical flexion, take this test. Put your reins around your saddle horn and use a lightweight string, such as the 6-foot progress string. Put this around the base of your horse's neck, and see if you can do all the prerequisites with nothing in your horse's mouth or around his nose. Back him up, ride him forward, ask him to side-pass. Bring one side of the string into your midsection or belly button and see if you can disengage your horse's hindquarters. Lead the front end through by stretching out your hand with the string.

Check out whether everything you've ever asked your horse to do with a halter or bit can now be done with a piece of string.

Until you can make your horse perform maneuvers with just the slightest suggestion of a string, you and he are not ready for the advanced concept of vertical flexion and total collection.

Here are some exercises to develop your horse's vertical flexion.

1/ Put your reins in one hand, and put that hand down in front of horse's withers. Then, take a rein in each hand and hold. You'll have a fairly short length of rein when you do this.

2/ Hold the reins taut and your hand steady. See if your horse will give you a soft feel; that is, relax his lower jaw and flex his poll to relieve pressure on the reins.

3/ As soon as he does, turn loose of the reins quickly. If your hands are slow on the release, the horse will learn to drag the reins away from you. He'll learn to fight your hands, not give to them.

4/ Walk your horse forward. Pick up on reins, hold them steady, and as soon as the horse flexes at the poll, turn him loose.

5/ Move into a trot. Close your fingers on the reins. When your horse is soft to you, be soft to him. In other words, when your horse gives you his head, open up your fingers, and release your hold on the reins.

6/ Opening and closing your fingers is an exercise designed to ask the horse for vertical flexion by flexing his poll. When you want your horse to give you a soft feel, close your fingers on the reins, and as soon as he does, open your fingers. Your horse will learn to be soft, and feel for that opening and closing of your fingers.

7/ Then release the reins and go to a loose or casual rein as a reward. Do 90 percent of your work on a loose rein. Go for short periods of time first. You don't want to hold your horse's head too long. That teaches the horse to lean into the hold instead of yielding to it. The vertical flexion position is a position for submission, communication, and engagement. It is not a control position.

To develop your horse's vertical flexion, take a rein in each hand and hold.

Hold the reins taut and steady. As soon as the horse relaxes his lower jaw and flexes at the poll, release the reins quickly. Soon your horse will learn to give you a "soft feel."

Trotting with vertical flexion.

8/ To move up into a canter, turn loose of your horse's head a little and let the horse take his lead. As you're cantering along, take hold of the reins for a few strides asking for head position. As soon as you get it, turn it loose. Over time and with much patient practice, your horse will learn to hold a vertical head position longer, and he'll be truly on the bit and collected. Note: Most humans make the mistake of looking to see if the horse is giving them vertical flexion. Check it out with feel.

You don't need draw reins, side reins, or other pieces of equipment to achieve vertical flexion. Don't tie up your horse's head in the vertical position for hours until he gets used to it. You can do this yourself with only your hands and by developing a soft feel.

Vertical flexion is something that helps the horse get strong over his top line. If he is strong over his top line, he'll be strung

Loping with vertical flexion.

like a bow, ready to spring into action at your suggestions. The horse will get softer and softer in your hands and more willing to follow them.

But if his attitude is wrong and you string him like a bow, with a tie-down or side reins, you'll get nothing but resistance and a hard feel. When you sacrifice quality for quantity, you won't have anything but quantity—a bunch of junk. Your horse should feel soft when you get that vertical flexion. It should feel like a willing partner's hand on the way to the dance floor.

TIME

"Just being with your horse is important, whether you are sitting on him or standing by his side. . . . Hang out with your horse. . . . Spend time with your horse."

IF YOU TAKE the time it takes, it takes less time. The flip side to that is, "I never have time to do it right, but I always have time to do it over and over and over."

Of the six keys to Natural Horse-Man-Ship, time is a key ingredient that is often overlooked or neglected. It takes time to become a Natural Horse-Man, just like it takes time to be good at anything. It's not possible to read this book or watch my video course and be a Natural Horse-Man overnight just because you have the information. You still have to put in the time that it requires.

There is the old adage about wet saddle blankets making good horses. It's true, especially if you do it with the right attitude, knowledge, tools, and techniques in putting in that time.

You can draw a parallel between becoming a Natural Horse-Man and becoming a pilot. You have to have at least 40 hours of instruction before you can get a pilot's license. But it takes a minimum of 400 hours before you are allowed to take a test for a commercial pilot's license. After that it takes somewhere around 1,000 hours for an instrument rating. Becoming a Natural Horse-Man has its own timetable, too.

Horse and Human Timetable

When it comes to riding horses, the best place to learn is on the horse's back. It will take the average person at least 1,000 hours horseback to be a green rider. When a person has put in that much time riding, he will have a whole different understanding about horses. He'll have developed some horse savvy.

After 1,000 hours of experience, the next plateau for a human comes when he develops the other five keys: the attitude, knowledge, tools, techniques, and imagination. It's the next 1,500 to 3,000 hours that tells whether or not a rider is really going to advance and become an expert rider from the horse's point of view.

A horse's timetable looks a little different from a human's. A horse who's had around 10 hours of riding can be called a green horse. It usually takes a horse 300 hours of riding to get to the next level of understanding. These are just approximate timetables, not hard and fast rules. The next plateau for a horse comes at about 1,000 hours. At that point, he is a fairly dependable horse for most riders.

Note the difference in timetables for human and horse. It's almost a three to one ratio. What takes a horse 300 hours to achieve takes a human 1,000 hours. Horses seem to be about three times as fast as humans when it comes to grasping concepts.

People often ask me how long it will take to become a Natural Horse-Man. It's realistic to say that if a person has 1,000 hours of riding as a foundation and then starts putting the six keys to use, he's got a good start with the Levels Program that is part of Natural Horse-Man-Ship. Most people can pass a Level 1 test after 20 hours of effort in assimilating the information that's in this book. But it will take up to 500 hours to reach Level 3. When you pass Level 3, then you can start calling yourself a Natural Horse-Man. Until then, you're just an apprentice.

I equate things in hours because it's like prop-time on an airplane. When you rent an airplane for 3 days, but only fly it for 3 hours, you have only 3 hours of prop-time in on that airplane, not 3 days.

Put an hour-meter on yourself and your horse. If you rode an hour a day 5 days a week, that's 20 hours a month. Multiply that by times 12 months and you have 240 hours. If you ride a few weekends, that might add an extra 10 hours for a total of 250 hours in a year. At that rate, 500 hours of riding time, you'd have to be involved in Natural Horse-Man-Ship for 2 years.

But riding is not the only thing you need to do in Natural Horse-Man-Ship. You must endeavor to develop all six of the keys, and that takes time.

That's why the first three levels in Natural Horse-Man-Ship are a hobby. The second three are a craft, and then everything after Level 6 is an art. It takes time and a strong commitment on your part to advance through the levels.

To become a sixth level horse-man, it's probably going to take up to 10,000 hours. It all depends on how far you want to go.

It would be a real achievement if you get to Level 3 in 2 to 5 years. You probably just raised your eyebrows and said, "2 to 5 years!" But think about this. In 2 to 5 years without this information, you'd still be where you are because if you always do what you've always done, you'll always get what you've always gotten. In other words, if you didn't have Natural Horse-Man-Ship, you'd still be doing all the normal things people do with horses and getting nowhere.

There are 8,766 hours in a year. Many people say they've been riding for 5 years, and really they've probably only put in a few hours each year. Even 100 hours a year is not much.

It's the same thing with horses. That's why so many of them are green and act like colts instead of becoming true blue, dependable partners. They may be 9 years old and really haven't had 300 hours worth of riding, let alone 1,000.

80-20 Concept

How much time should you spend riding a horse? How much is too much?

There are three things that are hard to overdo with a horse: 1/ Sit on your horse. 2/ Use lateral flexion. 3/ Use your horse for transportation.

There are three things that are hard to overdo with a horse: 1/ Sit on your horse. 2/ Use lateral flexion. 3/ Use your horse for transportation.

1/ Just being with a horse is important, whether you are sitting on him or standing by his side. Horses are social animals; they hang out together all day long. Hang out with your horse. Don't hurry up and saddle your horse, hurry and ride, then get off quickly, and put him up. Just sit on his

Laterally flexing your horse's neck is a great exercise for getting him under control mentally, emotionally, and physically.

Use your horse for transportation.

back and relax. Spend time with your horse.

2/ You can't do lateral flexion enough. Flexing your horse's head and neck is a great exercise for getting the horse under control mentally, emotionally, and physically. On the other hand, it's easy to overdo vertical flexion.

3/ Using your horse for transportation. If you go out trail riding for hours and hours, you'll wear out before your horse does in most cases. This is difficult to overdo, but not impossible. There are situations where a horse can be overtaxed when it comes to riding hard for long periods of time.

If riders would do the above three things 80 percent of the time and whatever it is they want to do the other 20

If you haven't got time to ride, you can laterally longe your horse over and around obstacles for only a few minutes. It isn't necessarily the amount of time you spend with your horse, it's the quality of time you invest to develop him mentally, emotionally, and physically.

percent of the time, they would get far better results with their horses. For example, if you want to rope, jump, rein, barrel race, etc., do that only 20 percent of the time and the above three things the rest of the time. The 80/20 concept is a great way to keep horses mentally fresh and willing to perform.

A horse is a lot like a child in that his attention span is short. Therefore, you should change the subject a lot. Work on one thing for 5, 10, or 20 minutes, then switch to another activity. One of the reasons *Sesame Street* is such a successful television program for youngsters is that the characters constantly do the same thing, but they do it in a variety of ways. This is where consistency is a good teacher and variety is the spice of life. But too much variety lacks consistency and too much consistency is darn boring.

It's been said that you should never work a horse for more than 20 minutes. But don't read into that statement that you've got to put him up after 20 minutes of work. That's not true. You can work on yourself and your horse for 20 minutes, but then change the subject and work on something else or rest.

How often should you play with a horse? Quality time is probably the key here. If you can only spend a little time with your horse, spend it on things that are worthwhile. In my situation with as many horses as I've got and with my busy schedule, I arrange it where my horses have to come into my environment daily to get their food and water. This way I spend time with them even if it's only superficially. They know I'm there and with them.

Another way to create quality time is to laterally longe your horse over obstacles for about 10 minutes. If you haven't got time to ride, this is better than doing nothing at all.

How often you should play with your horse is entirely up to you and the results

Horses live moment by moment. Human beings, on the other hand, live a couple of steps ahead into the future.

you want. If your goal is to really have your horse going well, you might want to spend an hour a day 5 days a week. Of course, this depends on his age and maturity. You'd be pleasantly surprised how much progress you could make if it was quality time.

If you are making so much progress with a horse that every 2 months he needs a 2-week rest, you're making as much progress as you can without overdoing it. If your horse doesn't need a rest for a year, you're probably not being progressive enough.

Moment by Moment

Horses live moment by moment. Human beings, on the other hand, live a couple of steps ahead into the future. For example, when you are driving your car, you might think about what you're going to do at work that day. You are doing what it takes to do at the moment (drive), but your mind is concerned with the future. Horses are not capable of projecting that far into the future.

My idea of a moment is that there are at least 4 moments in a second. A horse lives in the moment, so he's living not just second by second, but moment by moment, 4 of them in every second. This is a survival mechanism. Horses and other prey animals must live in the moment in order to survive. That's why a horse can be going along and all of a sudden, for no obvious reason at all, start spooking. The rider is not in sync with the horse's frame of mind, what's going on with him, and where he's going. The rider's thoughts might be on something totally different or in the future, and the horse's thoughts are on how he is going to survive the next moment. When something startles the horse, the rider might take 2 or 3 seconds to get in tune with it. The horse is going off like a firecracker, and the rider is just waking up to the fact that something was frightening to the horse.

Understanding how horses think and live in the moment puts a whole different perspective on handling them.

Timing

You must learn how to get in time with your horse, and later how to get him in time with you. When it comes to horses, it's not what you do, it's when you quit doing what you're doing that counts. If you pick up the reins to back your horse and he starts to back, release the rein pressure before he gets dull.

Like they say in the entertainment business, timing is everything. When it comes to a horse, he is symmetry in motion. He is an attitude with four feet and those feet are moving and they have different timing at a walk, trot, canter, gallop, and a back-up. Therefore, learning how to time everything and having good timing is an important ingredient. Where do you get timing? You need to go back to the qualities of a leader, which are attitude, feel, timing, balance, savvy, and experience. Basically, focus gives you feel, feel gives you timing, and feel and timing give you balance. Improve your timing by improving your focus.

Plan for Young Horses

Even though this isn't a colt-starting book, here's a timetable plan that might help many of you.

Often, you've heard that horses aren't really mature until they are 5 or 6 years old. But if you don't start them before that, all you've got is a 6-year-old rank bronc. Other people say to start them when they are young, but many times they are washed up by the time they are 3- or 4-year-olds because they were pushed too hard in the beginning.

I've come up with a plan that's down the middle of the road. It's a compromise that benefits both the horse and rider.

The best time to start a horse is in the spring of his 2-year-old year with a program that uses around 10 hours of quality time. Get the horse over the proverbial "hump," which is a pun, but also a reference to the horse becoming ridable. When he's over the potential trauma of having a rider on his back, turn him out until that fall. At that time, put another 10 to 20 hours on him. Turn him out again.

In the spring of his 3-year-old year, put in 20 more hours. Turn him out once more. Bring him back in the fall and put another 20 to 40 hours on him.

When your horse is a 4-year-old, he is physically more capable than he was when he was a 2- and 3-year-old. Mentally, he is still flexible and capable of learning things. Spend some time with him going on trail rides, cattle drives, or something that causes him to exert some energy, but still not overdo it. Put in up to 200 hours of time in the spring and summer with that horse. Give him a good long break in the fall. When he is a 5-year-old, have at him.

This is not a special formula. It's just a good common sense program. Many people give up long-term gains for short-term gains. The old adage is short-term gain, long-term harm. With this slow, but progressive program, your horse, when he is 15 to 20 years old, will not only be physically sound, he'll be a better horse than when he was 7 years old.

It all depends on what you're after, and I hope that by now, you're after developing a partnership for life.

IMAGINATION

"I'd like for you to understand that in order to become a horseman, you have to have the heart and desire, attitude, feel, timing, balance, savvy, and experience to get your horse's heart and desire, respect, impulsion, and flexion."

IMAGINATION PLAYS a part in the application of all the things that I've described and prescribed for humans and horses to get together and develop partnerships for life.

Everybody tends to have a different set of goals and interests when it comes to horses. You need to know how you are going to apply the 103 ingredients of Natural Horse-Man-Ship to your situation.

Although this is not a how-to book on cutting, jumping, reining, roping, gymkhana, dressage, or polo, at the same time to a large degree, it is. It takes imagination in order for the reader to see how having a horse with respect, impulsion, and flexion is going to apply to them.

I read a book by Maxwell Maltz titled *Psycho-Cybernetics.* This field or endeavor has to do with visualizing or practicing in your mind what it is you want to be or want to do before you do it. And this is what you can do in applying imagination to Natural Horse-Man-Ship. You can get almost religious about horsemanship. You think about it all the time. You become it; it becomes you. You pretend what you are doing and see it in your mind before you do it. For example, you can pretend there is a set of barrels in front of you and run them, or pretend there's a cow there and work it.

You can simulate real situations. Simulators are used to prepare people to go into outer space. Why can't we use simulation in our imaginations to practice the sports or interests we have? So many people say, "I don't have cattle, so I can't cut." Or "I don't have jumps, so I can't jump." You can do anything you want to do if you want

Simulation is a powerful way to develop yourself and your horse. Here, Pat simulates cutting with a friend.

to do it badly enough.

There are three types of games, exercises, maneuvers, or whatever you want to call them, that can help you use your imagination as a Natural Horse-Man: 1/ Imaginary Events, 2/ Simulator Games, 3/ Isolations.

1/ Imaginary Events

Think of whatever event or interest you have and learn how to practice this event mentally without any of the physical objects being there. For example, say you wanted to do gymkhana games. You can do barrel racing without barrels, pole bending without poles, keyhole race without the keyhole, etc. But you have to vividly imagine that they are there and how you have to go through them.

If you wanted to rope, you could practice all of the roping events without cattle. You could come out of the chute pretending you're the header and do all the things headers do. Or you could practice being the heeler. You could also use friends as part of an imaginary team roping scenario. One of you could be the header and the other the heeler. If you had a third person, he could ride his horse as if it were the steer.

You could ride an imaginary jump course or cross country course. Also, you could ride all the cow-working events without cattle. A friend could double as a cow if need be. Imaginary reining or dressage patterns are also fun.

But if you do imaginary events, concentrate and really pretend as though the cow is there, the jumps are there, the barrels are there, etc. Practice it perfectly in your mind and pretend perfectly with your horse.

2/ Simulator Games

Simulator games are different from imaginary events in that they actually break down a specific part of an imaginary event into separate components.

Here are some of the games you can do:

1. Shoot the Bad Guy—This is a game that helps you and your horse work on stops and roll-backs. By doing the quick stops and roll-backs, your horse learns to work off his hindquarters with maneuvers that he might use in such events as reining, cutting, and working cow horse.

Imagine that you're in a shooting gallery. There are two bad guys, one ahead of you and one behind you. In an arena, they can be at point A and point C, as described earlier in the cloverleaf pattern. (See Techniques—In the Saddle.)

Start at X, or the middle of the arena, and trot toward the bad guy at point A. Pretend as if you were shooting him with a gun in your right hand. Then, put your

Although this is not a how-to book on cutting, jumping, reining, roping, gymkhana, dressage, or polo, at the same time to a large degree, it is.

right hand in the middle of your reins. Stand up in your stirrups a little bit. Run your left hand down the rein and, as you sit down in the saddle again, look behind you and bring the indirect rein (left rein) toward your midsection at same time. Don't pull, just bring the rein to your middle. As you're sitting down, you're focusing behind and bringing that rein to your midsection. That action should cause your horse to put his hindquarters into the ground as you're looking around and focusing on somewhere else—point C. To get your horse out of the ground quickly, straighten your left arm and shoot the bad guy at point C.

Trot or canter about 25 or 30 yards toward that bad guy. Then stand up in your stirrups and run your right hand down the rein. Sit down and pull the rein toward your midsection as you're simultaneously looking at the bad guy at point A. That gets your horse into the ground again. As you're looking at the bad guy, straighten your right arm and shoot at him. This helps your horse get out of the ground.

This might sound silly, but it helps if you make bullet sounds as you're shooting. It sounds like clucking and your horse will really get out of the ground. The theory is if you turn a horse fast enough, he's got to stop somewhere in between.

2. *Sword Fight Side-Pass*—This is a great game for working on side-passing as a maneuver. Some events that use this as a component are dressage, polo, trail classes, and cow working.

Imagine that you are sword fighting on horseback with someone, and you have to side-pass to get over to him. You can side-pass toward him and away from him. This would create an offensive and defensive side-pass in each direction.

3. *Side-Pass War*—This is another side-pass exercise and is useful especially for young horses just learning this maneuver.

The game takes two people on horses. Stand with both horses facing a fence or arena rail. One person takes the offense and the other the defense. The offensive person takes his foot and tries to touch the defensive person's horse in the flank with his boot. Of course, if you're on defense, you try not to allow that person to get that close to you. This game gives you a reason to side-pass your horse quickly—either to tag somebody with your toe or to get out of the way.

4. *Horseback Bullfighting*—In this game you can practice turns on the forehand and hindquarters, just like you'd do in dressage tests or even team roping, if you're the header and your horse needs to turn on his hindquarters to face a steer.

Have someone on another horse trot toward you aiming for your stirrup. At the last moment, move your horse's hindquarters out of the way. As the fake bull goes by you, turn and face him. Make a 180-degree turn just like a brave bullfighter would do.

5. *Figure-Eight Cow Working*—This game takes two people. Have your partner trot a set of circles in front of you in the shape of a figure-eight. You hold a parallel line watching the person who is doing the figure-eights. Use your peripheral vision to draw a perpendicular line in front of them. Have your horse hold that line. To make the game more challenging, add more circles.

6. *Rodear*—In this simulation, you can practice holding a cow out of a rodear, which is a herd of cattle.

This game also takes two people. Put three or four barrels about 15 to 20 feet from each other in a circle. Have one person be the cutter and one person be the cow that is trying to get back into the rodear or ring of barrels.

3/ Isolations

Imagine that your horse is a motorcycle. God and Mother Nature gave him a frame and a set of wheels. But your job is to make sure his motor, brakes, steering wheel, transmission, and the clutch are put together and working right.

In isolations, you further break down the maneuvers mentioned in simulator games until your horse can do each particular movement in a maneuver perfectly.

1. *Departures*—(motor) Get your horse to perform his departures by squeezing your legs. If want your horse to go from a halt to a dead run (as in barrel racing), you should be able to this without kicking. Focus on a point in the distance and just squeeze your horse into a trot, a canter, and then a gallop.

2. *Stopping*—(brakes) The isolation for stopping is backing. If you feel your horse doesn't have good brakes, it's because your horse isn't backing well enough. So isolate your stopping by getting your horse to back up better.

3. *Turning*—(steering wheel) If you are not satisfied with the way your horse turns, make sure he is side-passing well. Make sure that it doesn't take more than 4 ounces to side-pass right and left.

4. *Gaits*—(transmission) You don't want your horse to change gaits without you wanting him to. So use games such as the trotting test (mentioned in Techniques—In the Saddle), which teaches your horse to hold his gait.

5. *Lateral flexion*—(clutch) Lateral flexion is what gives you the ability to engage and disengage your horse's transmission, his hindquarters. In this book, I've given you many exercises for lateral flexion on the ground and in the saddle.

By using isolations, you can go full circle with simulator games and imaginary events. If your horse doesn't do "Shoot the Bad Guy," or the "Horseback Bullfighting" well, then you need to go back to the isolations and practice each maneuver. Once you have the isolations down pat and can do the simulator games right, then you go on to the imaginary events.

Let's take barrel racing as an example of using these three types of games. If your horse has trouble getting around the pattern, isolate his problem areas. First of all, isolate the maneuvers and practice departures, backing, and side-passing to help your horse learn the cues for running, stopping, and turning quickly. Then use the following simulator games to practice those maneuvers: Shoot the Bad Guy, Sword Fight Side-Pass, and Side-Pass War. These should help you in teaching your horse to run, stop, and turn—all maneuvers he needs in a barrel race. After that, practice your runs with imaginary barrels. When you're through with all this preliminary work, you're ready for a real set of a barrels. Your horse should be prepared for the event without you having to burn him out practicing the sport the normal way. Most people just run around barrels constantly without proper training and conditioning, make tons of mistakes when they do, and wonder why their horses hate going into arenas, are uncontrollable at a run, and disrespect or hit barrels when they turn around them. Their horses are telling them that enough's enough, and they want out of there.

Once you have developed the principle, add purpose. Give your horse a job to do.

With these games, you save a lot of wear and tear on the both of you and accomplish what you want in the first place—a trained barrel horse who's fresh and ready to go.

I presented these three things (imaginary events, simulator games, and isolations) in the order that I did so you can see the large picture first, then dribble down to its smallest component. However, you have to master isolations first before you can get the simulator games right, and then be successful with the imaginary events to the point that you can turn around and actually perform the event of your choice.

The key in all of this (imaginary events, simulator games, and isolations) is that your horse has to really pay attention and take his cues from your body language. Your horse is using you as his leader and he is following your suggestions. This is what you want in a partnership for life.

Now that you have put all your six keys (attitude, knowledge, tools, techniques, time, and imagination) together, add in purpose because purpose gives meaning. Give your horse a job to do. If you have a rancher friend, help gather his cattle every chance you get. Mark trails for competitive or endurance rides or ride on one. Take your horse to contests, such as horse shows, gymkhanas, or ropings. Go out and do something with your horse.

From the beginning of this book to the end, I've tried to dispel the three big lies: 1/ Just saddle a horse and get on. 2/ Kick him to go. 3/ Pull back on the reins to stop. My goal was to replace those three lies with the truths and concepts of Natural Horse-Man-Ship. This is the foundation of all good riding.

I'd like you to understand that in order to become a horseman, you have to have heart and desire, attitude, feel, timing, balance, savvy, and experience to get your horse's heart and desire, respect, impulsion, and flexion. Combine these principles and qualities properly and you've got Natural Horse-Man-Ship.

Pat Parelli and friends.

Parelli-Isms

• Pat Parelli Proudly Presents his Provocative Programs and the Proclamation that Prior and Proper Preparation Prevents P-Poor Performance, Particularly if Polite and Passive Persistence is Practiced in the Proper Position. This Perspective is Patience from Process to Product, Principle to Purpose. The Promise that Pat Plans to Prove is that Practice does not make Perfect, only Perfect Practice makes Perfect and, it is Peculiar how Prey animals Perceive People as Predators.

• The better your horse backs up and goes sideways, the better he does everything else.

• Remember the four-letter word that starts with F! Fo.C.U.S.

• The four elements of success: Talent, Skills, Try, and Luck. Talent you are born with; Skills you develop; Try is intestinal fortitude or guts; Luck is spelled w.o.r.k. and is defined when preparation meets opportunity.

• Find out what happens before what happens happens.

• Mother Nature says: "Don't just stand there, do something." People sense is: "Don't just do something, stand there."

• If your horse is recreation for you . . . can you be recreation for your horse?

• Ask . . . Tell . . . Promise.

• Firm . . . Fair . . . Friendly.

• If he's blinking, he's thinking. If he's not, he's hot.

• If he's licking his lips, he's digesting a thought or he just tasted humble pie.

• Nobody has more feel than a blind man . . . he feels with his fingers.

• Normal is what everybody does that everybody else is doing when they've got half a mind to.

• Don't look at your horse . . . his ears won't fall off.

• Don't look where he (your horse) is going, that's his job.

• Horse sense is common sense with horses. People sense is the common sense thing to do in a human environment.

• Horse sense is stable thinking.

• "Horse sense is what horses have that makes them not bet on people." W.C. Fields

• Blood is thicker than water.

• Cause your ideas to become your horse's ideas, but understand his ideas first.

• To cause is to be as gentle as you can but as firm as necessary. When and if you become firm, don't do it being mean or mad. When you are gentle, do it without being a sissy.

• Trust that they will respond, but be ready to correct. Not more one than the other.

• Cause is less than make, and allow is more than let. Cause the undesirable things to be difficult and allow the desirable things to be easy.

• Define response, ill response, and reaction.

Response—has thought process, understanding, and respect.

Ill Response—has thought process, understanding, and disrespect.

Reaction—has fear and/or surprise and no understanding.

• Your legs should do exactly what your hands do.

- Forty, with four kids, full of phobias, never became famous, flubs up a lot, falls off, and followed everyone else into failure without a Fo.C.U.S.
- Direct, then support, if needed.
- The four most handicapping words in the English language: can't, won't, don't, yeah but.
- The only force that should be used on a horse is 4 ounces and a focus.
- Feel of, for, together.
- Everything starts in the mind, goes through the body, down the legs, and to the feet.
- Observe, remember, and compare.
- Attitude, feel, timing, balance, savvy, and experience.
- Get the horse to give, yield, and then turn loose.
- Respect, attention, direct, support.
- Exaggerate to teach, refine as you go along.
- The sum total of respect, impulsion, and flexion gives you natural collection.
- Your horse can only be as brave as you are.
- "Imagination is more valuable than knowledge." Einstein
- To err is human, but to blame the horse is even more human.
- Common sense has become a very uncommon thing.
- Every jackass thinks he's got horse sense.
- Go with the flow and flow with the go.
- The technique is not important; it is the respect that follows that matters.
- Smooth transitions, snappy departures.
- Allow your horse to soak.
- No horse is taller than the tips of his ears when his nose is touching the ground.
- Don't get mad, get even by taking a fresh start.
- When you want to learn as badly as you want air, then you'll be easy to teach.
- Put your horse away like he is your best fishing rod.
- Don't break any promises to your horse.
- I've got one rule. There are no rules.
- The horse doesn't care how much you know until he knows how much you care.
- Can you get firm without getting mean or mad?
- When you're green, you're growing. When you're ripe, you're rotten.
- Allow your horse time to digest your thoughts.
- The best way to make a crooked furrow is to look back and see if it's straight.
- Severe bits, martingales, and tie-downs are good excuses for bad hands and not enough knowledge.
- Do it for the horse, not to him.
- Natural Horse-Man-Ship is so old, it's new again; and it's so simple that even adults can do it.

LEVEL 1 TEST

Level 1 Test

EQUIPMENT NEEDED: 1/ Rope hackamore with 12-foot lead rope; 2/ Carrot stick; 3/ Progress string; 4/ Snaffle or bosal; and 5/ Saddle.

1/A. Walk up to your horse from at least 10 feet away carrying your halter and lead.

1/B. Put on the halter.

1/ Approach the horse and put on the rope hackamore.

Walk up to your horse from at least 10 feet away with your halter and lead in front of you and allow your horse to check it out with his nose. Organize your halter in your left hand and your lead rope over your right elbow. Place your right arm over his neck and place your halter under his neck and hand it to yourself. Use the fingers on your right hand to push his head towards you as you slip the halter over his nose. Adjust the halter with your left hand and tie it off with the Natural Horse-Man-Ship knot with your right hand.

In this segment, we are looking to see if your horse will accept your approach and the rope hackamore. You prove that you know how to put on and tie the rope hackamore correctly. This covers liberty work and knot tying.

1/C. Tie the Natural Horse-Man-Ship knot.

2/ Cooperation.

The first part of this segment is to show how gentle your horse is by touching him all over—mouth, ears, belly, legs, tail, etc. You ask the horse's permission to probe him all over with gentle, but firm movements, not abrupt or aggressive movements. In this segment, we would like to see you approach the horse gently and safely and have your horse accept your approach and touch.

The second part of this test is to be able to individually pick up all four of the horse's feet when you are standing on one side. This shows if your horse will cooperate with you no matter what side of his body you're on. Many horses won't coop-

2/A. Touch the horse's head all over: ears, mouth, eyes, etc.

2/B. Touch the horse's body all over.

2/C. Individually pick up the horse's feet when you are standing on one side.

erate in picking up their feet at all, much less on the opposite side.

We want to see if you can perform this easy, everyday task by using pressure points. Use the horse's chestnuts in getting him to pick up his front feet and cap of the hock to pick up hind feet. Simulate cleaning them with a hoof pick.

3/ Fingertip yielding.

The hot fingers exercises used in lateral longeing prove that you can maneuver the horse's body in all directions while you're on the ground. This segment shows that with just your fingertips you can move your horse's body backwards and sideways, and cause him to move his forequarters and hindquarters. We want to see you rub the correct areas on his body to prepare him to move, use steady stimulation to cause him to move, and then rub him again to cause him to stop.

Another part of this test is to get your horse to lower his head to the ground. If you are on the left side of the horse, put your left hand on the horse's forelock and your right hand on the horse's poll between the first and the third vertebrae where the halter crownpiece goes. Hold steady with your left hand to keep the horse's nose down. With your right hand, press your thumb toward your middle finger on the poll. When the horse drops his head even slightly, release the pressure of your hands and rub your horse back toward the withers. See if your horse can keep his head down for 30 seconds or more.

3/A. Use hot fingers to move your horse's body backward.

3/B. Cause your horse to move sideways.

3/C. Cause your horse to lower his head to the ground by pressing your right thumb and middle finger on his poll between the first and third vertebrae where the halter crownpiece goes.

4/ Six yields with 12-foot lead rope.

Use lateral longeing exercises to show how you can cause your horse to move in different directions without moving your feet, except in side-passing. First, have him move forward and backward. Next, move him right and left, a two-lap maximum each way. Side-pass along a fence both ways. Follow that with the come by exercise a half-lap each way, causing the horse to trot through a 3-foot gap between you and the fence. This exercise will help to prepare you to send him over the jumps and into the trailer. Finally, ask him to go over one jump.

Photos on the next three pages pertain to Test 4.

4/A. Have your horse move toward you.

4/B. Have your horse move backward.

4/C. Cause your horse to move to the right in a two-lap maximum circle.

Stop the horse.

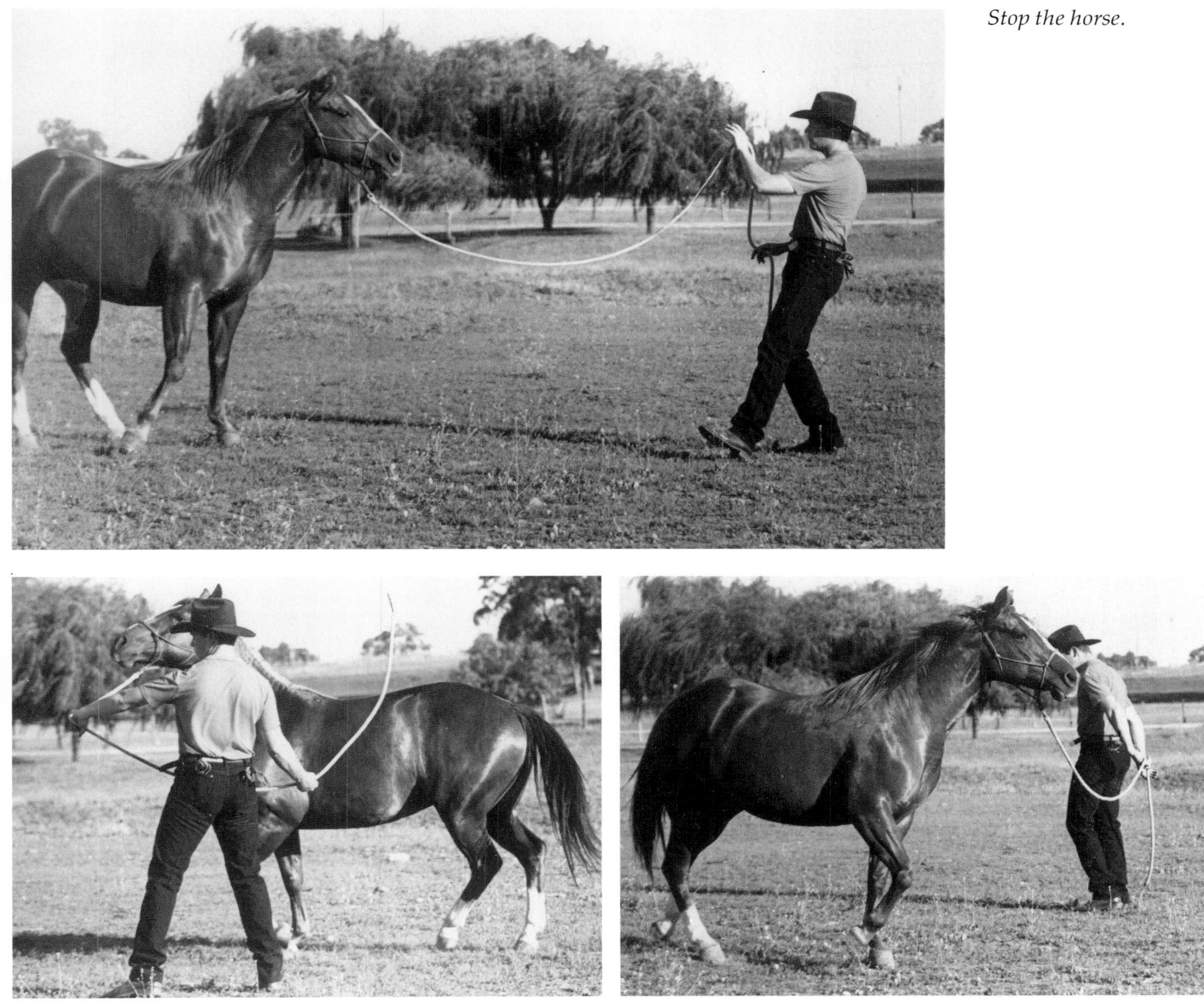

4/D. Cause your horse to move in a two-lap maximum circle to the left.

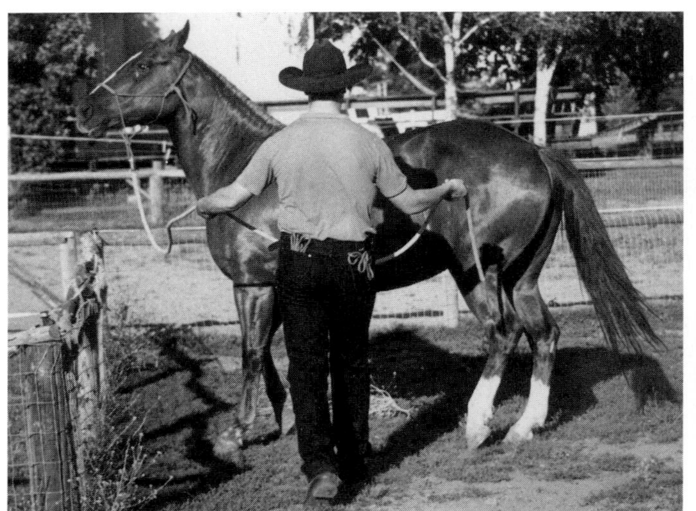

4/E. *Side-pass along a fence both ways.*

4/F. *Cause the horse to trot through a 3-foot gap between you and the fence.*

4/G. *Ask your horse to go over one jump.*

5/ Trailer loading.

Load your horse into a trailer by swinging the lead rope over the horse's withers as he loads. There is no aggressiveness in this or force on your part. You ask the horse to load and in a friendly manner throw the lead rope over his back, since you are confident he'll go in all by himself. The horse should step in smoothly and stay in the trailer until you ask him to come out. When he does come out, it should be without rushing.

6/ Mount bareback with help.

I'd prefer you get on bareback by yourself, but if you cannot, then use one or both of the following techniques:

1/ If you are being helped to mount on the left side, hold your left hand on the lead rope and the mane. Have your helper hold his left hand on the lead rope and the mane right behind yours, halfway up the horse's neck. While keeping your back straight, put your ankle into your helper's right hand. Your helper should do nothing more to help. You lift yourself on the horse with support from the helper.

2/ In mounting on the left, have your helper hold the rein in the mane right behind your hand. Then the helper should face the horse's neck and spread his legs slightly so that the left foot is perpendicular to the horse, like he is ready to do a jumping jack. He should then turn his right toe out and bend his right knee slightly to provide a step for the rider to quickly lift himself up on the horse.

Even if you can mount solo, learn the two techniques with a helper.

6/A. Mount bareback with your ankle in a helper's hand.

6/B. Mount bareback by stepping on a helper's knee.

7/ *Ride bareback with hackamore and progress string.*

Walk, trot, stop, and back up. Side-pass along a fence. Demonstrate lateral flexion by bending the horse's neck to the right and left with a string on each side of his neck. Then demonstrate an indirect and a direct rein. Trot one figure eight with the progress string on one side, then change it to the other side and ride a second figure eight.

This shows that you and your horse are natural enough together to ride without a saddle and that you can get your horse to turn to and from the progress string on each side.

7/A. Stop your horse and back up.

7/B. Side-pass along a fence.

7/C. Demonstrate an indirect rein.

7/D. Demonstrate a direct rein.

8/A. Saddle from the Indian or off-side with a hackamore on the horse.

8/ Saddle from the Indian or off-side with hackamore on horse.

This shows whether you are ambidextrous and that your horse can be handled easily from the off-side.

9/ Mount and dismount from both sides.

This, too, shows that you are ambidextrous and that your horse can be handled easily from both sides.

Get up and down in the stirrups three times on each side.

Mount in a three-step technique: 1/ Step up in the stirrup and face horse's ears. 2/ Rub horse's opposite shoulder. 3/ Put leg over horse's back.

9/A. Step in stirrup and face horse's ears.

9/B. Rub horse's opposite shoulder.

9/C. Put leg over horse's back.

10/A. Trot with a progress string on one side and a carrot stick on the other as a supporting rein—then reverse.

10/ Trot a figure eight with halter, progress string, and carrot stick.

Have the progress string on one side and the carrot stick on the other side and use it as a supporting rein, then reverse. This shows that you can get your horse to yield to pressure with just a progress string and from pressure with just a carrot stick.

11/ Bridle your horse while on your knees

You can use your snaffle bridle or bosal. This shows whether you have enough attitude, feel, timing, balance, savvy, and experience to get your horse to cooperate by lowering his head to accept the bridle.

While being bridled, many horses raise their heads as a form of resistance. If your horse will lower his head while you bridle him, it's a sign of cooperation. Also, demonstrate how to take off the rope hackamore from underneath the snaffle bridle or bosal.

12/ Casual to one-rein control.

Walk, trot, and canter on loose or casual rein. Then stop from the canter using one rein control. To stop, pump your hand up and down the rein three times before you bend your horse around. Hold the horse for 30 seconds.

This proves that you have control of your horse at a walk, trot, and canter on a loose rein, and that you can stop your horse with one rein.

11/A. Bridle your horse while on your knees.

12/A. Walk, trot, and canter on a loose rein.

12/B. From a canter, stop your horse using one-rein control.

12/C. Bend your horse until he stops and then hold him for 30 seconds.

13/A. *Trot a figure eight on a loose rein and show the following skills for 10 seconds each: bouncing on purpose, posting on each diagonal, sitting the trot, and standing in stirrups.*

14/A. *Pick up your reins and make a downward transition from a trot to a back-up.*

13/ Trotting skills for both horse and rider on a loose rein.

Trot a figure eight on a loose rein without changing gait. Show the following skills for 10 seconds each.

a. standing in stirrups.
b. sitting.
c. posting on each diagonal.
d. bouncing on purpose.

This proves that your horse will not change gaits or directions unless you tell him to. The horse should go on a loose rein and not have to be held back.

14/ Downward transition from a trot to a back-up in a straight line.

After riding the figure eight, pick a straight line and pick up your reins. Come down to a back-up, using the nine steps to a back-up.

14/B. *Use the nine steps to a back-up.*

15/A. Side-pass in each direction.

15/ Side-pass both directions.

See if you can cause your horse to move sideways or laterally in either direction. This shows that you and your horse have developed some proficiency in leg yielding.

If the horse's nose is turned in the opposite direction, as in the photo, this shows a need for more legs and less hands as you progress.

16/ Controlled catastrophe situation.

Have a friend approach your horse and move around the horse with a piece of plastic in his or her hands and show how you handle your reins in a scary situation. Your horse does not have to get scared for you to pass the test.

Prove that you can keep your eyes on the person who is creating the catastrophe. It proves your ability to focus and shows that your horse, through your handling, has become braver, less of a claustrophobic, less of a forward-a-holic. It also shows that your horse can follow a predator's suggestions even during a seemingly catastrophic situation.

16/A. Have a friend approach your horse with a piece of plastic or some scary object and show how you use your reins in a catastrophe.

The *Western Horseman*, established in 1936, is the world's leading horse publication. For subscription information and to order other *Western Horseman* books, contact: *Western Horseman*, Box 7980, Colorado Springs, CO 80933-7980; 719-633-5524.

Books Published by Western Horseman Inc.

BACON & BEANS by Stella Hughes
136 pages and 200-plus recipes for popular western chow.

BARREL RACING by Sharon Camarillo
144 pages and 200 photographs. Tells how to train and compete successfully.

CALF ROPING by Roy Cooper
144 pages and 280 photographs covering the how-to of roping and tying.

CUTTING by Leon Harrel
144 pages and 200 photographs. Complete how-to guide on this popular sport.

FIRST HORSE by Fran Devereux Smith
176 pages, 160 black-and-white photos, about 40 illustrations. Step-by-step, how-to information for the first-time horse owner and/or novice rider.

HEALTH PROBLEMS by Robert M. Miller, D.V.M.
144 pages on management, illness and injuries, lameness, mares and foals, and more.

HORSEMAN'S SCRAPBOOK by Randy Steffen
144 pages and 250 illustrations. A collection of popular handy hints.

IMPRINT TRAINING by Robert M. Miller, D.V.M.
144 pages and 250 photographs. Learn how to "program" newborn foals.

LEGENDS by Diane C. Simmons
168 pages and 214 photographs. Includes these outstanding early-day Quarter Horse stallions and mares: Barbra B, Bert, Chicaro Bill, Cowboy P-12, Depth Charge (TB), Doc Bar, Go Man Go, Hard Twist, Hollywood Gold, Joe Hancock, Joe Reed P-3, Joe Reed II, King P-234, King Fritz, Leo, Peppy, Plaudit, Poco Bueno, Poco Tivio, Queenie, Quick M Silver, Shue Fly, Star Duster, Three Bars (TB), Top Deck (TB), and Wimpy P-1.

LEGENDS 2 by Jim Goodhue, Frank Holmes, Phil Livingston, Diane C. Simmons
192 pages and 224 photographs. Includes these outstanding Quarter Horses: Clabber, Driftwood, Easy Jet, Grey Badger II, Jessie James, Jet Deck, Joe Bailey P-4 (Gonzales), Joe Bailey (Weatherford), King's Pistol, Lena's Bar, Lightning Bar, Lucky Blanton, Midnight, Midnight Jr, Moon Deck, My Texas Dandy, Oklahoma Star, Oklahoma Star Jr., Peter McCue, Rocket Bar (TB), Skipper W, Sugar Bars, and Traveler.

LEGENDS 3 by Jim Goodhue, Frank Holmes, Diane Ciarloni, Kim Guenther, Larry Thornton, Betsy Lynch
208 pages and 196 photographs. Includes these outstanding Quarter Horses: Flying Bob, Hollywood Jac 86, Jackstraw (TB), Maddon's Bright Eyes, Mr Gun Smoke, Old Sorrel, Piggin String (TB), Poco Lena, Poco Pine, Poco Dell, Question Mark, Quo Vadis, Royal King, Showdown, Steel Dust, and Two Eyed Jack.

NATURAL HORSE-MAN-SHIP by Pat Parelli
224 pages and 275 photographs. Parelli's six keys to a natural horse-human relationship.

REINING, Completely Revised by Al Dunning
216 pages and over 300 photographs showing how to train horses for this popular event.

ROOFS AND RAILS by Gavin Ehringer
144 pages, 128 black-and-white photographs plus drawings, charts, and floor plans. How to plan and build your ideal horse facility.

STARTING COLTS by Mike Kevil
168 pages and 400 photographs. Step-by-step process in starting colts.

THE HANK WIESCAMP STORY by Frank Holmes
208 pages and over 260 photographs. The biography of the legendary breeder of Quarter Horses, Appaloosas, and Paints.

TEAM PENNING by Phil Livingston
144 pages and 200 photographs. Tells how to compete in this popular family sport.

TEAM ROPING by Leo Camarillo
144 pages and 200 photographs covering every aspect of heading and heeling.

WELL-SHOD by Don Baskins
160 pages, 300 black-and-white photos and illustrations. A horseshoeing guide for owners and farriers. The easy-to-read text, illustrations, and photos show step-by-step how to trim and shoe a horse for a variety of uses. Special attention is paid to corrective shoeing techniques for horses with various foot and leg problems.

WESTERN HORSEMANSHIP by Richard Shrake
144 pages and 150 photographs. Complete guide to riding western horses.

WESTERN TRAINING by Jack Brainard
With Peter Phinny. 136 pages. Stresses the foundation for western training.